CLASSIC
GRAND
PRIX
CARS

 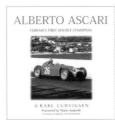  

What the critics said about *Classic Grand Prix Cars*:

'an excellent read'
Classic Cars

'highly recommended'
Car Graphic

'an impressive work'
Motor Sport

'amazingly detailed'
Historic Motor Racing News

'entertaining and informative'
Racecar Engineering

'fascinating reading'
Bugantics

CLASSIC GRAND PRIX CARS

THE FRONT-ENGINED FORMULA 1 ERA 1906–1960

Second Edition

KARL LUDVIGSEN

Haynes Publishing

First edition published by Sutton Publishing in 2000
Second edition published by Haynes Publishing in 2006 with new colour material

Karl Ludvigsen has asserted the moral right to be identified as the author of this work.

For
L. Scott Bailey

A 1926 Delage receives a servicing and refill. This was the final season for the first V-12-engined Grand Prix car.

A catalogue record for this book is available from the British Library

ISBN 1 84425 318 X

Library of Congress catalog card no 2005935261

Published by Haynes Publishing, Sparkford, Yeovil, Somerset BA22 7JJ, UK
Tel: 01963 442030 Fax: 01963 440001
Int.tel: +44 1963 442030 Int.fax: +44 1963 440001
E-mail: sales@haynes.co.uk
Website: www.haynes.co.uk

Haynes North America Inc., 861 Lawrence Drive, Newbury Park, California 91320, USA

Printed in Great Britain by J. H. Haynes & Co. Ltd., Sparkford

CONTENTS

Colour sections between pages 66/67 and 130/131.

INTRODUCTION

When I first became interested in cars and started to write about them, the cars in this book are the ones I knew about. I first learned about them in depth in *The Grand Prix Car* by Laurence Pomeroy, Jr., which my mother ordered for me for Christmas through the book department at Gilmore's in downtown Kalamazoo. Gilmore's ordered two copies; I always wondered who bought the other one.

Pomeroy's book, with its marvellous cutaway drawings by Leslie Cresswell, was an eye-opener and an inspiration for an American teenager. It is still an essential linchpin for any study of the evolution of the Grand Prix car up to the mid-Fifties. I referred often to Pomeroy in the preparation of this book and greatly value his insights and knowledge.

The cars of the Fifties, the first racing decade I experienced personally, will always have a special appeal for me. It was fun as well as a challenge, as technical editor at *Sports Cars Illustrated*, to write about the Ferrari, Lancia, Maserati, Mercedes, Vanwall and Aston Martin GP cars of that decade without actually having seen them. I relied on Jesse Alexander's photos, as did Clarence LaTourette, who produced our wonderful cutaway drawings. Later, in 1958-59, I had my first taste of the cars in action - just at the end of the era we celebrate in this book.

It seems an era well worth celebrating. Some wonderful Grand Prix cars were produced in these early decades of the 20th Century, cars that we now lionise and admire for their arresting appearance as well as their historic achievements. They are grouped by decades in the text – with a little loose logic leaving 1950–51 as part of the Forties – because this seems to be a convenient way to present their evolution over the first 60 years of the century.

The reader expecting a blow-by-blow account of the races of these years will be disappointed. I hope I've given a clear sense of the top dogs and lesser beasts of each period but the bare recital of racing results has not been my aim. Rather, the text and illustrations endeavour to provide a fresh view of the way the Grand Prix cars of each decade evolved, sometimes illuminated – perhaps unfairly – by what we have since learned about the cars and the men and companies that made them.

I've tried to put the Grand Prix cars, circuits, builders, teams, drivers and races in the context of the politics and economics of their times so that we can better understand their evolution. A table of specifications for selected cars gives an overview of that evolution technically, from the Gordon Bennett Mercedes of 1903 to the Lotus 18 of 1960, winner of the last race of the $2\frac{1}{2}$-litre Formula 1.

My hope, as well, is that this book will inform its readers about what might be called the 'pre-history' of Formula 1. With most aspects of Formula 1 now being dated from 1950, when the drivers' championship was established, the earlier years tend to be overlooked. I've tried to restore the balance with a portrayal of the origins and evolution of Grand Prix racing from 1906 – the year of the first Grand Prix organised by the Automobile Club de France – through the first decade of the drivers' championship and the establishment of the manufacturers' championship in 1958.

Much of the material between these covers was originally developed for publication in *Automobile Quarterly*. I'm most grateful to that excellent and valuable magazine for permission to use the material here. It has been substantially rewritten and expanded to fit comfortably into its new format and is newly accompanied by special texts dealing with people and subjects that are topical for each decade. As always, any errors of commission or omission are down to me alone.

Illustrations are from the files of the Ludvigsen Library, except where specially credited. When the book first appeared in 2000 it was under the imprint of Sutton Publishing, whose Rupert Harding helped fashion its content. This new edition, with corrections and greatly enhanced colour sections, is the work of Haynes, now the owner of Sutton, with the invaluable help of Mark Hughes and Flora Myer. My wife Annette has, as usual, borne the burden of my preoccupation with the writing of this book. Many thanks, Annette, for your love, patience and support.

Writing this book has given me the guilty pleasure of thinking about and picturing many of the racing cars that have given me the greatest technical and aesthetic satisfaction. We're depicting an era in which engineering knowledge and its application gained steadily in importance, but the pure art of the racing car was never very far behind. The result, happily, was the creation of some wonderful automobiles and the establishment of the rich traditions that power Formula 1 racing to its modern global success.

Karl Ludvigsen
Hawkedon, Suffolk
Spring 2006

After the Second World War a new marque, Ferrari, became a dramatic contributor to the excitement of Grand Prix racing. Ferrari's agile four-cylinder Type 500, seen here at the Nürburgring, dominated racing in 1952 and '53.

Opposite: If one car could personify the grace, excitement and drama of the front-engined era of Grand Prix racing cars it might well be the Alfa Romeo 158/159 'Alfetta'. It first raced and won in 1938 and was still capably serving as the mount of the Formula 1 world champion in 1951, as here in the Swiss Grand Prix at Bern.

Fritz Erle's big white Benz placed seventh in the 1908 French Grand Prix. Erle would be a mainstay of the Benz racing effort after the First World War.

CHAPTER ONE
GRAND PRIX BEGINNINGS

You had an engine in the front, the roads weren't good, they were very loose and when the cars came thundering by they didn't go straight even on the straights. When a fellow came up behind in a cloud of dust the crowd were on their feet and that was, of course, the glamour of motor racing. The driver was an enormous man ready to do anything, wrestling with the wheel – when he came to a corner the handbrake went on and he skidded round in a shower of stones. That was really exciting motor racing.

Rodney Walkerley

'At Lyons the smallest crowd ever seen at the end of a historic race was awaiting the winner,' wrote historian Gerald Rose. 'Charron afterwards said that it consisted of at least a dozen people, but other accounts give it as something less than a hundred.' This was the obscure and humble finish of the first race run to a regulation controlling the size of the cars, the race for the Gordon Bennett Trophy on 14 June 1900. From five official starters only two finished, both Panhards, with Fernand Charron driving the winner. From this small seed in French soil grew the modern phenomenon of Formula 1 racing for Grand Prix cars.

A Renault driven by Marcel Renault was the winner of the 1902 race from Paris to Vienna via Basle, Zurich and Salzburg. Marcel's death in a similar car in the 1903 Paris–Madrid race was one of the catalysts for change that led to the introduction of circuit races and the first Grand Prix race in 1906.

GORDON BENNETT BEGINNINGS

Although Grand Prix racing proper didn't begin until six years into the twentieth century,[1] the races for the Gordon Bennett Trophy were essential precursors. They were born in the spirit of intense and growing nationalism that swept Europe in the wake of the Franco–German war of 1870–71. From that conflict came the establishment of both the German Empire and the French Third Republic, as well as the unification of Italy. The hankering for revenge on the part of the French, losers in that war, would intensify the conflict in the First World War to come.

Into the midst of Europe's simmering discontent stepped a not-so-innocent American newspaper publisher, James Gordon Bennett.[2] Settled in Paris, Bennett took a keen interest in the burgeoning new forms of locomotion. None was dearer to the heart of the French than the motor car, in whose development and production French firms led the world. At her 1898 automobile salon 259 makers were represented. By 1900 France was home to 300 auto companies producing a total of almost 5,000 cars per year at a time when other nations were barely nudging triple figures.

Bennett conceived a new kind of automobile race that would pit nation against nation. Any country's recognised automobile club would have the right to enter three cars in the race for his trophy. Moreover, said the eighth of the twenty-four regulations, 'The cars must be entirely constructed and all their parts manufactured in the country which such cars represent.' The Gordon Bennett Trophy had much in common with the America's Cup yacht race in this respect, as well as the rule that the winning nation was to stage the race the following year.[3]

The rules required the cars to weigh at least 400 kg and not more than 1,000 kg, with an allowance of an additional 7 kg for a magneto. This came in all to 2,220 lb. They were weighed empty of tools and fuel; for electric cars the battery weight was not included. This was the first time an upper limit on any dimension of a car had been imposed for racing. Specific limits also came into force in 1901 for all types of racing to divide cars into four categories:

Fournier, Ferdinand Charron's riding mechanic, was grimly holding the water pump against the flywheel of their Panhard to keep water circulating as they roared across the finish line, winners of the 1900 Gordon Bennett Trophy. Charron's winning average speed was 38.6 mph over 353 miles from Paris to Lyons.

Unlimited	over 650 kg
Voitures Légères	400–650 kg
Voiturettes	250–400 kg
Others	up to 250 kg

1 For the pedant, five years after, since the new century began in 1901 and Grand Prix racing started in 1906.
2 Bennett's name is often hyphenated as Gordon-Bennett, either in emulation of the English phrase or as a modifier of his trophy, but this is incorrect.
3 In this respect it also resembled the Eurovision Song Contest.

The Gordon Bennett event was administered by the Automobile Club de France (ACF), which staged the first such race from Paris to Lyons in 1900. The honour of holding the race turned out to be a doubtful one for the ACF, which was immediately embroiled in controversy over the selection of the drivers who would defend the glory of *la belle France*. 'So far from having a number of prominent drivers all clamouring for the honour of driving in the race,' wrote Gerald Rose, 'the difficulty outside France was to raise a team at all.' Thus the field for the inaugural 1900 race was counted on the fingers of one hand.

Introduced with the Gordon Bennett competition was the concept of national colours for the cars: blue for France, white for Germany, yellow for Belgium, green for Britain and – at first – red for America. Run in parallel with the Paris–Bordeaux race of 1901, that year's race for the trophy was a washout, with only one French finisher. The same held true for the 1902 race, from Paris to Innsbruck, but this time Britain's Napier was the sole survivor. Although mainland Britain was inimical to racing on the public roads (the era of the dedicated racing track was still far in the future), a suitable road circuit was found in Ireland for the 1903 race.

FIRST CIRCUIT RACES

The fact that the race was held on a circuit in 1903 was significant. In May of that year a major race from Paris to Madrid had been halted short of the Spanish border at Bordeaux after numerous tragic crashes, including the deaths of several riding mechanics, spectators and driver Marcel Renault. The idea of all-out racing from town to town over public roads was seen as no longer defensible. It would survive only in such glorious anachronisms as the Mille Miglia, Carrera Panamericana and the South American road races.

To the disgust of France a Belgian, Camille Jenatzy, driving a white German Mercedes car was the winner of the Gordon Bennett Trophy in 1903. That year's race, held in Ireland, was won at an average of 49.2 mph by the 60 hp Mercedes.

The first-ever circuit race was a minor event run over two laps of 45 miles of French road, the Course du Catalogue of 18 February 1900. The idea was adopted for a major race in 1902 for the Circuit des Ardennes in Belgium, whose competitors lapped a 53-mile road course six times. This allowed much more effective policing of a closed road and eliminated the troublesome and controversial neutral zones through towns that plagued the town-to-town racers.

By 1903 interest in the Gordon Bennett Trophy was rising, so much so that elimination trials had to be held in England and America to sort out the eager contenders. The result was a triumph for the Mercedes driven by Camille Jenatzy, which headed the three French entries at the finish. With the end of the big town-to-town races all the world's motor-sporting attention fell on the 1904 Gordon Bennett Trophy. Elimination trials were held in Britain and in France, where no less than twenty-nine cars jostled for selection for the final trio.

The winner of both the French trials and the 1904 race was Léon Théry, driving a relatively new marque, Richard-Brasier. Originally known simply as

Wilhelm Maybach's original design for the radical 1901 Mercedes showed its steel frame rails, honeycomb radiator and cam-actuated inlet valves, features that set new standards for other automobile engineers. These made possible dramatic advances in the design of both racing cars and road cars.

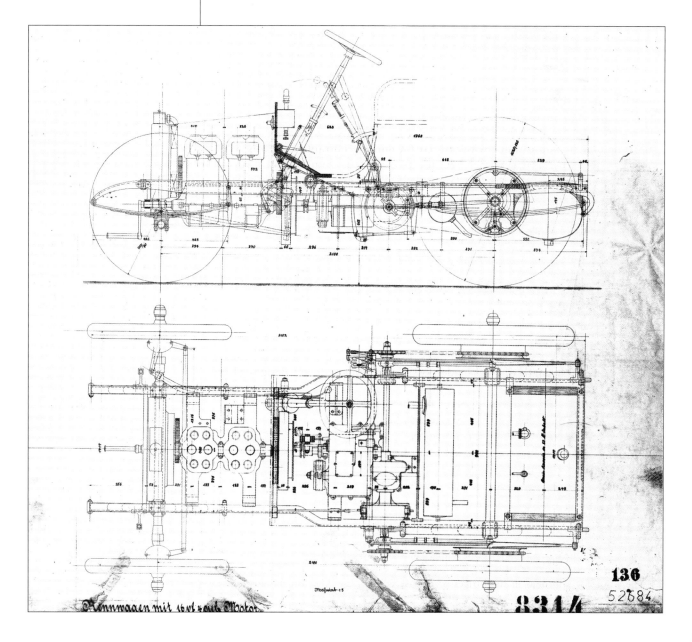

Richard, the firm obtained its hyphenated appendage in recognition of the success of Henri Brasier in building and managing the 1904 trophy winner. Remarkably, as well, Théry and Richard-Brasier repeated this success in 1905.[4] This was, however, destined to be the last race for Mr Bennett's trophy.

THE GRAND PRIX IDEA

The large number of potential competitors that they had mustered for these races (twenty-four in the 1905 trials) gave the French great cause for concern. Representatives of the Gallic car makers huddled at the automobile salon at the end of 1904 and formulated a proposal to the ACF. It was that the club should abandon its support of the Gordon Bennett race, which so constrained opportunities for French entries, and organise instead a Grand Prix de l'Automobile Club de France in which all firms entering would have an equal chance to win. The prize would indeed be grand: a purse to the winner of 100,000 francs (equal to $19,400 or £4,000), put up by the publisher of *l'Auto*.

The proposal was adopted and preparations for the 1905 Grand Prix were begun as an adjunct to that year's Gordon Bennett race – only to be suspended in response to a barrage of formal protests from all other interested nations.[5] The 1906 Gordon Bennett race lapsed in the absence of any challenge to the French holders of the trophy; it has never been revived, although suggestions to that effect have been made from time to time.

Thus the first Grand Prix race was held one year late – in 1906 instead of 1905. Equality of opportunity was assured by limiting entrants to teams of no more than three cars. The French would, as expected, dominate in terms of entries and would even win the first Grand Prix. But they would not have things all their own way in the early years of Grand Prix racing.

All the cars in the first Grand Prix were proud and powerful front-engined machines. Putting the engine in the front of a car had originally been the idea of Emile Levassor, the engineering chief of Panhard & Levassor in Paris, who broke with the industry's early pattern of under-floor power units by placing the engine of his 1891 models at the front. By doing so he unlocked the potential for increased automotive power, because engine size was no longer limited by the space available under the chassis.

The other major innovation was made in 1901 by Wilhelm Maybach with his design of the Mercedes car for Daimler. He introduced the honeycomb radiator and the use of pressed-steel frame members. Replacing the early wooden frames, the much greater strength of steel made possible the longer, lower designs of the early racing cars.

Thus Levassor and Maybach[6] between them prepared the ground for the evolution of the Grand Prix car as we came to know it through the fifties. There is much to admire about the modern rear-engined racing car. But few would deny the elegance and beauty of the front-engined racers that dominated the first five decades of the sport. It is those that we celebrate, decade by decade, in the pages that follow.

---

4   'Brasier's racing victories also were reflected in his firm's net profits for the years ending in 1905 and 1906,' wrote historian James Laux. 'They reached one-fifth of sales turnover and the company declared dividends of 20 per cent and 22.5 per cent in these two years.' These were short-lived profits gained from selling expensive cars to wealthy enthusiasts, who deserted the market in the 1907 slump. Brasier never recovered.

5   The trophy is still held in the offices of its last winner, the ACF, on the Place de la Concorde in Paris.

6   With a little help from Louis Renault, who introduced shaft drive to a live rear axle.

CHAPTER TWO

TUMULTUOUS ORIGINS

Most striking in appearance were the white-painted Mercedes, whose acute V-fronted radiators, straight line bonnet and dash, and curved pocket tail carrying the spare wheels and tyres gave them that complete-from-every-point-of-view appearance which gives such an individuality to war vessels of the British Navy and so many of the great railway express engines. One felt instinctively that these Mercedes would have to be reckoned with. They have lines which a camera cannot portray; a white marble model of one would be a priceless possession.

The Autocar, 11 July 1914

Grand Prix racing's first decade was strangely shaped. We can time it as beginning in 1906 and ending in 1914, punctuated by peculiar interruptions. As 'something new', an advanced form of motor sport that presented new challenges to its participants, it could hardly have been expected to have a smooth launch. Ironically, however, the French who were so active in creating it were also to the fore among those who almost brought Grand Prix racing to its knees. Then – as fate would have it – they revived it again.

THE POWER OF PEUGEOT

There were the many French car makers – and then there was Peugeot. A relative latecomer among the French heavyweight car producers, Peugeot plunged powerfully into racing at the end of the first decade of the twentieth century and thereby transformed Grand Prix competition both technically and economically. Thanks to Peugeot, Grand Prix racing's first decade divides neatly between the early years, when racing cars still resembled road cars, and the final years, in which the racing car took on a new and radically different configuration that was distinctly its own.

Although it had been among the successful marques in the early motor competitions of the 1890s, apart from token entries Peugeot vanished from the racing lists after the turn of the century. Based in the provinces, Peugeot had too long stayed faithful to the old style of under-floor engines while Daimler and Panhard were moving the engine to the front.

A quiet renaissance began in 1902 with the establishment of a Peugeot research and development centre near Paris at Levallois-Perret. In February of 1910, however, two formerly separate branches of the family firm were reunited to create SA des Automobiles and Cycles Peugeot – the forebear of the Peugeot company we know today. This made Peugeot France's second-largest motor company after the fast-growing Renault.

Heading the new company was Armand Peugeot, the family member who had been most eager to enter the automobile field. Although he died in 1915 at the age of sixty-six, Armand had time to give his company's racing activities a brisk acceleration. His ally in this was his second cousin, Robert Peugeot. Robert was a son of the company's co-founder, Armand's cousin Eugène, who had died in 1907. Robert was directly responsible for the implementation of Peugeot's racing programme, which was built on the foundation of the success of Lion-Peugeot racers in the Voiturette ('small car') categories late in the decade.

For the first time in the history of the industry, Peugeot's racing cars were built by an independent unit set up for this express purpose. 'The Peugeot Company,' related *The Automobile Engineer* in 1914, 'determined that it would make a great name in racing regardless of cost, and consequently the special racing factory was set up and the problem of racing car building dealt with as an entirely separate and complete business.' In this way Peugeot pioneered the economic organisation of racing as well as its technology.

Experienced engineers had built Peugeot's Voiturette racers. The veteran Gratien Michaux had headed the design of racing and road models for Lion-Peugeot. Louis Verdet had designed both aero and racing engines to be built by Peugeot at the Ateliers Aviation Rossel-Peugeot on the west side of Paris at Suresnes. But neither of these engineers was engaged to lead the work in the 'special racing factory', which in fact used the Suresnes workshops.

One of the most successful racing drivers during the early years of Grand Prix competition was Georges Boillot. In 1912 he won the French Automobile Club's Grand Prix at Dieppe driving an L76 Peugeot with 7.6 litres in four cylinders.

ENTER LES CHARLATANS

When word leaked out in 1911 that Peugeot was building a new racing car for the senior category, 'the project was the laughing stock of the city,' recalled journalist W.F. Bradley. Peugeot build a racing car? They did well enough in Voiturettes, but at the Grand Prix level they had been eclipsed for a decade. But the new project had strong support in racing drivers Jules Goux (Robert Peugeot's chauffeur), Georges Boillot and Paolo Zuccarelli, who had just come over from the successful Hispano-Suiza team. 'They all were bored with driving little cars,' said Bradley, 'and wanted to be in racing in the highest level.'

They had radical ideas for the design of such a car, as well as the backing of Roland Peugeot, who had been won over by a sober presentation by the serious Goux. Roland agreed to foot the bill for building a team of racing cars at an estimated cost of £4,000 each, and allocated space to the trio in the Rossel-Peugeot facility. There the cars would be assembled from parts made by skilled subcontractors throughout the Paris periphery.

Now the drivers needed an able engineer to interpret their ideas because the factory's own engineering staff wanted nothing to do with this notion of returning to racing. They found their man in a 26-year-old Swiss engineer, Ernest Henry. Although new to the car field, Geneva-born Henry had contributed to the

AIR TO GROUND TO AIR

As the main text of Chapter Two testifies, these were years of dramatic and rapid advancement in power-unit technology. Many of the techniques that helped Grand Prix engines perform better were also of value to the burgeoning industry of aviation – especially at a time when Europe's unsettled scores were openly threatening an outbreak of war. After the war as well, some of the advances made in aviation – such as supercharging – had their impact on the design of racing cars.

The close association between land and air was inevitable, with the same companies, and their engineers, designing and building engines for both aeroplanes and Grand Prix cars. Louis Coatalen at Sunbeam was active in both areas; Coatalen was no mean aviator. Peugeot built a V-8 aviation engine that had twin-cam heads and cylinders just like those of the successful Peugeot racing cars. Ettore Bugatti created a U-16 aircraft engine that was built both in France and, with modifications, by Duesenberg in America. The Duesenbergs had a V-16 aviation project of their own as well.

In Germany both Benz and Daimler were active in the development of aircraft engines. Both entered the Kaiser's 1912 competition for the best German aircraft engine, judged on the basis of low fuel consumption and high power from light weight. Although Benz was the winner, the more significant engine was the Daimler unit that placed second. It was a six, the only such to oust light, simple fours from the first five places. It achieved

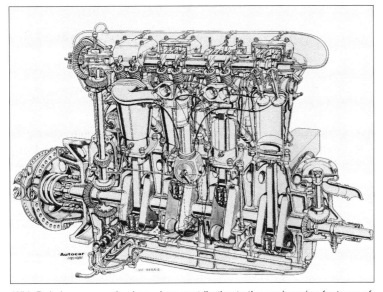

With Daimler aero-engine know-how contributing to the engineering features of the 1914 Mercedes Grand Prix engine, the British could hardly be blamed for taking a close look at its attributes when they designed their own aviation engines for use in the first global conflict. It was a robustly built unit capable of high continuous speed.

this with an exceptionally strong yet light form of cylinder construction for the 105 × 140 mm (7,250 cc) six that allowed it to weigh only 388 lb. An earlier six, of larger bore with cast cylinders, weighed 150 lb more and produced only 14½ more horsepower.

In the design by Paul Daimler, son of company founder Gottlieb, the new engine's cylinders were fabricated around a simple lathe-turned steel cylinder wall to which intake and exhaust ports were welded. A water jacket of thin steel sheet was oxy-acetylene-welded around each pair of cylinders.

Paul Daimler's designers chose the steel cylinder for its high strength as much as for its light weight. They felt that the usual cast-iron cylinders would be unable to contain the higher combustion pressures that they wanted to generate in the cylinder. Designated the DF80, their overhead-cam six developed 90½ hp at 1,400 rpm. Two of the four Mercedes racing cars entered in the 1913 Sarthe Grand Prix at Le Mans were powered by this very engine. One of these cars went to America in 1914, where it was inspected closely by the engineers of the famous Packard company – very much involved in aero engines.[1]

The DF80's design set the pattern for the highly successful Daimler sixes of the First World War, and indeed for the aviation engines produced then by NAG, Benz and BMW. Paul Daimler also seized on the welded-steel cylinder for his great 1914 Mercedes Grand Prix car, adding the refinement of four valves per cylinder for optimum

---

1 This came about because the car was entered at Indianapolis for Ralph de Palma to drive. As at Le Mans, so too at Indy the engine was troubled by severe vibration above 1,400 rpm, and the Mercedes was withdrawn from the 500-mile race. A consultant to Packard, de Palma arranged for the inspection by its engineers.

breathing. Like an aircraft engine, the racing Mercedes four also had duplicated (actually triplicated) spark plugs.

After the Mercedes victory in the 1914 Grand Prix de l'ACF, the winning car was displayed in Berlin and then shipped to London for display at the Milnes-Daimler showroom on Shaftesbury Avenue. The white car reached England on 8 August; Britain had declared war on Germany four days earlier. A prisoner of war, the Grand Prix-winning Mercedes was stored in the Milnes-Daimler service facility on London's Long Acre.

'I knew this,' wrote engineer W.O. Bentley about the car's presence in Britain at the outbreak of war, 'and immediately told Commander Wilfred Briggs, my chief at the Admiralty, about it. Without wasting any time, we went along to Long Acre and retrieved the hidden car before anyone could destroy it. We then had the engine sent up to Rolls-Royce at Derby who examined, vetted and tested it exhaustively.'

'It is common knowledge,' Bentley

Thirty-two exhaust stacks served the three-valve cylinders of the V-16 aviation engine built by Duesenberg during the First World War. It helped inspire the Duesenberg brothers to build their successful straight-eight racing engine of the postwar period.

continued in his memoirs, 'that all Rolls-Royce aero engines built during World War I were based quite closely on this engine.' Confessing that he was 'tremendously impressed' by the Mercedes engine, after the war Bentley freely adapted its valve gear and vertical-shaft cam drive to the first car bearing his name. Mercedes-type fabricated-steel construction was also adopted for the American Liberty V-12 aero engine.[2]

Although the eight-cylinder engines designed for aviation use were usually V-type, which ideally suited installation and cooling, the work done during the war on V-16 engines helped highlight the merit of the straight-eight engine. This contributed to its postwar adoption for racing and road cars by Bugatti and Duesenberg.

Supercharging, developed during the war for aeroplane altitude performance, was quickly adapted after the Armistice to racing-car use. While the Americans followed their own use of centrifugal compressors for racing, the Germans and Italians fitted their Grand Prix cars with the positive-displacement blowers that they had been testing in the air.

The next major aviation trend to benefit racing cars would be fuel injection. Injection systems were developed for aero engines during the thirties and put to use in the Second World War. In Germany, Bosch developed a system of injection directly into the combustion chamber; this was adopted for racing by Daimler-Benz in 1954. In Britain the SU fuel-injection system squirted fuel into the ports. SU systems began to be applied to racing cars in 1953.

In the forties and fifties, racing car design would also benefit from the great advances in the understanding of aerodynamics and structural design spurred by the engineering of aeroplanes for war. Disc brakes were also born in the air during the forties. In Britain both Lotus and Vanwall exploited these advances to improve the efficiency of their racing cars.

---

2   Daimler-Benz would continue to use this form of engine construction for all its purpose-built racing models up to the W196 Grand Prix car of 1955. The 300SLR sports-racing car of that year differed – for the first time – in having cast-aluminium cylinder blocks.

Mainsprings of the Peugeot racing effort are welcomed back from their trip to Indianapolis in 1913 at Paris's Gare St Lazare. Among those present are Ernest Henry (1), Paolo Zuccarelli (2), Georges Boillot (3) and Jules Goux (5). Also present is Peugeot director Lemoine (4).

advanced Swiss Picker engines that powered racing hydroplanes at Monte Carlo. Henry had come to Paris to represent Picker's engineering interests there.

The efforts of the men the Peugeot works engineers ridiculed as 'Les Charlatans' wrought a radical revolution in racing car design. Although essentially experimental cars, their first designs were stunningly successful. The 7.6-litre Peugeot L76 of 1912 and its Voiturette sister of the same year, the 3-litre L3, were the first cars of any kind to combine a V-inclined-valve cylinder head with four valves per cylinder and twin overhead camshafts – the hallmarks of most later high-performance engines.

Although in 1912 these were hugely elaborate and costly features, utterly impractical for production cars, Peugeot's rivals had no choice but to emulate them if they wanted to keep pace. 'Once let loose,' said *The Automobile Engineer*, 'upon a stem to stern design for racing and racing alone, almost every engineer turned to the overhead valve engine quite naturally. The real truth of the matter is that the overhead valve engine is theoretically more adaptable to the production of a very high hp than is the ordinary pocket valve type of motor, and this has been known for a very long time.' The cost had to be faced, said the journal's editor, because it had become 'essential that others who desired to run against Peugeots should spend equal sums of money'.

The explosion of activity triggered by Peugeot resulted in a record field of competitors for the last pre-war European Grand Prix in 1914, long considered by many experts to be the greatest motor race of all time. All the cars sparkled with new technologies, many of them prompted by the advancements that were being made in parallel on aero engines in preparation for the First World War. Thus Grand Prix racing ended before the outbreak of war at a peak of competitiveness and creativity that left its partisans eager for its early resumption.

HIATUS AT MID-DECADE

The bright picture of 1914 would hardly have been forecast in 1908, when Europe's leading auto makers banded together to stop making and entering these costly cars. Having created the Grand Prix to give more opportunities to their home producers than the Gordon Bennett rules afforded, the Automobile Club de France had to suffer an Italian victory in 1907 and a German triumph in 1908.

These discouraging defeats have often been cited as the reason for the subsequent Grand Prix hiatus. In fact, the high and rising cost of racing was the factor that led the car makers to agree to stop competing. During Georges Clemenceau's government of 1906–09 the CGT – the French labour union – then a feisty ten-year-old, started raising hob against the background of a sharp economic recession in 1907 that continued into 1908. Although, wrote historian James Laux, 'the situation was not at all critical for the industry as a whole, at the time the atmosphere reeked of gloom'.

For this reason Grand Prix racing came to a screeching halt in 1909 that lasted several years. After the 1908 race a dozen French and German auto makers signed an accord that barred them from entering races in 1909. It had teeth in the form of a 100,000 franc bond posted by each; anyone breaking ranks would forfeit his bond.[1] The pact held through 1910, and effectively 1911 as well.

In the latter year the Sarthe region's auto club mounted a Grand Prix race which was poorly attended when it was finally run after three postponements. The power of the Constructors' Syndicate – as it was known – to discourage entries was still strong. Unreadiness rather than discouragement was the reason for the absence of the maverick L76 Peugeots, whose bore and stroke dimensions of 110×200 mm had been pegged exactly to the figures specified by the Sarthe club for one of the categories in its race.

GRAND PRIX REVIVAL

In 1912 the ACF was again ready to stage a pukka Grand Prix – bringing with it the age of the Peugeot and the modern racing car. Largely supported by French and Italian makers, the race saw entries of massive chain-drive racers of 14–15 litres from Fiat and Lorraine-Dietrich, cars much like those of half a decade earlier. Although almost half its engine size, the new L76 Peugeot was very nearly as quick as the well-proven Fiat Tipo 14.

After two gruelling days of racing, helped by retirements, Boillot's Peugeot was the winner in 1912. Boillot won again for Peugeot in 1913, and was very nearly the victor in 1914 as well. By then others had emulated many of the features of the successful Peugeots. Indeed, if they wished to have a chance of winning they had little choice in the matter.

Georges Boillot's serial successes for Peugeot were exceptional achievements, pointed out Alfred Neubauer of Daimler-Benz: 'With so many firms competing in this "Race of Races", the French Grand Prix, it was very rarely that one

---

1   The amount was equal to £4,000, or almost $20,000.

individual driver achieved outright victory. It was even rarer for a driver to succeed in winning more than one Grand Prix.' The achievement of Boillot in that era was thus exceptional.

The role of racing-mad Peugeot had been significant in reviving the Grand Prix after its wilderness years, related Neubauer. He called this first decade the 'classical period' of Grand Prix racing, during which all the cars were entered by the factories themselves. Private entrants were unknown. At this level racing was a sport for the car makers, who took part in it as an inevitable and logical extension of their car-making and marketing activities.

In the first Grand Prix years many makers could state with confidence that their racers were prototypes for next year's production cars. Replicas of their racing cars were built and sold as high-powered sports models. By 1914, however, this was no longer possible. The racing car and the road car had diverged, never again to converge – apart from a brief period at the beginning of the fifties.

Men at the Wheel

Another implication of the factories' involvement in the 'classical period' was a change in the backgrounds of the drivers. Wealthy amateurs frequented the sport in the Gordon Bennett years. With the prestige of a factory at stake, these now had to step aside to favour the professional. Often a works engineer or tester, building up his skills with frequent stints behind the wheel, the factory driver became a mainstay of the sport.

Although this trend had been evident in the early years of the twentieth century, it was accelerated by the Automobile Club de France in its rules for the

With its shaft-driven rear axle, four valves per cylinder and twin overhead camshafts, the 1912 Grand Prix Peugeot was the first of a new generation of Grand Prix cars that departed sharply from conventional touring-car design. Winner Georges Boillot carried number 22 in the 1912 Grand Prix of the French Automobile Club at Dieppe.

Grand Prix, which it was 'determined to make . . . the finest test of men and motors that had ever been held', said contemporary observer Gerald Rose. To this end the ACF forbade outside assistance to the driver and mechanic – previously made freely available – and required them to do all the refuelling, retyring and repairing.[2] Dilettantes were definitely not required.

The professionals had begun to make their mark in the Gordon Bennett era, when the reputation not only of a marque but also of a nation was at stake. Earliest among them were Léon Théry, whose consistent speed earned him the nickname 'The Chronometer', and Belgian Camille Jenatzy, whose red hair and beard combined with a forceful style to brand him the 'Red Devil'. Both were gone before the end of this racing decade – Théry dying of tuberculosis in 1909, and Jenatzy in 1913 of a gunshot wound on his estate, where he was tragically mistaken for a wild boar.

Nor did two of the three Charlatans long survive. Paolo Zuccarelli was killed while testing a car in preparation for the 1913 Grand Prix, and the superb Georges Boillot, who was credited by a contemporary as representing 'the spirit of France in motor racing', was killed in 1916 when his Nieuport Scout was attacked by German Fokkers near Verdun. Only Jules Goux weathered these risks. He used a Peugeot L76 to win the Indianapolis 500-mile race in 1913. Driving for Bugatti in the twenties, Goux won the hollowest victory in the history of Grand Prix racing in the 1926 French Grand Prix, as Chapter Three reveals. He died in 1965 at the age of eighty.

Although the 6.2-litre Delage was the quickest car in the French Grand Prix at Amiens in 1913, Albert Guyot (here at the wheel) suffered tyre problems while leading and had to settle for fifth. A similar car won the Indianapolis 500-mile race in 1914.

---

2 An additional two men could be delegated to twist the crank to start each car.

CHRISTIAN LAUTENSCHLAGER

Towards the end of this first decade Georges Boillot was twice a Grand Prix winner, a remarkable achievement. But against this we must set the accomplishment of Christian Lautenschlager in winning the Grand Prix de l'ACF at the beginning and the end of the era: first in the years of the great chain-drive cars, and second in the final race of the decade when racing cars had become much more sophisticated.

When he won at Dieppe in 1908 Lautenschlager was already thirty-one years old. An employee of the Daimler Motoren Gesellschaft since 1899, the richly moustachioed Lautenschlager was born on 13 April 1877 in Magstadt near Stuttgart. He apprenticed as a locksmith and worked for a maker of bicycles before joining Daimler, where he earned the responsible post of a foreman, inspector and, by 1905, car tester. This brought him into the Stuttgart firm's racing activities.

Lautenschlager rode as mechanic to Otto Salzer in the 1906 Ardennes Races, in which they ran second before falling back down the order. His pluck and skill in testing won him the wheel in 1908 for the Grand Prix – his first race, and his first success. 'I am overjoyed over the great triumph my firm has achieved with this victory,' he said afterwards. 'We have earned this success, for the cars have been thoroughly tested for a long time before and the labours of preparation have been very thorough and have lasted a long time.'

Knowing his cars and engines through and through was hardly a handicap to the racing career of Christian Lautenschlager, seen here at the wheel of his winning car in the 1914 French Grand Prix. Lautenschlager also drove a Mercedes to victory in the same event in 1908.

To say that his win was unexpected was to express the obvious. He was described as 'Herr Lautenschlager, surname unknown and until now equally unknown to fame.' He was also called 'a typical German, with a makeup apparently without nerves and splendid judgement'. In his defeat of the massed French forces, mirroring the result of the Franco–Prussian War, he was credited with 'the same solid, patriotic and obedient character of man at the head of the mechanical invasion as the man in panoply of war'.

Not until 1913 did Lautenschlager return to the wheel of a racing car in anger. This was in the 'Grand Prix de France' organised by the AC de l'Ouest at Le Mans. Finishing sixth in his chain-drive Mercedes racer, Lautenschlager was third-placed among the four entries from Stuttgart, all of which completed the race. This was a good foundation for the 1914 Grand Prix effort, which resulted in another outright victory for Lautenschlager.

In that great race, observers remarked on his implacable speed and concentration. *The Autocar* found him 'impassive but determined, part of his car, in fact', and remarked on his approach to a corner 'at a tremendous speed, braking at the last minute and yet sitting on the road like a duck upon water'.

When he returned to racing for Daimler in 1922 Christian Lautenschlager was forty-five years old. In that year he was tenth overall in the Targa Florio in an updated version of the 1914 Grand Prix car, one of which Count Giulio Masetti used to win the Targa outright. Lautenschlager was a member of the Mercedes team that tackled the Indianapolis 500 in 1923, but spun off on the fourteenth lap and incurred injuries (not serious) to himself and his riding mechanic.

Christian Lautenschlager's last major race for Mercedes was the 1924 Targa Florio, in which he was tenth. The other Mercedes team cars were driven to first place by Christian Werner and to fifteenth place by a newcomer to Daimler named Alfred Neubauer.

After retiring from competition Lautenschlager remained a Daimler-Benz employee. He died in 1954 – just as a new racing initiative by his company was beginning to bear fruit.

Others among the French drivers who distinguished themselves in this era were Louis Wagner, Victor Rigal, Henri Fournier, Paul Bablot, Arthur Duray,[3] Albert Guyot and Henry Farman. Two who left France behind to throw in their lot with Benz in Germany were Victor Hémery and René Hanriot. They were second and third for Benz in the 1908 Grand Prix, with Hémery the moral victor after falling out of contention with an eye injury, not at all uncommon on the rocky roads on which they raced.

Representing Italy with speed and style in the early Grand Prix years were Felice Nazzaro, who placed second in 1906 and first in 1907, and Vincenzo Lancia – both driving Fiats. Dario Resta, Ralph de Palma and Alessandro Cagno were among Italy's other representatives.

German drivers enjoyed disproportionate success in the first Grand Prix decade. Not many took part. Carl Jörns was Opel's stalwart, and Fritz Erle drove for Benz. Max Sailer and Otto Salzer raced Mercedes cars for Daimler, and would continue to do so in the twenties. But no other German matched the astonishing success of Christian Lautenschlager, who won the Grand Prix of the ACF in both 1908 and 1914 for Mercedes – matching Boillot with two wins in this era, and the only driver to enjoy victory in both cusps of the decade.

Ironically, in this 'classical period' the driver whose name will always be prominent in history as the winner of the first-ever Grand Prix came from none of these great motoring nations, but instead from Hungary. To be sure, Ferenc Szisz soon became known as 'François' after he arrived in France in 1900 at the age of twenty-seven.

Joining Renault, Szisz was riding mechanic to founder Louis Renault in the early town-to-town races, and soon moved into the driving seat. 'His mechanical skill and calm temperament,' wrote historian Cyril Posthumus, 'helped to develop a deliberate, machine-like style of driving, totally in sympathy with the big, powerful, intractable racing cars of the time.'

ENGINES ON WHEELS

For François Szisz (often misspelled 'Sisz' at the time) these qualities were of special value in the first Grand Prix, which was held over two days on 26–27 June 1906. Raced over a 64-mile triangular road course east of Le Mans, six laps each day, its total distance amounted to 770 miles – akin to the distance from Paris to Berlin. The surface was dirt that had been coated to a width of 18 feet with 500 barrels of *goudron* (a heavy, tarry mineral oil) to suppress dust, except for two turns near towns that were temporarily wood-paved.

The race attracted a handsome entry of thirty-four, most teams fielding three cars. Their marques provide a profile of the era: Clément-Bayard, Darracq, De Dietrich, Fiat, Gobron-Brillié, Grégoire, Hotchkiss, Itala, Mercedes, Panhard, Renault and Richard-Brasier. Another entry came from a new marque, Vulpès. Although little more than an engine on wheels, unusually attached to an underslung chassis (one in which the frame passed under the axles instead of above them), it was unable to sneak under the maximum weight limit of 1,007 kg.

The idea of an upper limit on weight, and indeed the specific metric tonne value used, was carried over to the Grand Prix from the Gordon Bennett Trophy races. In these years, said Gerald Rose, the limit served to concentrate the minds of designers and builders:

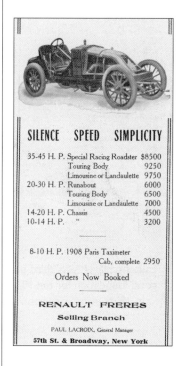

---

3 Although Duray was American-born, he was naturalised as a Frenchman and conducted his automotive career in France.

Having led convincingly after the first day, François Szisz started in pole position on the second day to drive his Renault to a convincing victory in the first French Grand Prix, held at Le Mans in June 1906.

Manufacturers were forced out of the groove into which they were rapidly falling, and throughout the whole history of the movement the story has always been the same. Impose some restriction on designers, and they at once set to work to obtain from their new vehicle results equal to those which they achieved with their unrestricted car. With a restriction in one direction, it becomes necessary to find some other way by which the car can be made to attain that same speed and that same reliability under its new limitation. The rapid improvement of the design of the racing car, and hence that of the touring car, may certainly be attributed in great part to the weight limit imposed in 1902.[4]

When the 1,000 kg limit was first decreed in 1900, the engine size of a racing car (almost invariably of four cylinders) was typically 5–6 litres. By 1901, however, Mors had built a 10.1-litre racer, and in the following year Panhard upped the ante to 13.7 litres with its '70' model. By 1905 typical displacements were Fiat's 16.2 litres and the 14.1 litres of Mercedes. In 1906, for the first Grand Prix, Panhard contrived to meet the weight limit with an engine of 18.3 litres.

4   Gerald Rose, *A Record of Motor Racing – 1894–1908*, Motor Racing Publications, Abingdon-on-Thames (1949 reprint of 1909 book). Rose's observations about the response of racing engineers to the challenge of regulations continued to hold true throughout the subsequent history of Grand Prix racing.

This took some ingenious engineering. Laurence Pomeroy Jr wrote: 'it was a commonplace to have cast-iron cylinders with open sides covered by copper water jackets only 1 millimetre thick; for pistons and connecting-rods liberally to be drilled and for crankshaft diameters to look like knitting-needles by modern standards'. Panhard's engines were so delicate that a special mounting had to be devised to isolate them from the twisting of the car's frame. Aluminium, then an exotic new material, was widely used for crankcases and gearbox housings.

Thus most of the awesome automobiles lining up for the 5 a.m. start of the 1906 Grand Prix had massive engines mounted on exiguous frames and axles. Renault represented a significant exception to this school of engineering. Brothers Louis and Marcel Renault had participated keenly and successfully in the early town-to-town races, but Marcel's death during the aborted 1903 Paris–Madrid race cast a pall over this activity. Louis vowed never to race again.

In 1904 Renault allowed his company to build a racing car with a 12.1-litre engine for a customer, and in 1905 Renault took part unsuccessfully in the Gordon Bennett selection race with a team of 13.0-litre racers. This remained the relatively modest (by the standards of the day) capacity of the four-cylinder side-valve engines of the 1906 Grand Prix Renaults.[5]

Also differentiating the Renaults from their rivals was thermo-syphon cooling. When heated in the engine, the cooling water's density reduced and the warm water rose to the top and into the radiator. Cooled therein, it sank to the bottom of the radiator and returned to the engine without the bother and complication of a water pump. The system worked perfectly in the 1906 race, which was run at the height of summer in what one observer called 'Senegallian weather'.

Perversely, Renault also placed the heavy and bulky radiator behind the engine, adjacent to the dash and footboards. All the rest positioned their radiators at the front of the chassis, ahead of the engine. Logical though this was,

Thanks to the positioning of its massive tubular radiator behind the engine, the 1906 Renault Grand Prix car made relatively moderate demands on its tyres when cornering. This greatly extended the longevity of these vital components.

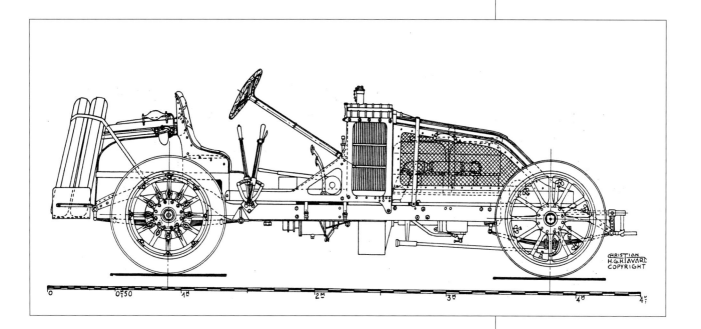

5   Renault had built the industry's first side-valve engines in 1902, engines in which the inlet and exhaust valves are placed along one side of the engine with the camshaft beneath them. This is also known as the 'L-head' engine.

Christian Lautenschlager's 13.5-litre Mercedes is being given a tyre change on its way to victory in the 1908 French Grand Prix. The race took place on a very fast road circuit at Dieppe.

it had the disadvantage of shifting even more mass above the front wheels, which were already burdened enough by the huge engines. The Renault's front wheels were much less heavily loaded.

At a time when tyre survival was crucial to racing success, another advantageous feature of the rear-mounted radiator was that more of the car's mass of machinery was concentrated centrally in the frame. This was an important 'speed secret' of the 1906 Renault. The Renault could be said to have a low polar moment of inertia, meaning that the concentration of its main masses near the centre of the chassis made it easier to turn – just as a ball is easier to start in rotation than a dumb-bell of the same weight. This reduced the cornering demands on the tyres, especially those at the front.

SAVING AND CHANGING TYRES

With negligible exceptions, the front and rear wheels of the 1906 Grand Prix cars were 87 mm (34¼ inches) in diameter with 3½-inch rims. Tyre sections were 4¾ inches. Over this decade the sizes changed little; diameters remained much the same in 1914. The rear tyre sections stayed as in 1906, but front sections typically fell to 4 inches. Tyre suppliers included Michelin in the early years, and later Continental, Dunlop and Pirelli.

Both wire wheels and so-called artillery wheels, traditional wood-spoked designs, were available. Wheels were not quickly detachable; the state of the art did not yet suggest that this was a good idea. Early designers were more concerned with ensuring that the wheels did not part company with their axles.

Tyre changes were inevitable during these long races, both voluntary and involuntary, with covers being cut by stones and failing because of overheating at the speeds of 100 mph of which these cars were capable. Tyres were changed by slashing off the old cover with knives and then levering on and inflating a fresh tyre. During 1905 this was handled by pit staff, except for failures on the circuit, but not in 1906 under the new Grand Prix rules. 'Wrestling with heavy covers in a tropical heat,' wrote Gerald Rose, 'with his eyes inflamed by the tar and dust, and with the strain of driving upon him as well, the lot of the driver in the Grand Prix was not a happy one.'

Not long before the 1906 race, however, so late that pre-race reviews didn't mention it, a solution to this problem was engineered and fitted. Several companies developed a means of detaching a steel rim, complete with tyre, from the wheel and fitting a new one. Renault, Fiat and Itala used these new rims, the French car featuring a system developed by Michelin that relied on eight bolts to wedge the rim in position. Other systems were developed by Houdet and Vinet; the latter had the Renault's rims impounded after the race to investigate possible patent infringement by Michelin.

Only those car makers whose racers were underweight could take advantage of these new wheels, because each of them added 17½ lb to the weight of the car. Although Renault practised with wire wheels, it fitted artillery wheels for the race and used the detachable rims at the rear only, since these were the tyres that took the most punishment. The new rims brought the huge advantage of requiring as little as 1¼ minutes for a tyre change instead of at least 5 minutes for the old slash-and-lever method.

The new rims helped François Szisz win the 1906 Grand Prix; he led by no less than 26 minutes after the first day, and improved this to 32 minutes over Nazzaro's Fiat by the second day's finish. But Nazzaro, with 136 bhp to the Renault's 105, also had the detachable rims. The Renault succeeded by virtue of its fine balance, good preparation and the metronomic piloting of Szisz.

Removable rims were widely adopted for the 1907 Grand Prix, in which Szisz was a close second behind Nazzaro's Fiat. In 1908 Renault (with Panhard) adopted built-in pneumatic jacks to lift the car for tyre changes. Less fortunate was its fitting of new single-bolt Michelin detachable rims. These detached themselves prematurely, putting Szisz out of the race and delaying the other Renaults.

Mercedes had taken the precaution of using steel twice the normal thickness for its single-bolt Michelin rims; these stood up much better. It also inflated its tyres to the exceptionally high pressure of 100 psi. In spite of having to change a dozen tyres, Lautenschlager won in his Mercedes. By the end of the race he and the rest of his five-car team had used up every tyre in their inventory.

In 1908 Britain's Napier was refused an entry in the Grand Prix because its car had detachable wheels; these were still considered too risky.[6] By the time Grand Prix racing resumed in 1912 the Rudge-type splined hubs were widely used, held on by a nut cinched by a special wrench. They were universal by 1913, when Peugeot introduced the final innovation that completed the design of the Grand Prix wheel for the first half of the century: an eared wheelnut that could be knocked on and off with a hammer.

BRAKES ON ALL FOURS

The thrusting Peugeot team also advanced the art of Grand Prix car braking. Throughout these years the normal braking kit employed a hand lever that applied drum brakes on the rear wheels. A foot pedal applied a drum brake that was mounted on the propeller shaft. Some of these had bands that contracted on the drum, but the general trend was towards internal-expanding shoes and finning of the drums for cooling.

Braking the propeller shaft had the merit that the brake was carried on the chassis as sprung weight, and also that its retarding force was balanced between the rear

---

6   Published on 8 January 1908, the rules for that year's Grand Prix expressly forbade the use of detachable wheels of the Rudge-Whitworth type (Rule 17). Napier whipped up anti-French spirit in the British press – no difficult task – over its exclusion but doubts have been raised ever since as to whether it really intended to enter the Grand Prix.

A 1914 Delage shows off its new front-wheel brakes, operated by a short shaft to each brake assembly according to the Perrot system. The year 1914 marked a breakthrough to four-wheel braking for Grand Prix cars. The Delage brakes were also finned to aid their cooling.

wheels by the differential gears. Some cars, like the Renault, did without a differential altogether. A frame-mounted brake could also be given total-loss water cooling, which Fiat used. The brake pedal was interlinked with a valve which opened and poured water on the brake whenever it was operated.

Opinions in these years were deeply divided over the possible merits of braking the turning front wheels. Front-wheel brakes had been introduced on some touring cars but had resulted in front-wheel skids that caused accidents. Both car buyers and makers were wary. In 1913, however, one of Peugeot's Charlatans, Georges Boillot, tried a four-wheel-braked Argyll during a visit to Brooklands and was impressed by its stopping power. This, he decided, was what Peugeot needed for the 1914 Grand Prix, to be run on a course at Lyons on which one leg had forty-five turns over just ten miles.

In 1913 Isotta Fraschini had fitted front brakes of its own to a racing car; Boillot tried one of these and recommended the last-minute fitting of the Isotta system to the new Grand Prix Peugeots that were then under construction. Brakes on all four wheels were now under foot-pedal control. *The Automobile* reported three months before the race: 'Boillot declares that he can approach turns at a much higher speed than is possible with any other kind of brakes, thus saving several seconds per lap, and that the car is under more complete control than with brakes on the rear wheels only.'

In what was becoming a pattern, Peugeot's initiative was aped by others. The French Perrot front-brake system was adopted by Delage, Fiat and Piccard-Pictet in time to equip their cars for the 1914 race. Peugeot's brakes contributed to a good performance in the Grand Prix, with Boillot holding the lead in the mid-race period but finally succumbing to the more reliable Mercedes of Lautenschlager. He was the last driver to win a Grand Prix with brakes on his rear wheels only. When Mercedes raced these same cars after the war it equipped them with front-wheel brakes.

SUSPENSIONS UNDER STRESS

These were early days for the effort to comprehend the best way to engineer the handling characteristics of a racing car. In the 1914 Grand Prix, Peugeot was plagued with handling problems that caused numerous pit stops to change tyre tread patterns and pressures to try to improve cornering stability. In fact, the source of the problem was Peugeot's adoption of a long, streamlined tail that contained two spare wheels placed longitudinally, hung out well beyond the rear wheels. This overhanging mass raised the centre of gravity of the rear of the car and degraded its handling in corners.

During this natal decade of Grand Prix racing, chassis design made only modest progress. It might have been otherwise, had an ambitious Renault design been successful. Renault brought a team of three radical machines to the start of the French elimination race for the 1905 Gordon Bennett contest. Ultra-low, they had a ground clearance of only 4½ inches thanks to the use of an underslung frame – a concept tried earlier for racing, by Britain's Wolseley, in 1902.

With its radiator placed at the firewall like the 1906 winner, the 1905 Renault had a sharply streamlined prow. Moreover, half the height of the bodywork at the front was shaped and riveted to the frame in such a way as to add to its stiffness – an early form of monocoque construction. A low-placed fuel tank at the rear helped keep the centre of gravity very low.

Although cooling problems slowed the Renaults, the reliable Szisz brought his home fifth, missing the top three 1905 Gordon Bennett qualifying spots. Observing the Renaults on the twisty Auvergne course, Léon Théry praised their stability and speed, saying that they would be ideal for a faster circuit. The 1906 Grand Prix was run on just such a course, but by then Renault had abandoned the radical 1905 design that could have advanced the art of the racing car chassis by several decades.

Renault was a firm adherent of the shaft-driven rear axle at a time when many still relied on chains to drive the rear wheels. Few controversies burned at whiter heat in the early racing years than the arguments over the merits of drive by shaft

Elegant though it was as a means of stowing spare wheels, the elongated tail of the 1914 Peugeot contributed to handling and tyre problems which were attributed to the overhung weight of these wheels and their mountings at the extreme rear of the chassis.

Low, clean-lined and with a semi-monocoque frame structure at the front, the 1905 racing Renault was a remarkably advanced vehicle for its time. Some two decades would pass before a low build was perceived to be an important advantage for Grand Prix car design.

A classic chain-driven Grand Prix car was the 1908 Benz with its 12.1-litre four-cylinder engine developing 120 hp at 1,500 rpm. The work of a team of French designers at Mannheim, the Benz was capable of a top speed of 100 mph.

versus chain for a powerful racing car. Crude though they looked, and noisy and dirty though they were, chains had three important advantages for racing:

· The rear axle was little heavier than that at the front, reducing the rear unsprung weight and thus improving rough-road traction.
· Drive ratios could be quickly changed to suit the circuit with new sets of sprockets and chains.
· All the drive torques were taken by the chassis, eliminating the live axle's tendency to lift the right wheel on acceleration.

In 1907 *l'Auto* summed up the state of play. In the 31 major races run since 1901, it found, victories went to chains 17 times and shafts 14. The 1906 Grand Prix was contested by 14 cars with chains compared to 20 with shaft drive; the proportion in 1907 was 16 chain versus 17 cardan shaft. Most tellingly, considered *l'Auto*, in the 1906 Grand Prix the finishing ratio was 57 per cent for chains and only 15 per cent for shaft drive (although that included the winner). It concluded that at high power levels, 'transmission by bevel pinions on our roads appears to us clearly inferior to that by chain'.

Panhard was among the ditherers. An early advocate of shaft drive, it reverted to chains in 1908, when the Grand Prix-winning Mercedes was chain-driven. By 1913, however, all the entries in the Grand Prix had adopted shaft-driven live rear axles. Mercedes very nearly drove its 1914 racers with chains, but rejected them after an analysis showed that shaft drive would be the lighter system overall.[7]

---

7   In search of perfection, the 1914 Mercedes axle had separate ring gears and pinions for each axle so that the rear wheels could be given a slight positive camber to suit crowned road surfaces. Each ring gear was machined in one piece with its axle shaft.

In many of the racers the need to absorb the drive and braking torques of a live rear axle was met by enclosing the propeller shaft in a stiff tube pivoted to the frame, known as a 'torque tube'. This was heavy, however. In 1902 Renault had found that it was sufficient to let the rear leaf springs take the torque reactions. This was the simple system used by Hotchkiss on its 1905 racing cars, leading to the layout being dubbed the 'Hotchkiss drive', as indeed it has been known ever since. Renault, however, used torque tubes on its racing models.

By 1907 only a few cars entered the Grand Prix without some form of damper to suppress unwanted oscillations of their road springs. All used multiple-leaf springs, within which friction between the spring leaves introduced a crude form of damping. Most cars had various forms of friction dampers which could be adjusted for stiffness. Here again, Renault was different: it was the first to use double-acting hydraulic dampers. In 1913, British Sunbeams raced with Derihon hydraulic dampers. These then disappeared until Mercedes-Benz brought back hydraulic dampers almost twenty-five years later.

Solid front axles carried by semi-elliptic springs were universal; in rare instances a transverse leaf was used. A rear-mounted steering box was connected to the steering arms by a drag link and tie rod. By the 1910s, when engines could be more strongly built, it was customary to bolt the crankcase solidly to the channel-steel frame members to add stiffness to the front of the chassis. Knowing this, we can better understand the remark of 1914 winner Christian Lautenschlager: 'at 3,500 [rpm] the vibration was pure hell'.

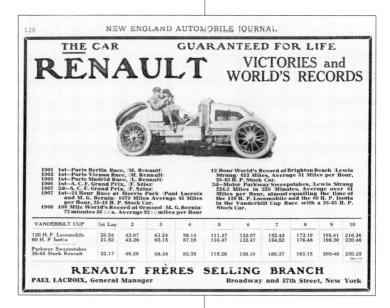

IMPRESSIVE ENGINE PROGRESS

The fact that 3,500 rpm could be reached in 1914 was pretty impressive. The Mercedes fours exceeded that on down grades, and took the punishment thanks to their counterweighted five-bearing crankshafts and the robust design of their plain bearings. Their maximum power of 106 bhp[8] from 4½ litres was reached at 3,100 rpm, the highest speed reported by any 1914 contestant. With their twin-cam valve gear, the 1914 Peugeots developed 112 bhp at just 2,800 rpm. Like the Peugeots, the Mercedes had four valves per cylinder, but these were operated by a single overhead camshaft – a system that was also put to good use in the Mercedes aero engines of those years.

Engine speeds were higher than ever with the 1914 limit of 4½ litres on engine displacement for the Grand Prix, the first time any outright capacity limit had been applied to the premier racing class. 'The average crankshaft speed in a race may be put down at 2,600 to 2,700 revolutions per minute,' W.F. Bradley informed his readers. 'Not a few motors will run at 3,000 revolutions per minute and over, and it is quite the exception to find motors to run below 2,500 revolutions per minute.'

---

8   The figure of 115 bhp is often quoted for the 1914 Grand Prix Mercedes. It did attain this power, but only after modifications were made to it for racing after the First World War.

With individual steel cylinders on an aluminium crankcase, the 1914 Mercedes Grand Prix engine was built to operate reliably at very high engine speeds for the era. It was the first engine to develop its peak power at a speed in excess of 3,000 rpm.

In terms of firing frequency and the operation of valve gear and other systems, this represented remarkable progress in only a few years. The victorious Renault in the first Grand Prix developed its peak power of 105 bhp at only 1,200 rpm. The winning Fiat of 1907 (16.3 litres) was capable of 1,600 rpm and an output of 130 bhp. In 1908 the victorious Mercedes produced 135 bhp at 1,400 rpm, and its great rival in that race, the 12.1-litre Benz, revved to 1,500 rpm to deliver 120 bhp. Thus the engines of 1914 were operating at twice the rpm of those of only six years earlier.

There is an obvious reason for this. The earlier engines, in some cases more than three times as big as those of 1914, simply could not move as fast. To put it another way, if their pistons were moving at the same speeds, the crankshafts of the smaller 1914 engine would have to spin much faster. Even so, this should not underestimate the challenge that the designers of 1913–14 were facing, following the lead of Peugeot, in order to create ignition systems and valve gear that could cope with these doubled crankshaft speeds.

The first builders of Grand Prix engines saw no compelling reason why their bores and strokes should differ greatly. Representative engines in 1907 measured as follows:

Marque	Bore (mm)	Stroke (mm)
Darracq	180	150
Panhard	185	170
Richard-Brasier	165	140
Lorraine-Dietrich	180	170
Mercedes	175	150
Fiat	180	160

Among these leading manufacturers there was unanimity that, if anything, the bore should be bigger than the stroke. The bore was, after all, the surface upon which the expanding gases pressed in order to make the wheels go round. They reckoned that this should be large rather than small.

This assumption was valid through 1906 and 1907. Introduced in the latter year was a fuel-consumption formula for the Grand Prix. Cars could consume no more than 30 litres of fuel for every 100 km travelled (equivalent to 9.6 miles/ Imperial gallon). Although this was a substantial reduction from 1906, when 40 litres/100 km was typical, *The Autocar* considered it 'a much too liberal allowance'. Controls on the fuel systems were stringent, *The Autocar* continued:

All competitors must send eight days before the date of the race a model of the tank they propose to use upon their car, and the piping leading the spirit from the tank to the carburettor. Makers are strongly recommended to use simple and easily verifiable forms of tanks. All the unions and connections must be of a special type, of which a pattern will be furnished to the competitors by the Sporting Committee.

Only one first-rank competitor fell foul of the fuel limitation: Vincenzo Lancia, driving a Fiat, was third on the final lap, but pulled up with a dry tank. Felice Nazzaro's Fiat was the winner, followed by the Renault of Szisz, less than seven minutes behind after almost seven hours of racing over 478 miles at Dieppe. At the flag Szisz still had 6.8 gallons in his tank against the 2.4 of Nazzaro; one observer remarked that Szisz would have won had the race been twenty miles longer. Rigal was awarded a gold medal for finishing with the most fuel – 9.3 gallons – in the tank of his Darracq.

The car that upset the French industry's applecart, the Italian Fiat, was powered by an engine of unusual and ingenious design. The chamber at the top of each of its cylinders was shaped like a hemisphere. This provided a clean and compact combustion-chamber shape that would allow rapid burning of the fuel/air mixture, combined with the minimum loss of productive heat to the cooling water.

Set into the Fiat's hemispherical chamber were two valves, both inclined from the vertical at 30°, hence being symmetrically disposed at an included angle of 60°. Above the tips of their stems was a pivoted rocker arm that opened first one valve, then the other, at the command of a rod at the side that both pushed and pulled the rocker. When the rod was pulled down by a coil spring it opened the inlet valve, and when it was pushed up by the cam it opened the exhaust valve. A transverse-leaf spring acted on both valves to close them.

This system was good enough at a time when engineers did not see a need to open the inlet valve before the piston passed top dead centre on its suction or intake stroke. In fact, the idea of an advanced inlet opening, or of overlap between the inlet and exhaust valves at top dead centre, did not take hold at all during this first decade of Grand Prix racing.

Responding to a general impression that engine sizes were becoming excessive, the ACF took a new tack with its regulations for the 1908 race – fortuitously promulgated before the full impact of the 1907–08 recession was felt. Piston area was limited to 117 square inches, which meant a bore of 155 mm for a four-cylinder engine and 127 mm for a six. Instead of a maximum weight, a minimum weight of 1,150 kg (2,536 lb) was now imposed.

Strokes naturally became longer to gain more displacement when a bore limit was imposed – but not excessively so. A popular stroke for four-cylinder engines was 170 mm, which produced a 12.8-litre capacity. This was bracketed by the winning Mercedes (180 mm, 13.5 litres) and the second-place Benz (160 mm, 12.1 litres). Later Benz would lengthen the stroke of its engine to 200 mm and increase its bore

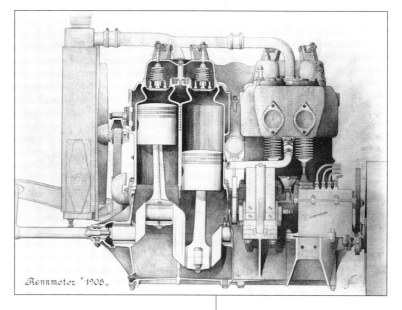

Rennmotor "1908.

A section drawing of the 1908 Mercedes Grand Prix engine revealed its pushrod-operated overhead inlet valves, the heads and seats of which were of annular design. The exhaust valves were side-mounted in what was later known as an 'F-head' configuration.

Pushrod-operated overhead valves were used in the Benz racing engine of 1908. As seen here, the big Benz was enlarged to 21½ litres to develop 200 hp as power for a Benz that was capable of breaking the world land speed record at speeds in excess of 140 mph.

to 185 mm to create the famous 200 hp 'Blitzen Benz' of 21.5 litres that was capable of more than 140 mph in 1911 – the world's fastest vehicle of any kind.

VOITURETTES SHOW THE WAY

This, then, was the state of the engine art when Grand Prix racing was ended by the manufacturers' pact after the 1908 event. Quietly, however, in the subsequent hiatus both the major and minor car makers carried on competing in the Voiturette races organised by the magazine *l'Auto*. Like the 1908 Grand Prix rules, these events placed limits on the cylinder bore diameter, limits that spawned some long-stroke engines so tall that the drivers had to look around rather than over them.

By 1911 most competitors for the Coupe de l'Auto had settled on four-cylinder engines with displacements of around 3 litres. But they configured them in wild and wonderful ways. 'The 1911 l'Auto Cup drew 43 entries,' wrote historian Griff Borgeson, 'made up of 17 marques from seven countries. It was a feast of novel mechanical ideas.' Included were entries from Peugeot, for whom Les Charlatans were already building a big 7.6-litre car to compete in the 1911 Grand Prix – although that car was not ready to race until 1912.

The ferment of engine design ideas shown by the Voiturettes included a Grégoire with four overhead valves per cylinder operated by a single overhead camshaft, and an Alcyon with four overhead valves worked by pushrods and rockers. In building four-cylinder engines, these and other makes were following the lead set by Hispano-Suiza with its winning 1910 Coupe de l'Auto entry, driven to victory by Paolo Zuccarelli – the very engineer-driver who was now one of Peugeot's renegade Charlatans.

American driver David Bruce-Brown stands to the fore next to the big 14.1-litre Tipo S.61 Fiat, with which he led after the first day of racing in the 1912 French Grand Prix at Dieppe. Although he finished third on the road after repairing a fuel line, he was disqualified for taking on fuel away from the pits.

Four valves per cylinder were not, as such, a novel idea. Many early engines had what was known as a 'T-head' valve arrangement, after the end-on view of the cylinder and its valves. Each side of the engine carried a camshaft which opened valves at the sides of the cylinder. One side had the inlet valves and the other the exhausts, each opening onto a chamber set at the sides of the piston, forming a T-shape.

Against the T-head was its meandering combustion chamber. In its favour was the ample space available for the valves and ports at each side. Some makers, such as Napier for its Hutton racing cars of 1908, took advantage of this by fitting two valves at each side, for which there was ample room. This significantly improved the T-head engine's breathing ability.

Nor were overhead-cam-operated quadruple valves a new idea in racing engines. The 1908 S61 Fiat had them, with a single camshaft running the length of the big four-cylinder engine's head. Instead of being paired along each side of the engine, however, the valves were paired laterally, so that one cam lobe could press down on a transverse bar and open two inlet valves, for example. Although this engendered some inelegant porting, it worked well enough to power the Tipo 14 racing Fiat that won the American Grand Prize[9] in 1911 and very nearly won the 1912 French Grand Prix.

All these influences were combined by Les Charlatans to create the large and small Peugeot racers of 1911–12, the first cars to have twin overhead camshafts operating four valves per cylinder. These raced in both 7.6-litre form (winning the Grand Prix) and in 3-litre form (less successfully) in 1912, with a vertical shaft at the front of the engine driving the overhead cams. Both were converted to gear drive to the camshafts for the 1913 season, when with 5,655 cc (100 × 180 mm), Georges Boillot drove a Peugeot to victory in the Grand Prix de l'ACF for the second year in succession. Thus was completed the establishment of the configuration of the classic automobile racing engine.

For the 1913 race the ACF brought back the idea of a fuel consumption limit, setting an allocation of fuel of 40.3 Imperial gallons for a 570-mile race – 20 litres/100 km or 14.1 miles/Imperial gallon. Immense trouble was taken over the inspection of the fuel lines and the tanks, which were all built to a standard cylindrical design that included two baffles to keep the fuel from sloshing laterally on turns. The day before the race, the tanks were filled precisely with the complete fuel allocation[10] and the cars locked up for the night. The Peugeots that placed first and second averaged an excellent 16-plus miles per gallon at an average speed for the winner of 72.1 mph.

---

9   Noting that most nations express 'Grand Prix' in their own languages when titling their races ('Grosser Preis von Deutschland', for example), and that America did it in the early days as well, the author campaigned for a return to the title 'Grand Prize' for the American event in the early sixties when he was editor of *Car and Driver*. This was one of his less influential initiatives.

10   Officially 183.3 litres.

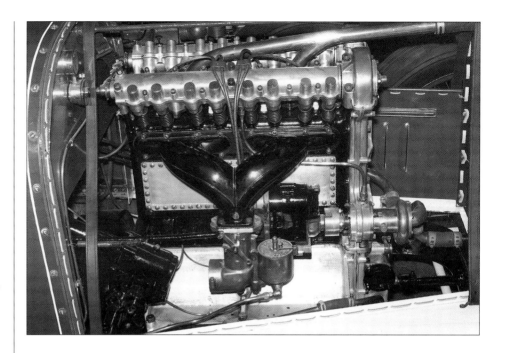

As embodied by a 1913 model, which used gears rather than a shaft to drive its twin overhead camshafts, Peugeot demonstrated beyond question the power potential of a cylinder head using vee-inclined overhead valves. All but a handful of subsequent Grand Prix engines of the twentieth century owed something to this pioneering design.

A maximum weight of 1,100 kg applied in 1913 as well. Most cars coped easily with this, but the Italas were found to be some 80 kg overweight. 'This incident provided quite a lot of excitement,' *The Autocar* reported:

> Out came all the water and all the oil, all the grease from the gear box, and every fitting that could be done without. Another trial showed them still too heavy, but by a very little, so then the grease was washed out from the universal joints, the dirt cleaned from off the tyres, and in one case the handle for screwing down on the spare wheels was shorn of its arms. Then another trial on the scales disclosed the exact weight: not an ounce either over or under.

EXPERIMENTATION WITH VALVE SYSTEMS

Itala was unusual among the entrants in having rotary valves. A single rotary valve driven at one-quarter engine speed by a vertical shaft sufficed to feed and exhaust a pair of cylinders; its engine had two such cylinder pairs.

In 1913 great pains were taken over carburettors, in some cases with water-jacketed manifolds, to get the best fuel consumption. Most had French Claudel carburettors, M. Claudel then being regarded as 'the high priest of carburetion'. Sunbeams from Britain fitted roller blinds to their radiators so their drivers could keep the engines running as warm as possible to reduce consumption. One of the Sunbeams placed a respectable third, a harbinger of the company's postwar successes.

For the 1914 Grand Prix, Itala was not present but unconventional valves were represented by Piccard-Pictet from Switzerland. Its entries had sleeve-valve engines, using a sleeve between the piston and cylinder to control the port timing.[11] Sleeve valves would reappear in the twenties (Voisin) but would never manifest an advantage for racing.

---

11 Each sleeve both reciprocated and rotated in accord with Argyll patents.

Otherwise the 1914 Grand Prix entries reflected an almost universal adoption of the four-overhead-valve cylinder head. This was used by 9 of the 13 makes entered. Peugeot's lead in providing two overhead cams as well was followed by Nagant, Sunbeam, Vauxhall and Delage. Single overhead cams were used by Opel, Mercedes, Fiat, Alda and Th. Schneider.

Among these, two makers had taken a bold step forward: they had eliminated the springs that were used to close the valves. These were, after all, still the formative years of the automobile and its technology. Only thirteen years earlier Wilhelm Maybach had transformed the auto engine by providing a camshaft to open the inlet valves. Until then, inlet valves had simply been sucked open against spring pressure by the vacuum created by the descending piston. Maybach's 1901 Mercedes was the first to put the inlet valves under positive control.

The next step seemed logical enough to the engineers who designed the cars entered in the 1914 Grand Prix by Delage (Arthur-Léon Michelat) and by

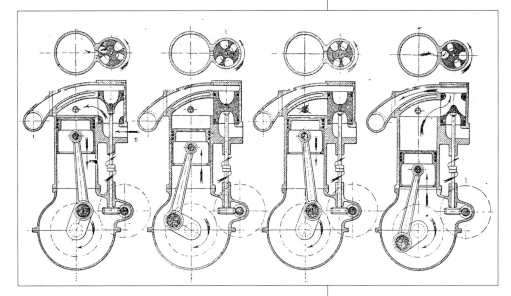

This section drawing shows the ingenious functioning of the single vertical rotary valve that served a pair of cylinders in the Itala which competed in the 1913 French Grand Prix. From left to right, the engine phases seen here are induction, compression, ignition and exhaust.

Louis Delage had every reason to express great confidence in the potential of his 1914 Grand Prix car, with its four-wheel brakes and desmodromic valve operation. However, none of his three team Delages figured significantly in the French Grand Prix of that year.

INTRODUCING DESMODROMY

One of the most dramatic technical innovations near the end of this decade was the introduction of positively closed valves by Delage and Th. Schneider for their 1914 Grand Prix cars. At its inception this was called 'desmodromic' valve gear, after a classical Greek expression which means 'I run in a halter or leash' – fully under control, in other words – for such a system positively controls the actions of the valves at all times.

This idea was 'in the air' at the time. The case for springless valves was put by *The Automobile* of 22 April 1915:

> However carefully valve springs are made, they never have a very long life, as can readily be perceived when it is remembered that the set of valve springs absorb and give about 4 horsepower on a 130-horsepower Grand Prix motor. With the finest possible steel valve springs which have to withstand 2,000 vibrations a minute cannot possibly have a long, useful life. Sooner or later, the metal shows signs of fatigue, and in consequence the timing is modified and the valve no longer closes correctly. On this account it has been sought to abolish the valve springs in motors capable of 4,000 rpm and, by means of a light spring having but three-tenth millimetres stroke, ensure the closing of the valve and its gas-tightness.

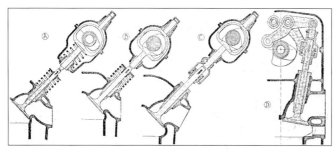

These drawings give a schematic indication of the manner in which positive valve closing was achieved in the 1914 Delage Grand Prix engine. Drawing C gives the closest approximation of the final design, although it does not show the bridge piece that allowed each cam unit to close two valves. Drawing D shows the desmodromic system designed by Michaux for the 1914 Th. Schneider four-cylinder engine.

The camshaft serving four of the inlet valves of a 1954 Mercedes-Benz Grand Prix engine shows two cam lobes for each valve – a conventional lobe to open the valve and a D-shaped lobe for closing it. The inventors of this system were unaware of its many French and Italian precedents.

Designers had been cogitating over the best way to eliminate the springs since engine speeds began to rise under pressure from the advancements made by Peugeot. Attention had already been given to various methods of mechanically withdrawing the tappet or cam follower to relieve the spring of the task of returning it. The precise design of the 1912 Peugeot valve gear is unclear but it is likely that in at least an experimental version it had this feature. Now all that remained was to connect the follower to the valve stem and pull the valve shut as well.

The engine designed for the 1914 Grand Prix by Arthur-Léon Michelat for Louis Delage followed Peugeot practice with its four valves per cylinder operated by twin overhead camshafts. Above each pair of valves, however, he placed only a single opening cam lobe. It opened the valves by pressing on a steel shoe at the bottom of a stirrup which fully encircled the cam. At the top of the stirrup were two rollers which were contacted by two closing cam lobes athwart the opening lobe. Thus the stirrup's movement was fully controlled between the two sets of cam lobes.

Integral with the bottom of the stirrup was a shaft which extended down to an H-shaped bridge piece through which the two valve stems protruded. Adjusting screws in the top arm of the 'H' set the point at which the valves would be opened. Screw adjustments at the top of the valves themselves set the closing clearance. Short, stiff springs between the stems and the bottom arms of the 'H' bridge assured a good seal when the valves were closed.

This ingenious system allowed Michelat to use more severe valve accelerations than were then normal, to improve cylinder filling. Made to very fine tolerances, its cam lobes were keyed to the camshaft to allow the valve gear to be assembled. The engines worked reliably enough, as the subsequent racing careers of the Delages in America demonstrated. Barney Oldfield placed fifth in one in the 1916 Indianapolis 300-mile race.

Former Peugeot engineer Gratien Michaux was credited with the elegant design of the 1914 Th. Schneider Grand Prix engine, with its desmodromic operation of two valves for each cylinder. Inclined at an included angle of only 20° above a cylinder of 94 mm bore, both valves had a 60 mm head diameter – very large indeed – and robust stem diameters. Fully enclosed by a rocker cover was a single gear-driven overhead camshaft, running in ball bearings like those of the Delage.

Michaux neatly controlled each valve by a single rocker arm that was attached by a pair of pivoting links to the top of the valve stem. One link pushed the valve open, while the other closed it through the medium of a sleeve around the stem that housed a small clearance-reducing spring. Roller tips on the rocker rode on the two side-by-side cam lobes: one for opening and the other for closing the valve. Th. Schneider reported that one of the small springs had broken during the Grand Prix without degrading the valve gear's performance.[1]

Of the other contenders for Grand Prix glory, Fiat came closest to introducing a desmodromic engine before the First World War. In 1914 it prepared a layout of a four-

The Mercedes-Benz desmodromic system was closely inspected by the designers of the Reventlow Scarab Formula 1 engine. To shape its final components they made oversized patterns for the cam lobes and a single-cylinder test rig.

cylinder racing engine with two valves per cylinder operated by a valve gear conceived by Giustino Cattaneo. He operated each valve by a pivoted lever which carried a roller near the valve stem. A camshaft above the roller opened the valve, and another camshaft below the roller pushed it closed. There is no indication that this engine was ever completed.

After the war attention turned to rotary disc-type cams as a means of positively operating valves. In France, Bignan built a sports-car engine with such a system. Fiat patented a comparable (but quite different) valve gear in 1919, and indeed laid it out in detail for its Type 801 racing car of 1921. Although this 3-litre four-cylinder racing car had been built to compete in the 1921 French Grand Prix it failed to come to the starting line. French firm Rolland-Pilain experimented with positive valve closing in its 1922 Grand Prix cars.

Thereafter, desmodromics faded as an art of the racing car, although some production-car applications were essayed. Engineers had not yet fully mastered the technology of materials and their application that was needed to make the concept work. Meanwhile, valve-spring steels improved enough to make positive valve closing a luxury rather than a necessity.

The idea was successfully reinvented by Mercedes-Benz for its 1954–55 Grand Prix cars. Mercedes mastered the dynamics of the system and found an ingenious way to ensure its precise adjustment. Others, among them BMW, Porsche, Maserati, OSCA and BMW, tested desmodromic valve gear but never competed with it.

The American Scarab Grand Prix car raced briefly and unsuccessfully with desmodromic valve gear in 1960. Cosworth in the eighties and Ferrari in the nineties also tried but rejected desmodromic valve control. Only Ducati with its famous 'Desmo' motorcycles has kept faith with the principle of positively closed valves. First used for racing by Ducati in 1956, desmodromic valve closing has since become a hallmark of the company's road as well as racing motorcycles.

---

1   Mercedes-Benz had the same experience when it began testing its first desmodromic systems, which also had a small spring to effect final closing. Thus emboldened, Mercedes eliminated the springs from its final 1954 designs. This had the small disadvantage that the Mercedes engines had no compression when they were at rest, as Stirling Moss and Denis Jenkinson discovered during a recce of the Mille Miglia in 1955, when they parked their 300SLR 'in gear', only to see it start rolling away. They didn't make that mistake twice.

Th. Schneider (Louis Ravel and Antoine Jaubert).[12] This was to eliminate the springs that were used to close the valves, instead placing the complete cycle of opening and closing under positive control. The French firms that originated this technology called it *commande desmodromique de soupapes*; it became known in English as 'desmodromic' valve gear.

Desmodromy was only one of the innovative forms of valve gear that were being experimented with in these early years of auto engineering. We have already seen Itala's rotary valves and the use of sleeve valves, which were also fitted to production engines by Mercedes and Th. Schneider, among many others. Using positive valve closing seemed to point the way to higher engine speeds with reliability at a time when valve-spring steels were still variable in quality.

The principle failed to prove itself in the 1914 Grand Prix. The Th. Schneiders were never in the hunt, two retiring early and one placing ninth. The Delages were hugely fancied, not least by Louis Delage himself, who very precisely accorded his team a 48 per cent chance of winning. They had been quick in practice, but before the race they were retuned to eliminate a backfiring problem.[13] The tweaks seemed to rob all the Delages of their pace except for Arthur Duray's car. He held third in the early laps, but finally slipped to eighth ahead of the Th. Schneider.

In these years designers also began experimenting with new ways of supporting the crankshaft, again to cope with rising engine speeds. For its traditional plain-bearing crankshaft Fiat introduced dry-sump lubrication in

Under the bonnet of the 1914 Delage was this four-cylinder engine with its twin camshafts and positively closed valves. Although seen here with a single updraft carburettor, the Delages actually raced in 1914 with twin dual-throat Claudel carburettors.

---

12 Laurence Pomeroy Jr, whose writings on Grand Prix cars command immense respect, identified the Belgian firm Nagant as the 1914 entrant which joined Delage in offering positively closed valves. This is supported neither by contemporary sources nor by an authoritative history of the Th. Schneider automobile. In fact, in photos of the twin-cam Nagant engines their valve springs are exposed to the view of all and sundry.

13 The nature of the changes made has never been made clear. Another 'speed secret' of the Delages was their use of two twin-throat Claudel carburettors, one throat to each cylinder – the first time this advanced technique had ever been used. Novel as they were, these carburettors may have given trouble. Delage would have protected his valuable relationship with M. Claudel by blaming – as he did – the magnetos instead.

The 4.5-litre Mercedes of Otto Salzer (left) and André Pilette await the start of the 1914 French Grand Prix. A sister car driven by Christian Lautenschlager was the winner of this event, judged to be one of the greatest Grand Prix races ever held.

1914.[14] This used two pressure pumps, one to extract oil from the sump and the other to deliver it to the crankshaft and connecting-rod bearings. Introducing as it did a separate reservoir in which the oil could cool and in which a large supply could be carried, dry-sump oiling would become the future norm for Grand Prix cars. It also allowed engines to be built lower to the road.

The other new technique introduced in these final years of the first decade was the use of so-called 'anti-friction' bearings for the crankshaft. This term refers to roller or ball bearings, usually the latter in the early years of the industry. Ettore Bugatti (about whom we will hear more in Chapter Three) began using them in 1910 and Delage adopted them in 1911. The 1914 Grand Prix Delage not only carried its crankshaft in five large-diameter ball bearings, but also used ball bearings to support its twin camshafts.[15] In 1913 Peugeot too began using anti-friction bearings for its crankshafts. This would become common practice in the twenties.

DENOUEMENT

The 1914 Grand Prix de l'ACF took place on Saturday 4 July. On the following Monday the tennis finals were played at Wimbledon; Norman Brookes was the men's winner and Dorothea Chambers the women's. Late in the morning of the preceding Sunday, 28 June, in the capital of Bosnia, Sarajevo, an assassin shot and fatally wounded the heir to the throne of Austro-Hungary and his wife. Seizing this as an opportunity to enhance its prestige in the Balkans by subduing Serbia, which was thought complicit in the assassination, Austria declared war on the Serbs a month later. By August the tumult of armed conflict engulfed Europe.

Racing continued for two years in America. In 1915 the Indianapolis 500-mile race was won by one of the 1914 Mercedes Grand Prix cars. In 1916, when the race was curtailed to 300 miles, the cars that placed first and third were 1914 Grand Prix Peugeots – cars that represented the state of the art of the first decade of Grand Prix racing. When racing resumed in America and Europe after the First World War, their influence would be obvious.

---

14 The sump is not literally 'dry', but instead of carrying all the oil the engine needs, the sump or oil pan only carries the oil that is thrown off by the crank and valve gear before it is sucked away by the 'scavenge' pump.

15 In the next decade Delage would outdo all rivals in its mass consumption of ball bearings.

GERMANY'S VICTORY IN GRAND PRIX OF FRANCE

Mercedes Redivivus, then Benz and Benz Again, with Clement Fourth Followed by More Germans—Italy Fails to Figure Dangerously

By A. G. BATCHELDER

DIEPPE, July 7.—France to-night isn't exactly sure that automobile racing pays. "Made in Germany" it a label that does not find extraordinary favor in the land of the fleur de lis. To have had one Lautenschlager the winner of the Grand Prix were sorrowful enough, but to have had his Mercedes chased by two Benz racers and the nearest French contender a fourth, added to gloom still further intensified by the subsequent arrival of three more Germans. Think of it! Six cars out of the first ten bearing the hated label and that tenth one from Belgium! No wonder that the departures from the grandstand began before the elated Lautenschlager had completed his tenth round. Yes, he received some cheers—there were a goodly number of Germans present—but the enthusiasm of the multitude evoked that same quality of joy which may be expected when the home team loses out in the ninth inning and there is no consolation.

Mercedes presumably had been placed on the shelf by the French makers, and as for Benz, that car had been heard of in the early days of automobiling. Opel was a name unknown. And to have these intruders survive the ordeal in superb manner, and only a single French car intermingle with them, was cause for lamentations prolonged and undisguised. Last year it wasn't quite so bad to have Nazzaro of Italy win with French runners close up, though that blow gave the racing advocates a jolt that benumbed them for the whole year intervening.

The Gordon Bennett, with all countries participating having five cars each, didn't give France as much chance for victory as she thought her automobile importance entitled her to, and so that event had to give way to the Grand Prix, wherein every maker can have three cars each. For like reason the Vanderbilt, being similar to the Bennett, received the kibosh from the French club and its European satellites.

But this Grand Prix is not working out as satisfactorily as anticipated—France with a preponderance of the entry list has met defeat twice in three years, and the one to-day is a crusher. Automobile sport is most uncertain—and, alas! it is grounded in commercialism. No longer do the multi-millionaires pay the bills and drive the cars. Now 'tis the maker who pays the freight—with rare exceptions—and the expenses are heavy when three entries become advisable, once the plunge is made. France is the only European country which now conducts a real big race, and to hold it with the inevitable risk of losing prestige is chilling the ardor even of those who think racing a good advertisement for the industry.

But there is also sorrow of a different sort to-night, and the

Lautenschlager, the Mercedes Winner.

startling death of Cissac and his mechanician has called attention to the great risks now associated with high speed contests. Tires can only stand so much, and the Dieppe circuit has been unusually severe this time on the wind-shod shoes of the hard-driven autos. Stretches of road there were which hacked tires as though the rubber was pulp, and it became the usual thing to have car after car limp to the replenishment depots in front of the grandstands and take on fresh supplies of pneumatics.

As was demonstrated in the practice work, the limiting of the piston area so that a four-cylinder had 155 mm. and a six-cylinder 127 mm. per cylinder did not prevent an increase in the speed. Last year fuel consumption—30 liters for 100 kilometers—was the basis of limitation. Nazzaro then accomplished an average of 70.61 miles per hour for the entire run.

For a single round to-day Salzer on a Mercedes averaged 78.5 miles, and if tire troubles had not multiplied, the winner's average of 69.5 for the entire distance would have been miles ahead of a year ago. Another factor which interfered with the speed was the inadequate tarring of the first day did not improve places reeked with dust that penetrated the goggles of the drivers and made them suffer intensely and use no small amount of caution. The voiturettes race of the first day did not improve the course, which, however, did not impress me any too favorably during a Sunday journey over it. Excellent stretches there were, but one also encountered rough spots and more dust than I have ever seen on any Vanderbilt course. It is only fair to say that thousands of autos visited the triangle on the days preceding the races and unquestionably were greatly responsible for its disappointing condition.

But there is a widespread feeling to-night evident that high speed racing has reached its climax. France can hardly quit now with two successive defeats chalked up against her, and this means that there must be a 1909 race at least. After that—well, one can't state positively. Charles Jarrott even ventures to say that it is now ended, but the English have not been keen on the road racing proposition since the Gordon Bennett in Ireland. Marquis De Dion asks: "What's the use of it? It does not prove anything except that it is easy to endanger life." The Marquis, however, has been opposed to racing for some time, though it is to be noted that he no longer stands practically alone in his attitude among the French builders of prominence.

There were 48 starters, 23 of them being French, and 25 supplied by other nations. There were 23 finishers, only 10 of which were furnished by the home country. Germany put in 9 cars and finished with 7. Italy had 6 starters and 2 finishers; Belgium had 3 starters, 2 finishers; England had 6 starters, 2 finishers.

America sought experience and did not hope a single instant for victory. The Thomas entry was known to be nothing more or less than a partially remodeled stock car, of less power than any other racer engaged, and participating for the purpose of gaining experience for future use and incidentally to demonstrate reliability. Harry Houpt had a hard task cut out for him from the moment he landed in Dieppe and took charge of the Thomas interests. He labored indefatigably to overcome hurried preparation and the usual handicaps following in the train of doing things in a country where the American way is at times impossible and impracticable. And the Thomas started in its turn, persistently pursued its progress for four rounds, after suffering from tire difficulties in profusion. Then a leaky gasoline tank on the fifth round brought Strang's ride to its conclusion. Many others had fallen by the wayside in the meantime—some of them possessing international reputations.

One cannot resist asking, however, as to whether it is worth while for the American maker to seek international racing glory in Europe. There will be no market of much account for American cars in Europe for years to come—if ever—and unless an American can "cash in" a European victory, what is the good of seeking a useless asset. Furthermore, the work of preparation must be thorough and planned not less than a year in advance.

And it might be said right here that several European makers who have been much in evidence heretofore in American racing are doing some careful calculation as to whether it is worth while. Since they race their cars for advertising purposes, they are inclined to compete in the most important event, which, of course, means the Vanderbilt cup. If through some hocus-pocus or other, this is impossible, they are not charmed with the idea of going any distance from New York City, even to accommodate a club which has been over friendly to foreign makers generally and only as recently as last winter had the French ambassador as the guest of honor at its annual dinner. But the present administration of the Automobile Club of America prizes highly its "foreign relations," to "protect" which Dave Hennen Morris, formerly president—and a good one, too—came over for the Grand Prix and a session of the "Recognized Clubs," in the running of which figures dictatorially Rene de Knyff, managing director of a French automobile company and chairman of the racing board of the French club. Of course, the "Clubs" will stick by the A. C. A. through thick and thin, and thereby hangs a tale which will be set forth in these columns in due course of time. Self-preservation is said to be the first law of Nature—and also of "national" automobile clubs. But 'tis good guessing that until America has a real voice and vote in the international proposition, there will be no acceptance by American makers of international racing conditions. If the foreign makers do not fancy our rules, then they can stay away—or compete in a special event arranged for them by their particular friend, the automobile club of "foreign relations" fame. But, alas! Now they are not sure at all that it is remunerative to race cars in America, for the American market is not what it once was for foreign cars.

W. K. Vanderbilt, Jr., was among those who saw the race, and incidentally he made clear to those who cared to know that it is the A. A. A. and not the A. C. A. which promotes the Vanderbilt Cup race and controls racing in America. Robert Graves, who has a Mercedes entry in the Vanderbilt and may have an American candidate also, was another in evidence who made known the American situation, which only now is being understood for the first time. John S. Worden, who drove in the 1905 Vanderbilt, was to be seen. He now lives at Nice. James Butler, owner of the Empire City track, enjoyed the sport immensely, and regretted that the "stars and stripes" didn't have more speed. Cortlandt Field Bishop, president of the Aero Club of America; J. C. McCoy, also of aeronautical fame; J. Harvey Lanning, of the Wilkes-Barre Automobile Club; Hart O. Berg, now foreign manager of the Wright brothers; and A. E. Lumsden, London manager of the B. F. Goodrich Company, were among the American contingent in Dieppe which witnessed the race.

A COMPLETE TABLE SHOWING THE TIMES MADE BY EACH CAR THROUGHOUT THE CONTEST.

No.	Car	Driver	1st Round	2nd Round	3rd Round	4th Round	5th Round	6th Round	7th Round	8th Round	9th Round	10th Round
1	AUSTIN	Brabazon	44:48	1:31:00	2:17:00	3:04:08	3:55:32	5:00:54	5:53:47	6:54:05	7:48:27	8:46:50
2	MERCEDES	Pæge	38:25	1:28:38	2:11:47	2:56:30	3:47:20	4:30:36	5:13:59	5:59:24	6:45:49	7:23:32
3	MOTOBLOC	Courtade	43:19	1:31:26	2:13:32	Abandoned.						
4	RENAULT	Szisz	37:06	1:22:05	Damaged rim.							
5	LORRAINE-DIETRICH	Duray	38:58	1:08:00	Clutch seized.							
6	BENZ	Hemery	37:55	1:19:02	1:58:22	2:39:58	3:24:49	4:10:42	4:50:26	5:34:42	6:19:58	7:04:24
7	F. I. A. T	Lancia	38:58	Broke water-pump shaft.								
8	BRASIER	Thery	37:06	1:17:17	2:04:21	2:47:46	3:33:35	4:15:15	4:59:19	5:44:58	6:40:46	Abandoned.
9	PORTHOS	Stricker	46:15	1:31:02	2:27:12	3:18:27	4:13:13	5:16:45	6:04:07	7:00:47	8:05:32	Abandoned.
10	OPEL	Fritz Opel	44:59	1:28:40	2:27:03	3:16:41	4:09:50	5:00:12	6:39:00	7:06:01	8:11:05	9:08:11
11	BAYARD-CLEMENT	Rigal	43:46	1:33:05	2:18:15	3:01:22	3:46:05	4:30:17	5:20:03	5:57:31	6:44:40	7:30:36
12	ITALA	Cagno	39:26	2:00:48	2:46:05	3:31:00	4:18:37	5:52:07	5:49:32	6:37:29	7:18:26	8:07:56
13	WEIGEL	Laxen	48:36	1:44:05	2:23:54	3:19:04	4:04:40	Overturned.				
14	MORS	Jenatzy	41:31	1:27:05	2:20:31	3:08:21	4:02:12	4:53:23	5:50:55	6:47:10	7:36:30	8:24:44
15	THOMAS	Roberts	53:44	1:57:30	2:54:17	3:52:18	Punctured gasoline tank.					
16	PANHARD	Heath	41:37	1:22:50	2:05:18	2:45:12	3:36:22	4:28:26	5:13:22	5:56:12	7:03:43	7:53:36
17	GERMAIN	Degrais	53:39	1:44:55	2:38:03	3:29:52	4:20:56	5:23:12	6:22:40	7:25:40	8:24:42	9:13:34
18	AUSTIN	Wright	47:34	1:37:41	2:27:22	3:11:55	4:06:10	5:00:19	6:07:15	6:58:46	7:45:40	8:42:50
19	MERCEDES	Salzer	36:31	1:36:05	Abandoned.							
20	MOTOBLOC	Pierron	41:28	1:26:18	2:12:27	3:00:05	3:59:55	4:53:26	5:41:02	6:23:14	7:09:49	8:19:56
21	RENAULT	Caillois	39:20	1:27:19	2:10:44	2:59:58	3:47:25	5:13:48	5:59:04	6:49:04	7:32:40	8:19:56
22	LORRAINE-DIETRICH	Rougier	39:37	Magneto trouble.								
23	BENZ	Hanriot	38:43	1:18:56	2:03:51	2:44:34	3:26:43	4:11:15	4:53:40	5:38:16	6:20:50	7:05:13
24	F. I. A. T	Nazzaro	37:48	1:15:51	1:59:15	Broke crankshaft.						
25	BRASIER	Baras	37:44	1:24:06	4:00:51	Cams worked loose on shaft.						
26	PORTHOS	Gaubert	Did not complete first round.		Smashed wheel on turn.							
27	OPEL	Jorns	41:14	1:24:11	2:09:28	2:52:47	3:35:25	4:23:42	5:05:31	6:00:44	6:46:41	7:39:10
28	BAYARD-CLEMENT	Gabriel	38:48	1:50:05	2:48:32	3:29:10	4:20:36	5:02:59	5:55:19	6:37:10	7:27:25	8:11:44
29	ITALA	Fournier	38:55	1:22:32	2:44:17	3:54:31	4:38:25	5:25:50	6:09:00	7:11:25	7:58:20	8:47:20
30	WEIGEL	Harrisson	53:03	1:50:24	2:38:53	Overturned.						
31	MORS	Robin	40:13	1:30:37	2:28:01	3:18:34	4:13:30	5:04:00	6:10:12	6:55:42	7:51:55	8:39:20
32	PANHARD	Farman	46:10	1:30:52	2:19:28	3:13:15	5:59:22	4:43:33	5:35:22	6:42:44	7:53:15	9:24:40
33	GERMAIN	Roch-Brault	44:50	1:29:30	2:22:00	3:07:23	Abandoned.					
34	AUSTIN	Moore-Brabazon	43:35	1:27:47	2:14:47	3:00:38	Engine seized.					
35	MERCEDES	Lautenschlæger	38:29	1:16:55	3:21:56	2:41:36	3:21:56	4:06:34	4:49:35	5:30:53	6:09:35	6:55:43
36	MOTOBLOC	Garcet	42:30	1:29:42	2:12:22	3:13:08	3:54:49	4:41:20	5:31:31	6:26:13	7:24:31	8:12:43
37	RENAULT	Dimitri	44:31	1:27:00	2:33:03	3:15:38	3:57:39	4:50:22	5:33:10	6:17:27	7:05:42	7:54:12
38	LORRAINE-DIETRICH	Minoia	39:59	1:18:48	4:11:42	Abandoned.						
39	BENZ	Erle	45:35	1:27:59	2:10:10	2:59:05	3:45:51	4:32:01	5:19:17	6:10:09	6:55:48	7:43:21
40	F. I. A. T	Wagner	37:13	1:17:38	1:56:25	Abandoned.						
41	BRASIER	Bablot	36:40	1:21:19	2:07:35	2:49:48	3:59:48	4:54:18	5:38:24	6:24:26	7:11:17	Abandoned.
42	PORTHOS	J. Simon	43:31	1:33:43	Overturned.							
43	OPEL	Michel	46:51	1:33:43	2:22:45	3:07:17	4:00:48	4:56:57	4:45:00	6:52:04	8:29:18	Abandoned.
44	BAYARD-CLEMENT	Hautvast	42:05	1:29:03	2:09:42	2:51:33	4:48:51	Abandoned.				
45	ITALA	Piacenza	1:51:23	Abandoned.								
46	WEIGEL	Shannon	49:55	Broke a wheel.								
48	PANHARD	Cissac	39:37	1:22:51	2:09:46	2:50:34	3:39:11	4:22:37	5:07:18	5:57:07	Abandoned.	
49	GERMAIN	Perpère	46:44	1:33:39	2:21:02	3:07:26	3:58:36	4:49:05	5:36:25	6:23:06	7:13:35	7:59:07

Jenatzy, Now a Mors Pilot, Replenishing.

Hemery and His German Benz Obtain Lead.

On the completion of the fourth round Hemery, the French driver of the German Benz, was in first position, with a lead of two minutes on Lautenschlager, the Mercedes conductor. Hanriot, also on a Benz, was third, with Thery running a very close fourth. Heath, who was driving his Panhard with remarkable dash, was in fifth place, Bablot on the Brasier in sixth, Cissac's Panhard seventh, and Hautvast, Clement, eighth.

Owing partly to the forcing of the pace, and in a certain measure to the fact that the road was exceptionally hard, tire trouble was abundant. At the end of the first, second, and fourth rounds Strang put into his station to change a punctured tire and take on replacements for those lost on the course. Guichard, the mechanician of the Thomas car, showed remarkable agility by climbing out to the bracket behind the gasoline tank and unstrapping the tires as the car was running down to the station. With the single fastener Michelin rim and prompt responses from those at the tire and gasoline station the changes were all made with remarkable speed.

Tire Changing Became an Important Factor.

Tire changing being an important factor in the race, it was interesting to notice the various arrangements adopted and methods of work of the different teams installed in the dugout "ravitaillement." Renault and Panhard both had pneumatic jacks which could be put under the axle of the car and the vehicle raised in less time than it often took to place the old type in position. Dietrich had a long double lever about seven feet in length by which the entire front or rear could be lifted off the ground on one pull. Half a dozen firms maintained their gasoline under pressure in a large tank with a long connection. The Englishmen at the Austin stand distinguished themselves

Cissac's Last Appearance Before His Fatality.

by unusual slowness in making tire changes, filling tanks, etc., sometimes as much as five or six minutes being lost waiting for appliances which ought to have been at hand or loitering around for no apparent reason. In view of the fact that the cars were running excellently it was hard to understand such indifference.

Lautenschlager to the Fore in the Fifth.

During the fifth round Lautenschlager on the Mercedes managed to wrest first place from Hemery on the Benz and to secure for himself a margin of three minutes. Hemery took second place, his companion Hanriot retained third, and Thery kept in fourth position. There was now something like consternation in the French camp, for unless Thery could wear down the three fast cars in front of him victory was assured to Germany, and, in any case, the home industry would be poorly represented in the first half dozen. Heath and Cissac, each on a Panhard, were running well, but could not be expected to secure first place except by accident, and the two Renaults handled by Caillois and Dimitri were too far down to get to the front.

On the termination of the sixth round the Mercedes-Benz duel was still in progress, Lautenschlager leading by four minutes on Hemery and five minutes on Hanriot (Benz). Thery, in fourth position, handled his car magnificently, the big blue Brasier whizzing past the grandstand as if on rails, the veteran driver slipping from third to fourth speed at a fixed spot opposite the grandstand with a sharp touch of the lever.

Thomas and Its Leaky Gasoline Tank.

While the leaders were on their sixth round Strang pulled into the station at the end of his fourth round with the gasoline tank leaking badly. It was quickly filled, fresh tires taken, and a start made for a fifth round, Strang believing that he could run on gravity with his large supply and keep sufficient fuel to get around the course. In other respects the car had shown satisfaction, and, though not as fast as the Germans and French, seemed capable of going the entire distance.

Hemery managed to close up on Lautenschlager during the seventh round until the difference between the two men was barely a minute. Hanriot was four minutes behind the leading Mercedes, and Thery was ten minutes in the rear. During this round Hemery was struck in the eye by a flying stone which broke his goggles and caused some of the glass to enter the eye. Though suffering intensely and only seeing with one eye, the Frenchman stubbornly refused to allow his car to be taken over by a reserve driver. One side of his head was horribly swollen, the effect of the tarred surface and dust aggravated the evil, but still the killing pace was maintained. Lautenschlager managed to draw away from Hemery one minute and from Thery four minutes, but the respective positions of the four leaders remained unchanged during the eighth round.

Victorious Mercedes on Its Final Round.

Down in the tire and gasoline pit the Mercedes assistants were in a frenzy of excitement as the last round commenced with Lautenschlager in the lead. Before starting off on what promised to give him the victory the German ran in to change front and rear tires, replacing the smooth one by non-skids, and to take a hasty drink of coffee. With a roar from a hundred German throats the white Mercedes was off again in pursuit of Hemery, who, having started thirty minutes earlier, was still leading in position but not in time.

Hemery finished first with his left rear tire flat and his left eye probably useless for the rest of his life. But he had started earlier than Lautenschlager carrying No. 35, and had to be content with second place, nine minutes behind the Mercedes. Hanriot, who had struggled hard to wrest second place from his mate, had to accept third, less than one minute behind.

At the commencement of the last round fourth place had seemed certain for Thery; it was even imagined by his supporters that a supreme effort could be made to run up to third or second position, first place being manifestly beyond his reach

Thery (Brasier), Whose Star Was Dimmed.

except in case of accident. Henry Brasier wandered up and down the track with a worried look on his face and glancing every few minutes at the announcement board for news of the passage of his crack driver. Louis Renault strode up and down nervously and anxiously, stopping now and again to explain how Caillois had been delayed by trouble with his dismountable rims. The minutes passed, but no reports came in of the approach of Thery. The time necessary to secure first place elapsed, then the cruel truth burst upon them that Thery, long looked upon as superior to breakdowns and accidents, had met with defeat. It was not, however, until an hour later that it was learned that the Brasier car had completely broken down during the last round, a cylinder having cracked.

Rigal, who earlier had been delayed by trouble with his dismountable rims, made a supreme effort and finally brought his Bayard-Clement into the fourth place vacated by Thery. Poegge, who had undone the first Renault, brought his Mercedes into fifth place; Joerns on the Opel secured sixth place, Erle on the Benz took seventh, and Dimitri, Renault, was classed eighth.

Heath, First Vanderbilt Winner, Unofficially Ninth.

Though George Heath was unable to officially finish the race, his car took ninth position. The winner of the first Vanderbilt

Fournier (Itala), Who Fought Unsuccessfully.

race had suffered severely from the effects of the tar on his eyes all through the race. At the end of the ninth round he declared that it was impossible for him to continue, and immediately Artois, who was in the gasoline station, jumped onto the road and was off with the car. During the final round the mechanic was thrown out of the car on one of the turns, the rear wheel passing over his left hand and severely crushing it.

Twenty-three out of the 48 starters finished the race, the only teams complete at the end being Benz with all three cars well placed and Mors with their two cars, sixteenth and seventeenth.

Henry Fournier, one of the several veterans who have returned to racing this year after a long absence, was delayed by tire and slight mechanical trouble early in the race, and later suffered intensely from the action of the tar on his eyes. On completing the course in twentieth position he had to be led away to the doctor, his eyesight having temporarily left him. Moore-Brabazon and Resta, the English drivers, were similarly in a pitiful condition, while Heath had to take to bed.

The Double Fatality of the Race.

A little time after the winner had been announced, and while the stands were comparatively empty, the rumor spread abroad

Map of the Triangular Course.

that Cissac, the Panhard driver who had set out in sixth position to make his ninth round, had met with a serious accident. For at least an hour no exact information was available, but about 3 o'clock the sad truth was made known that both driver and mechanic had been killed. The real cause of the disaster is not quite clear, for the only eye witness was a soldier who is able to supply but meager details. The probability is that while running on a straightaway between 80 and 90 miles an hour a front tire burst or the steering gear broke.

How Cissac Met His Unhappy End.

The spot where the accident took place was at Sept Meules, the road slightly descending and perfectly straight. The soldier declares that a fire burst, the machine swerved suddenly to one side, struck two trees, bounded to the opposite side of the road, then rolled over on itself two or three times. Cissac, who was 31 years of age, had graduated from the bicycle to the motorcycle, and from the motorcycle to the voiturette. The race in which he found his death is the first big automobile event in which he had participated.

CHAPTER THREE

THE TWENTIES

*Imagine a clean, well-planned town of wide spaces, green lawns and white stone
buildings, bedecked gaily with coloured flags and bunting. Brilliant, hot sunshine,
streams of the world's best cars, wonderfully dressed women and men who talk only of
the Grand Prix. That was Tours. By night, Tours was as brilliant as by day. Clusters of
glow-lamps helped a limpid moon to extend the hours of waking. Visitors, drivers, team
managers, and everyone thought not of bed until 3 a.m. The townspeople coined money.*
The Motor at the 1923 French Grand Prix

B y the time the First World War stopped play only 12 races had been held
in broad accord with the Grand Prix rules – 7 in France and 5 in
America. Promising though this new concept was, especially after the
epic race at Lyons in 1914, Grand Prix racing was still only an infant. It
managed to survive through the twenties – but these
were the trying and tortured years we associate with the
growth of any adolescent.

The twenties saw radical transformations of Grand
Prix racing cars and their environment: adoption of
high-speed multi-cylinder engines, advanced fuels,
supercharging, elimination of the riding mechanic, new
starting methods and the first purpose-built road
circuits. Yet chassis design and aerodynamics stagnated,
a promising start for hydraulic brakes was ignored,
works teams fell by the wayside and private teams using
'production' cars rose to prominence. In a decade of
contrasts, Grand Prix racing mirrored the turbulence of
the twenties' politics and economics.

*After experimentation with radical
aviation-inspired 'freak'
aerodynamic shapes in the Grand
Prix races of 1922 (here a Ballot
leads a Bugatti) and 1923, Grand
Prix designers settled for body
designs that were more
conventional, practical and, above
all, marketable.*

CONSTRAINTS ON ENGINE SIZE

One innovation of the twenties was the consistent
adoption of a limit on engine displacement as a means of
establishing some parity among the cars taking part.
Previous limits had covered maximum weights, maximum
cylinder bore size and the amount of fuel that could be burned. The idea of an
engine-size limit was first tried in 1911 by the editors of the periodical *l'Auto* for its
race *Coupe des Voiturettes*. The limit they set, 3 litres (183 cubic inches), was used
in 1912 and 1913 as well.

Engineers were starting to experiment with superchargers. These used rotary
blowers of various kinds to defeat displacement limits by packing in more air than
the engine could inhale naturally. Such devices were prohibited for the only pre-war

Grand Prix that was contested under a displacement limit: the 1914 French Grand Prix for cars of 4½ litres (275 cubic inches). For 1915 the Indianapolis 500-mile race was first run under an engine size limit, slightly larger at 300 cubic inches.

Logically enough, the same limit applied when engines first revved up again at Indy in 1919, but the Speedway management said that for 1920 it would adopt the new 3-litre engine size set by the international authority, the International Association of Recognised Automobile Clubs (AIACR, the acronym derived from its French name) for future Grand Prix racing. This 39 per cent size reduction was aimed, they said, to slow the cars and to facilitate international competition. It was more successful in the latter sense than the former.

Auto makers in both France and Britain took an anti-motor-racing stance in 1919 and 1920, refusing to field cars in European Grands Prix. This didn't prevent them sending cars to race at Indianapolis in those years, however. The striking feature of the 1919 500-mile race was the entry of French Ballot and American Duesenberg cars powered by in-line eight-cylinder engines. This marked the beginning of a trend that would sweep Grand Prix racing in the twenties. By the end of the decade no top-line contender would be powered by anything other than a straight-eight engine – a prime contributor to the long-bonneted look that makes the cars of this era look so magnificent.

STRAIGHT-EIGHTS SUPREME

As so often happens, the new eights were not successful in their first Indianapolis appearance. Neither did an eight win at Indy in 1920, the first year of the new 3-litre limit, when three such cars were entered by Ballot and four by Duesenberg. However, behind the winning four-cylinder Monroe, finishing places

Designed along Peugeot lines, Ralph de Palma's 3-litre eight-cylinder Ballot was the class of the field at Indianapolis in 1920. De Palma's riding mechanic was his nephew Peter De Paolo, who later became a famous driver and Indy winner in his own right.

TWO-STROKE EXPERIMENTS

Racing-car designers have often been intrigued by the idea of making their engines work twice as hard by the simple expedient of having a power-producing explosion every time the piston goes down, instead of every other time. The four-stroke cycle 'wastes' three of the four strokes over two revolutions of the crankshaft in getting ready for the fourth stroke, the one that produces power. With a two-stroke cycle, in contrast, power is produced by every piston downstroke.

In no era of the classic Grand Prix did the two-stroke engine receive more attention than in the twenties. Justifiably, engineers were preoccupied by the problems attendant upon making their engines run faster and faster to

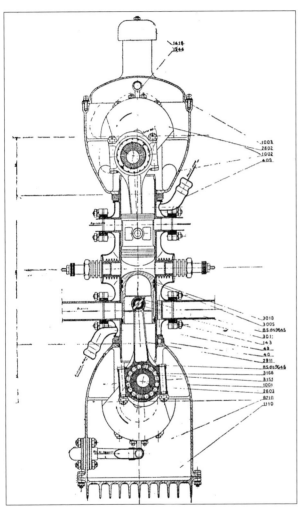

Fiat's Type 451 two-stroke engine of 1925–26 was one of the most audacious concepts ever proposed for Grand Prix racing, with its six long cylinders each containing two pistons. The Porsche office proposed a similar engine, but with its cylinders laid horizontally, for Mercedes-Benz in 1938.

meet the challenge of the new smaller displacement limits: 2 litres from 1922 and then 1½ litres from 1926. Higher speeds posed even more difficulties for the valve gear; most two-stroke designs avoided these by having no valve gear as such.[1] Instead, the entering and exiting gases were controlled by the movement of pistons past ports in the cylinder walls. The fresh charge was forced into the engine by an external blower.[2]

One of the most creative Grand Prix car builders, Delage, was also one of the first to evaluate the potential of the two-stroke. Delage experimented with an eight-cylinder two-stroke engine before deciding that a four-stroke V-12 would be the better solution for the 2-litre formula.

Not long thereafter, in America Fred Duesenberg took up the two-stroke's cause. As a base, Duesenberg used the crankcase, crankshaft and centrifugal supercharger of his twin-cam straight-eight 1½-litre engine. His new cylinder block had piston-controlled porting, with the added refinement of a rotary valve to control the timing of the incoming charge. The piston crown carried a deflector to kick the fresh charge upwards and to chase out the exhaust gases.

On his test bench at Indianapolis Duesenberg succeeded in getting his engine to 4,800 rpm with an output level similar to that of his 2-litre engines of 1924, which would have been around 150 bhp. Unlike any of the others of this decade he also succeeded in testing his engine in a car. Pete De Paolo drove the two-stroke Duesey in private trials at the Speedway before the 1926 race, finding it not geared well enough to exploit its power potential.

A two-stroke Duesenberg might have entered the 1926 '500' had it not been for the difficulty the engineer and his team had in starting the engine. It needed to have its blower running at a good clip before

---

1   A Miller modified by a customer was entered in the 1926 Indianapolis race. Its cams and valves were retimed to make it operate on a two-stroke cycle. 'I know there was considerable trouble with the valves,' Harry Miller told the Society of Automotive Engineers. 'They had to work twice as fast as in an ordinary engine and it was hard to keep them all in one piece.' It did not start in the race.

2   Simple two-strokes use the compression that takes place in the crankcase to provide the pressure needed to deliver the fresh charge. No Grand Prix two-stroke engines used this procedure.

Cooling by air was provided for the eight pairs of radially placed cylinders powering the front-drive Trossi-Monaco Grand Prix car of 1935. Regrettably it was never brought to raceworthiness.

it could be cranked to start, so Duesenberg equipped the blower drive with an overrunning clutch so it could be brought up to speed by an electric motor. Contrary to the confident representations of its vendor, the clutch couldn't cope with the blower-drive load and failed. 'For that reason,' said Fred, 'we were inclined to give up the idea of having any two-cycle engines in the 1926 race.'

His unusual initiative attracted world-wide attention, said Duesenberg: 'We have had a great many inquiries from different States, from England and, in fact, from all parts of the world about our two-cycle-engine racing car.' One such inquiry could very well have originated in Turin, Italy, where a team of Fiat engineers was test-running a radical 1½-litre two-stroke racing engine intended for the new Grand Prix formula starting in 1926.

Based on a concept by Tranquillo Zerbi, the Fiat two-stroke had six vertical cylinders, within which two pistons faced each other crown-to-crown and were connected to two crankshafts, one at the top of the engine and the other at the bottom. The two cranks were geared together at the rear of the engine, where the lower crankshaft drove the clutch. The layout gave the maximum possible area for the ports; the upper pistons opened and closed the inlet ports, fed with air/fuel mixture by a Roots blower, and the lower pistons uncovered the exhaust ports.

Design work on this Type 451 engine began in 1925. 'The development and experimental testing of this engine constituted a bold endeavour,' wrote Gino Cabutti, 'but one which was not a joy to everyone. Rosso, who was assigned to the test cell, was deafened by it.' It ran to the remarkable speed of 6,500 rpm and produced a verified 152 bhp; Scipione Treves, who also worked on the project, said that a peak of 170 bhp was achieved. Any value between these numbers would have been respectable power for the first year of the new 1½-litre formula. But the Type 451 never reached a level of serviceability that allowed it to be installed in a car, let alone raced.

Two-stroke engines then lapsed into quiet obscurity with the withdrawal from Grand Prix racing of the big battalions of the likes of Fiat. Two-stroking surfaced again in 1934–35 as a result of the efforts of a Swiss engineer, Arnold Zoller, and the deep pockets of a fine driver, Count Carlo Felice Trossi. Both projects used a two-stroke concept that placed two cylinders side by side and connected them with a common combustion chamber. One cylinder had the piston-controlled inlet ports and the other the exhaust ports.

Zoller's effort was an in-line engine of 1½ litres with six pairs of cylinders and two geared-together crankshafts. In his single-seater it made some Voiturette appearances, but without great success. The Trossi-Monaco was a full Grand Prix racer for the 750 kg formula with eight paired radial cylinders at the front of the car, air-cooled, driving the front wheels. Although it was tested, it never raced.

In later years the excellent performances achieved by small-displacement two-stroke engines in motorcycle racing prompted some engineers to think of scaling them up to automobile size. The engines only worked well at small displacements, however, and the task of clustering them to power a Grand Prix car – a 24-cylinder 3-litre? – was uninviting.

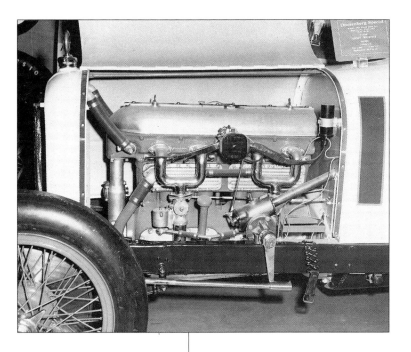

To European eyes the straight-eight engine of the 1921 Duesenberg had a sober simplicity, with its enclosed single overhead camshaft. However, its compactness, lightness and high rpm capability were distinct advantages.

two to seven were filled by straight-eights. The handwriting was on the walls of the Gasoline Alley garages.

Eights as such were not novelties. V-8 engines had been built for both aeroplanes and cars. Bugatti had built some in-line or straight-eights and had paired two of them to make a sixteen-cylinder aero engine, while the Duesenberg brothers had designed straight-eights for marine service and produced a V-16 aviation prototype. As a concept, in-line eights were in the air; Ballot and Duesenberg introduced the straight-eight to Grand Prix racing in 1921, the year in which the European auto makers finally rescinded their ban on racing participation.

Although 11 of the 1921 French Grand Prix's 13 starters on the Le Mans circuit were straight-eights, including the winning Duesenberg, some observers were still unconvinced that this more complex engine would have the legs of the fours that had hitherto dominated racing. 'Despite the fact that the Grand Prix was expected to settle the question in its favour,' opined *The Autocar*, 'the superiority of the straight eight engine remains unproved.' It based this conclusion on the third-place finish achieved in the race by a four-cylinder Ballot of only 2 litres.

This was in fact a fair enough assessment of the state of the art of the 3-litre cars raced in 1921. Multi-cylinder-engine technology was still in its natal phase. Most races to date had been won by four-cylinder engines. These were seen as light, robust and adequately powerful. Best of all they had short crankshafts, which helped keep at bay the twisting or torsional vibrations that could easily destroy longer crankshafts. This had harmed the durability of the few six-cylinder engines that had been tried in racing.

Now engineers saw the introduction of the straight eight, with its even longer crankshaft, as a possible step too far. In favour of an increased number of cylinders for the same displacement, however, was the possibility of reaching even higher engine speeds with safety. By subdividing the capacity into smaller units, each individual piston-and-rod assembly is made to weigh less. Less weight means lower stresses and bearing loadings at the same rotational speed – hence higher speeds are possible. And an engine's power rises in proportion to its torque and revolutions in combination.

Designers of the new in-line eights were not all in agreement. The contrast was striking between the Ballot, Talbot (British) and Talbot-Darracq (French) eights raced in the 1921 French Grand Prix – all with twin overhead cams, four valves per cylinder and multiple main bearings – and the winning Duesenberg engine with its single overhead cam, three valves (one inlet, two exhaust) and only three main bearings, a construction which, with its smaller bore (63.5 mm versus 65.0 for all other eights) made it strikingly shorter, lighter and simpler than the engines of its rivals.

Most striking of all was the speed the Duesenberg engines could reach. Before the war only one Grand Prix engine, the Mercedes, developed its peak power at more than 3,000 rpm. In sharp contrast the eight manufactured in Indianapolis attained its power peak at 4,250 rpm and was capable of revving to an astonishing 5,000 rpm even before, later in 1921, its cam profiles were refined by

Colonel E.J. Hall of the Hall-Scott Engine Company in California. Observers remarked that the engines seemed 'infinitely flexible', which was a help with their less versatile three-speed gearboxes against the four-speeders fitted by others.

'It was noticeable that the Duesenberg engines seemed to misfire a good deal just at the first opening of the throttle after cornering,' *The Autocar* noted, 'but within a few yards they settled down again to an acceleration which soon became remarkably good.' From the standing start (in 1921 cars were started in pairs at thirty-second intervals) the white Dueseys regularly out-accelerated their heavier French and Anglo French rivals.

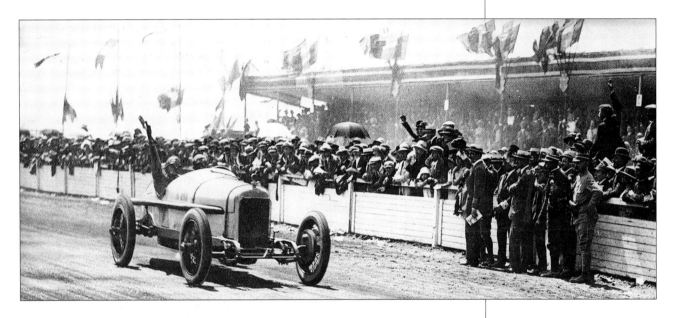

Riding mechanic Ernie Olson waved as Jimmy Murphy crossed the line as the winner in the 1921 French Grand Prix. Clean-lined and light, the Duesenberg also benefited from its hydraulically operated four-wheel drum brakes.

A 32-valve Henry-designed straight-eight powered the 3-litre Talbot Darracq Grand Prix car of 1921. Like the Duesenberg, it carried no spare and relied on limping to the pit to change tyres. René Thomas, partnered here by Albert Divo, retired in the 1921 French Grand Prix.

With an advanced six-cylinder 2-litre car, the 804, Fiat was victorious in the 1922 French Grand Prix at Strasbourg. Felice Nazzaro was its successful driver.

FIRST HYDRAULIC BRAKES

Although by now all Grand Prix cars had mechanically operated four-wheel brakes, the Duesenbergs impressed on the rough Le Mans circuit with their pioneering hydraulically actuated four-wheel brakes developed by Lockheed. These were literally hydraulic, the operating fluid being a mixture of glycerine and water. Later, of course, hydraulic brakes used an oil-based fluid.

Effective though they clearly were, the hydraulic brakes of the Duesenberg were not immediately emulated. Against their use was the need to pay licence fees to Lockheed in America, a burden the Europeans were unready to shoulder. Besides, they were still developing their own four-wheel brakes, which had only been introduced in Grand Prix racing in 1914. Thus throughout the decade all other Grand Prix contenders would rely on mechanically operated brakes, with the sole exception of the hydraulic front brakes of the 1921 Bugatti. Not until 1933 would Maserati reintroduce four-wheel hydraulic brakes to Grand Prix racing.

Ballot, Fiat, Sunbeam and Delage would provide gearbox-driven servo-motors to augment the driver's leg muscle. In 1924 Bugatti would introduce unique cast-aluminium wheels which were combined with the brake drums. These improved heat dissipation and allowed brake shoes to be changed easily at pit stops.[1] Alternatively, at a pit stop a Bugatti team could fit new wheels that had slightly smaller brake drums to compensate for the wear of the linings. Otherwise brake technology remained static in the twenties.

AERONAUTIC INFLUENCES

Another Duesenberg feature that excited comment was its clean-lined body form. Called 'streamlined', bred in America for the fast tracks that prevailed there, the white cars were indeed sleek with their low cowls, long tails and fully enclosed undertrays. Unlike their rivals they eschewed the on-board carrying of spare wheels for changes out on the course; their successful strategy was to limp to the pits to change a flat tyre if necessary.

In the next two years of Grand Prix racing, streamlining, spurred by the advances made in aeronautics in the First World War, became a major theme of new designs. In any case, all-new cars were needed for the 1922 races because the AIACR changed the rules to require engines of only 2 litres (122 cubic inches) and a minimum weight of 650 kg (1,433 lb), well down from the 800 kg minimum set for the 3-litre cars.

A poorly supported first Italian Grand Prix at the end of 1921 had marked the reappearance of a contender in this class of racing: Turin's Fiat.[2] For 1922 Fiat was better prepared with an exquisite six-cylinder racing car, the Tipo 804. Although sixes had been raced before, most successfully by Britain's Napier, this Fiat would be the first car in Grand Prix history to demonstrate that a six could be a competitive racing engine.

Noting the 1914 Grand Prix success of Mercedes with its engine cylinders welded of sheet steel, Fiat adopted this labour-intensive form of construction for all its subsequent racing cars. The six's seven main bearings and its connecting-rod big-end bearings all ran on low-friction rollers, a feature aiding both reliability and performance which had been pioneered in Grand Prix racing by

---

1   They also improved Bugatti's bank balance. The wheels were cheap to make in his own foundry, and commanded high prices as much-needed spare parts.
2   This was the season for which the Fiat Tipo 801 was built, the four-cylinder car for which Fiat had proposed a desmodromic valve gear. The type numbers given are those of the cars; the engines proper had different type numbers.

Pietro Bordino at the wheel of the new Tipo 804 six-cylinder Fiat of 1922. The elegant lines of its body and enclosed exhaust piping – aerodynamic without 'freakishness' – were to the credit of Fiat's aeronautical engineering department.

Fiat's 3-litre cars of 1921. So novel was this technology that Fiat had to develop precision techniques for making its own rollers. Others, such as Delage, had used ball or roller bearings to support the crankshaft in the previous decade, but not for the connecting-rod big-end bearings as well.

Although conventionally laid out, the Tipo 804's trim and well-profiled body form had been lofted by the company's aeronautical department. Its radiator air inlet was small, and although external, its exhaust pipe was contained in a faired shrouding. Much more radical were the entries from French firms Ballot and Bugatti. The former rebodied three of its Type 2LS sports cars with completely cylindrical bodies tapering to pointed tails.[3] A rounded nose with its circular air inlet was made just big enough to house a spare tyre and rim – certainly the oddest place in which a Grand Prix car has ever toted a spare.

CAMS, SPRINGS AND TAPPETS

The 1922 race was to prove to be Ballot's last Grand Prix entry. This Paris-based company had streaked like a meteor across Grand Prix racing's firmament. Ballot was the direct inheritor of the advances in engine design created by Les Charlatans for Peugeot before the war. Already established and active as a maker of engines for marine, aviation and automotive use, Ballot accepted a challenge to design and build a team of cars to compete at Indianapolis in 1919.[4] Its straight-eight cars of 4,817 cc (294 cubic inches, to meet the Indy limit of 300 cubic inches) were designed by the architect of the Peugeots, the Swiss Ernest Henry.

Using as a basis a 1914 racing 2½-litre four he had designed for Peugeot, Henry simply reduced the bore by 1 mm and doubled the number of cylinders to

---

3 Powered by a four-cylinder 2-litre twin-cam engine with four valves per cylinder, the 2LS Ballot may be the first twin-cam vehicle to have been produced in series for road use. About one hundred were made between 1921 and 1924, according to Griff Borgeson.

4 Griff Borgeson speculated that the building of the team of four Ballots, said to cost $120,000, was covertly sponsored by the owners of the Indianapolis Motor Speedway in order to bring more foreign glamour to their first postwar 500-mile race.

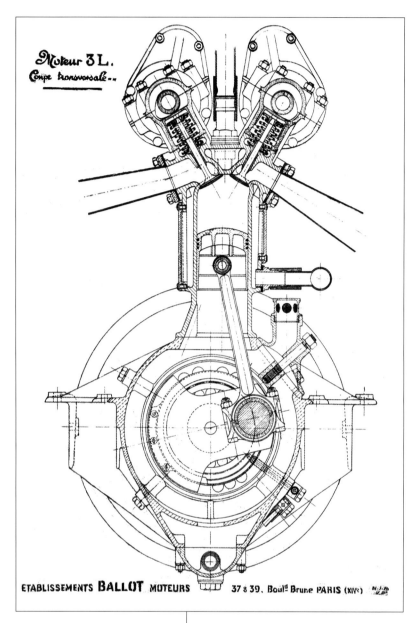

Moteur 3 L.
Coupe transversale

ETABLISSEMENTS **BALLOT** MOTEURS   37 & 39, Boul^d Brune PARIS (XIVe)

With its adoption of inverted-cup-type cam followers, the 3-litre Ballot of 1920 adopted a type of valve gear that is instantly recognisable by students of modern engines. Massive anti-friction bearings carried its crankshaft.

create the Ballot's engine. In doing so, however, he introduced a historic innovation. As tappets interposed between the cam lobes and the valve stems – needed to absorb the lateral wiping force of the cam lobe – the Peugeots used a flat steel rectangle atop a shaft that extended down to the end of the valve stem. At one end of the rectangular tappet, at the side of the cam, a short shaft ran upwards from it into the cam cover to provide a positioning guide for the tappet. Below the shaft was a small coil spring to help return the tappet. The coil valve springs were exposed below the cam carriers.

Although in all other respects his eight followed the principles of the Peugeot fours, Henry innovated significantly in the big Ballot's valve gear. He enclosed the valve springs, unifying the cylinder head's structure. Gone were the rectangular tappets with their finicky guides and springs. In their place was a simple inverted circular cup which surrounded the valve springs and presented its flat top to the cam lobe. Here for the first time in an overhead-cam automobile engine was the piston- or cup-type tappet that came into wide use thereafter and is still a feature of many modern racing engines.[5]

Two other types of tappets or cam followers came into use for overhead-cam racing engines in the twenties. One was a finger interposed between the lobe and the valve stem, pivoted from the side of the cam case. This was used by Fiat, Mercedes, Benz,[6] Delage, Bugatti and Maserati. The other was the simple notion of screwing a circular disc onto the end of the valve stem. In this solution, patented in 1915 by Marc Birkigt of Hispano-Suiza and used in his superb aero engines, the valve stem itself takes the side thrust from the wiping motion of the cam lobe. It was used by some Fiat and Mercedes racing engines, and in adapted form by Alfa Romeo for its Grand Prix cars of the twenties.[7]

---

5   This type of tappet was patented by Albert Morin in France in 1916 and in Britain in 1918. Engineer Harry Mundy conjectured that Morin may have been employed during the war at Ballot, where Ernest Henry could have learned of his idea and licensed its use for the Ballot racers. Morin's paternity for this simple and effective tappet seems secure.

6   They did not join to form Mercedes-Benz (actually Daimler-Benz) until 1926.

7   Alfa Romeo's Vittorio Jano redesigned the Birkigt tappet in order to avoid having to license the design from Hispano-Suiza.

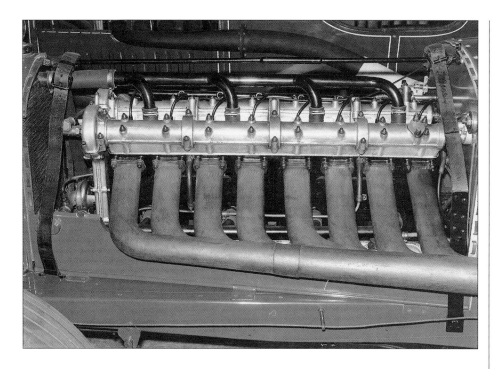

The beautiful straight-eight engine of the 1920 3-litre Ballot fully integrated its camshaft carriers with the cylinder head. The gear train driving the camshafts was located at the front of the block.

BUGATTI APPEARS

Symbolically, in the 1922 Grand Prix de l'ACF Ballot handed the French baton to a firm competing in the Grand Prix for the first time: Bugatti. Italian-born, the ambitious and fertile Ettore Bugatti was just getting into his stride at his well-equipped motor works in Alsace,[8] located a scant four miles from the roads between Molsheim and Strasbourg on which the 1922 French Grand Prix was run. One of Bugatti's small cars had impressed with its pace in the Sarthe Club's 1911 Grand Prix, but only in the twenties did Bugatti take up front-line motor sport.

Like Ballot, Bugatti adopted a tapering cylindrical body, with the added refinement of an exhaust pipe that ran inside the body to emerge at the tip of the tail. This was sound aerodynamically, but not much liked by the drivers. Chassis dimensions were 2,400 mm (94.5 inches) for the wheelbase and 1,200 mm (47.2 inches) for the track. With one bizarre exception, these classic proportions, with the wheelbase precisely double the track, were used by Bugatti for all his racing cars throughout the twenties.

Under the new Bugatti's hood was another classic work of engineering: the first appearance in a racing car of Ettore's straight-eight engine. The engine's avant-garde architecture, with the crisply squared lines of its aluminium crankcase, its paired cast-iron blocks and its engine-turned or 'damascened' cam housing, created the new standard for elegance that characterised all Bugatti engines of the twenties.

Measuring 60 × 88 mm, its cylinders were fed by vertical valves, two inlets and one exhaust (the opposite of Duesenberg), operated by a shaft-driven single overhead camshaft. Twin side-draught carburettors created the mixture. Like

---

8   The Alsace and Lorraine regions, a major bone of contention between France and Germany, were returned to France under the terms of the Armistice.

ETTORE BUGATTI

No armchair engineer, Ettore Bugatti was fully capable of piloting his own creations at racing speeds. Bugatti is seen at the wheel of one of his earliest racing creations.

A novelist would have found it quite impossible to invent a character with the startling originality, creativity and eccentricity of Ettore Bugatti. He littered the twenties and thirties with new ideas in Grand Prix car design and engineering, and created some of the most beautiful racing cars ever made – some say *the* most beautiful. And they were extraordinarily successful, not least because they were reliable and numerous, racing throughout the known world in the hands of both aces and amateurs.

Ettore was the youngest son of a Milanese artist and furniture designer, Carlo Bugatti. Born on 15 September 1881, he came into the world just in time to be captivated by the new age of speed. Ettore combined an artistic sensitivity with an appreciation of mechanics that was – and so far remains – unique in the history of the automobile. Addicted to speed after racing motorised tricycles, at the age of twenty-one he was already designing cars that were made under his name.

In 1910 Bugatti settled in Molsheim in Alsace, where he set up workshops of the highest quality and lived the lifestyle of a landed seigneur. He had a base in Paris as well; he built aero engines there during the First World War, and in the thirties retreated to Paris when he felt unappreciated by his restless Alsatian workforce. Bugatti died in Paris in 1947 after creating some of the most mouth-watering fast cars ever made.

Although engineering experts declared astonishment at the strange induction arrangements and lack of cylinder-head cooling of Bugatti's Type 35 Grand Prix car, the car itself didn't seem to mind. His engine technology took a leap forward with the Type 51 of 1931, with its twin-cam cylinder head inspired by the designs of Harry Miller. Bugatti's chassis looked disarmingly simple – but his cars won many races by virtue of their superb handling and remarkable cornering grip.

Like Henry Ford, Bugatti designed by inspecting and correcting the three-dimensional sketches and wood models of key parts made by his craftsmen. A spate of failures was traced to a period when the correction in his spectacles had been made too strong; the parts were not actually as big as he perceived them to be. Behind the scenes, labouring anonymously, were capable engineers like Antonio Pichetto – later with Gordini – who provided the technical foundation that Bugatti lacked.

From left to right are Ferdinand Porsche, Count Alexander Kolowrat and Ettore Bugatti. In the twenties Bugatti was beginning to enjoy great commercial success not only with his touring cars but also with his successful Type 35 Grand Prix cars.

Bugatti's use of the Miller technology had been encouraged by his son Jean, whose influence in the firm increased in the thirties. Together they produced the beautiful Type 59 Grand Prix car of 1933–34. Able though it was, the Type 59 was no match for the Italians, let alone the Germans, and Bugatti cars gradually faded from the Grand Prix scene. A final effort before the Second World War, the Type 50B monoposto, was well driven by Jean-Pierre Wimille, but without success.

As strikingly individualistic in his dress and style as the cars he made, Ettore Bugatti mastered the art and economics of making racing cars for sale far better than anyone else of his era. Without his tough, versatile cars raced by private teams and drivers, the state of Grand Prix racing in the difficult years between 1928 and 1934 would have been even worse – unthinkably so. In addition, so easy were they to make that there may well be more Grand Prix Bugattis running today than ever left that remarkable factory-cum-estate at Molsheim.

Duesenberg, Bugatti carried the crankshaft in only three main bearings, but fitted each with double-row ball bearings which required only a low-pressure feed of lubricating oil. To feed oil to the rod big-end bearings Bugatti squirted it into circular gutters – known as 'slinger rings' – in the crankshaft. From these the oil flowed by centrifugal force to the bearings.

In the 500-mile 1922 French Grand Prix, which was the first to begin with a massed start,[9] a low-speed rolling start paced by a motorcyclist, the Bugattis were 'best of the rest'. They placed second, third and fourth behind Felice Nazzaro's winning Fiat, which after 6 hours 17 minutes' racing had a margin of nearly a full hour over the first Bugatti. Nazzaro, winner of the 1907 French Grand Prix, was one of the few top drivers who both survived the war and proved able to revive his career after it.

So overwhelmingly daunting was the Fiat performance that the huge prospective entry for the subsequent Italian Grand Prix simply melted away. Only Bugattis, Diattos and Heims opposed the Fiats, which won as they pleased. The race took place on the first track ever to be expressly built for Grand Prix racing: a road circuit in the Monza Park north of Milan.[10] This marked the final phase in the evolution of Grand Prix racing venues. The first had been very long open-road circuits. Next shorter real-road circuits were used; indeed, some like

The start at Monza in 1923, showing the high standard of spectator seating and information services provided by this purpose-built road circuit in parkland north of Milan. Motor racing was becoming well enough established to warrant dedicated circuit construction.

9   The first Gordon Bennett Trophy race of 1900 began with a massed start, but it was not much of a mass – only five cars.
10 The first purpose-built racing track of any kind was the banked oval at Brooklands in England, erected in 1907.

Installed here in a Type 35, the 2-litre Bugatti straight-eight exhibited the remarkable symmetry and purity of its external design. This normally aspirated engine is fitted with two downdraft carburettors.

Monaco and Spa are still on the modern calendar. Evolution then led to purpose-built racing facilities. Monza, among the latter, is still in use today.

In the meantime Fiat's restless racing engineers had been building an even more awesome Grand Prix car. Giulio Cesare Cappa led the design of a new 2-litre straight-eight, the Tipo 805, similar in detail design to the Tipo 804 except for its use of a gear train at the rear of the engine, instead of a shaft, to drive the two bevel shafts to the overhead cams. The idea of placing the gear train at the rear was to help overcome the torsional vibration problems of the long crankshaft by concentrating all the main loadings at just one end. The eight sat in a chassis that was similar to that of the 804 except for an extended wheelbase to take the longer engine.

THE RISE OF SUPERCHARGING

On Cappa's engineering team, Tranquillo Zerbi was especially identified with an engineering breakthrough that Fiat brought, with the Tipo 805, to the 1923 French Grand Prix on a twisty circuit near Tours: supercharging. After the war the racing authorities had neglected to reimpose the ban on forced induction that they had applied in 1914; Fiat was among the first to exploit this loophole.

Fiat chose a Wittig vane-type compressor for its racing cars, driving it from the nose of the crankshaft. It brought the 805's power to 130 bhp at 5,500 rpm, well up from the 804's 92 bhp, in an engine that could rev to 6,000 if needed. In the French race the new car showed stunning speed, lapping at 88 mph and clocking 122 mph on the straight. All three entries took turns leading.

However, the road dust and grit, then so common, was inhaled by the blowers and wrecked the engines of all the Fiats. Immediately, Zerbi set to work on a type of blower that was less easily damaged: the twin-lobed Roots supercharger. Named after the Roots brothers of Connersville, Indiana, who developed the configuration in 1860 for industrial purposes,[11] the most common Roots blower has two figure-eight-shaped lobes that counter-rotate on parallel shafts to shift liquids or gases around the periphery of their housing. Blowers with three or even four lobes are also used to smooth the flow of the medium being pumped.

Newly Roots-blown, Carlo Salamano led a team-mate to victory in the 1923 Italian Grand Prix at Monza. He thus scored the first Grand Prix success for a supercharged car. In another Tipo 805 Pietro Bordino set the fastest lap at a whisker under 100 mph.

Fiat genius in the form of expatriate engineers Vincenzo Bertarione and Walter Becchia stood behind the winner of the 1923 French Grand Prix: the British-built

---

11 A British inventor named Jones had created a similar device twelve years earlier, but the higher profile and global activity of the bearded Roots brothers, Philander and Francis, ensured their indelible association with this type of blower. In any case, the term 'Jones blower' doesn't have quite the same appeal.

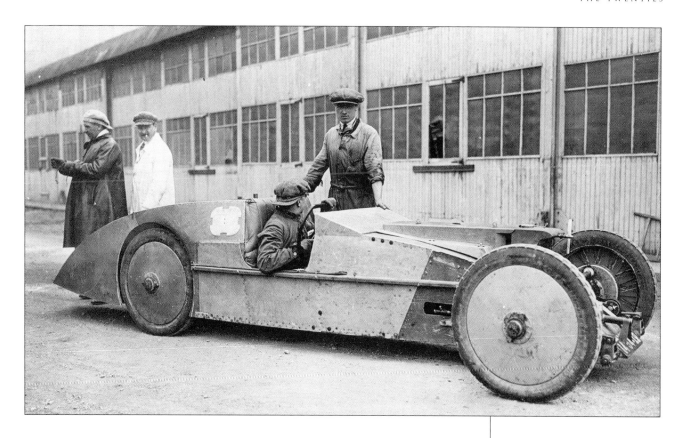

Sunbeam driven by Henry Segrave. Following the failure of his four-cylinder cars in the 1922 French race, Sunbeam major domo Louis Coatalen engaged the two Fiat men to design his 1923 contender.[12] 'Not much time had been lost on drawings,' wrote W.F. Bradley, 'for the engineers came with a complete set of blueprints.'

Logically enough, both the Sunbeam's engine's architecture and the car's shape closely resembled the 1922 six-cylinder Fiat 804, albeit with gear drive to the camshafts (already being prepared by Fiat for the 805) and, oddly, a gearbox with three instead of four speeds. Coatalen's combination proved adept, for after almost 500 miles and more than 6½ hours his three cars were first, second and fourth in the 1923 race.

Here was a triumph for orthodoxy after the failure of the blown Fiats. Heterodoxy in the 1923 Grand Prix season was also represented, and gloriously, by radically streamlined entries from Bugatti, Voisin and Benz. They carried to new extremes the advances in aerodynamics that had been seen in 1922.

RADICAL NEW SHAPES

'Tank; tortoise; dish cover; beetle; slug and roller-skate – all these names were given them in turn,' said *The Motor* of Bugatti's three cars. Their fully enveloping bodies were ruthlessly slab-sided and curved up and over from nose to tail in profile. With an ultra-short wheelbase (Bugatti's sole departure in these years from his ideal chassis

Seen at the Voisin works, one of the unsupercharged 2-litre racing cars built by the Parisian firm in 1923. Gabriel Voisin was more successful in his entries for races for modified touring cars than he was with his 'Laboratoire' at the Grand Prix level.

---

12   Acknowledging the superiority of the 1913 Coupe de l'Auto Peugeot design, Coatalen had acquired such a car and directly copied its engine (enlarging its displacement from 3.0 to 3.3 litres) for his 1914 entries in the Isle of Man Tourist Trophy. One won the race.

proportions) the eight-cylinder engine intruded into the cockpit and forced the driver and riding mechanic far apart. 'Tank' became the enduring nickname of these bizarre Bugs, one of which filled the last podium place behind the two Sunbeams.

Observers commented on the very small dust swirls left behind the Bugattis compared to conventional cars, as well as behind the four creations of Gabriel Voisin. This brilliant if eccentric French engineer called his new design the 'Laboratoire' in honour of its many new and untried ideas, including a sleeve-valve six-cylinder engine, semi-monocoque frame and a narrow 30-inch rear track for the rear wheels, which were differential-less and shrouded by bodywork. One of these gloriously outrageous Laboratoires was piloted to the fifth and last finish among 1923's seventeen starters by the designer of its engine, André Lefebvre.

The third streamlined entry of the 1923 season was the Benz RH, a teardrop-shaped rear-engined racing car that also introduced independent rear suspension by swing axles and inboard rear brakes. In spite of the modest output of its unsupercharged six-cylinder engine the Benz Tropfen-Wagen performed respectably in its only Grand Prix outing, the 1923 Italian Grand Prix at Monza. There W.F. Bradley noted that 'the car gave a very curious impression as it went over the bumps at speed, for the first suggestion as the wheels rose and fell independently of one another was that the axle was going to buckle up on itself'. One Benz was classified fourth and last finisher, and another was running at the finish but not classified.[13]

American Jimmy Murphy, the 1921 French Grand Prix winner, proved he was not a one-shot road-racing wonder by placing third at Monza in an unblown eight-cylinder Miller, only five minutes behind the winning supercharged Fiat after 5½ hours of racing. Americans and Europeans were still criss-crossing the Atlantic thanks to the use of the 2-litre Grand Prix engine size limit by the organisers of the celebrated 500-mile race at Indianapolis.[14] The substantial prize money offered by the fabled 2½-mile Speedway was a powerful attraction for European competitors in spite of the high cost of crossing the Atlantic to compete.

Semi-elliptic leaf springs were cantilevered at both front and rear from the filigreed steel frame of the 1923 Benz RH. It had independent rear suspension by swing axles and a solid front axle, although the original prototype had independent front springing as well. (Also see p. 180.)

13 Their performance was not convincing enough to encourage others to attempt a rear-engined car. But the efficiency of the Benz would be remembered by Ferdinand Porsche's business partner, Adolf Rosenberger, when it came time to design a racing car for the 750 kg Formula of 1934. The Auto Union racing car would be the result.

14 Indianapolis would remain in step with the Grand Prix Formula through 1929 – two years longer than Europe in terms of 1½-litre cars – then adopt rules of its own. It came back into line with the Grand Prix rules in 1938. The CART racing rules at the end of the twentieth century were remotely derived from the 1938 formula.

The only difference was the abandonment of riding mechanics by the Americans in 1923, a step the Europeans would delay until 1925 (though they would require cars with space for two until 1927). Bugatti exploited this in a four-car team he prepared for the 1923 Indy 500 by refitting his 1922 Grand Prix cars with narrow single-seater bodies. The sustained speed demanded by the Indianapolis track played hob with his centrifugally lubricated plain-bearing connecting-rod big ends; only one Bugatti finished in ninth place. Subsequently, Bugatti would fit roller bearings to his rod journals as well as to his main bearings.

Also at Indy in 1923 was a team of three white Mercedes cars, with their four-cylinder twin-cam engines, the first supercharged autos to race at the American speedway. They placed eighth and eleventh. In the improved form in which they won the 1924 Targa Florio, these Mercedes competed only once more at Grand Prix level, at Spain's San Sebastian in 1924. In wet conditions they proved to have the speed to match both Sunbeam and Delage, and led until stopped by engine failure.

DELAGE'S V-12

Speaking of Delage, the ultra-conventional body of Louis Delage's entries in the 1922 French Grand Prix hid a development that would give a further impulse to higher engine speeds under the 2-litre Formula: a V-12 engine of 51.3×80 mm, the first of this configuration ever to be built to power a Grand Prix car. The sound of its exhaust, said *The Motor*, 'is exactly like the roar of a lion at feeding time'.

SUPERCHARGING THE GRAND PRIX CAR

Mounted for museum display, an early twenties Mercedes Roots-type blower shows its lubrication feed, at top, and the multiple-disc clutch at the bottom that permitted the blower to be used on demand.

Supercharging of Grand Prix engines came out of thin air – the air at the high altitudes that aeroplanes were trying to reach in the First World War to gain an advantage over their rivals. Some engineers, like those at BMW, coped with this by building over-dimensioned engines with such high compression ratios that they could only be run at full throttle at altitude. Others, like those at Stuttgart's Daimler, equipped their engines with pumps that could pack in enough air to cheat the engine into thinking it was operating nearer sea level.

In peacetime the idea of trying this 'super-charging' to improve the performance of ground-based engines was seductive. Daimler first supercharged a car engine experimentally late in 1919. In parallel it then began developing supercharged road cars as well as boosted racing cars. Three of its entries in the April 1922 Targa Florio were supercharged. Although the Mercedes trio were not especially successful in the Sicilian race, theirs was the first racing entry in Europe for supercharged cars.[1]

When Daimler designed a new four-cylinder 2-litre Mercedes to suit the current Grand Prix Formula, it was supercharged from the outset. This engine, which would be the last new four-cylinder engine designed to a Grand Prix Formula until after the Second World War, powered the Mercedes team cars that went to Indianapolis in 1923, the first blown cars ever to compete in the famous 500-mile race. Not fully developed, their engines suffered from mismatched boost and valve timing that manifested themselves in a loud exhaust and mechanical failures. But Americans of the twenties had had their first good look at a supercharged racing car.

Just after the cars had been crated for the trip to Indianapolis, a new chief engineer came to Daimler: Ferdinand Porsche. His first chore after their return was the development and improvement of this 2-litre engine. Porsche supervised the design of a new Roots blower for it, larger and with a finned casing. He also improved the engine's performance by drastically cutting back its compression ratio from 7.5:1 to 4.5:1 and filled the hollow stems of its exhaust valves with mercury to improve their cooling. The Porsche touch helped Christian Werner's 2-litre win the Targa Florio in April 1924.

The seeds sown by Paul Daimler's pioneering supercharging work fell on fertile soil in America's Indiana. As soon as he had time, intrigued by the performance of the 1923 Mercedes, Fred Duesenberg started thinking about a blower for his 1924 Indianapolis cars. From his wartime work on V-12 and V-16 aviation engines and on the King-Bugatti double-eight engine, Fred had come to know many people at McCook Field, an aviation development centre, which was only a hundred miles east of his Indianapolis plant. Early in 1924 Duesenberg asked McCook's David Gregg – then deeply involved in development of gear-driven aircraft centrifugal blowers – to design a supercharger for his 2-litre straight-eight.

Gregg worked out a neat and reliable installation of a centrifugal compressor with a 5½-inch impeller, placing it flat against the left side of the block and driving it by a cross-shaft through an existing hole in the middle of the block. Gregg decided it would be best to have the blower draw from the carburettor instead of blow into it, making the Duesenberg one of the first such automotive supercharging systems. With efficiencies that were low, in retrospect, and a boost pressure of no more than 3½ psi, the blown Duesenberg of Joe Boyer was still sufficiently superior to win the 500 in 1924.

In the meantime Europe had gone compressor-crazy. It was the fault of Fiat as well as Mercedes. As in Germany and America, so too in Italy, aircraft experience contributed to the Fiat work on racing-engine supercharging that began late in 1922 for the Turin firm's entries both in 1½-litre Voiturette racing and in the 2-litre Grand Prix series.

Fiat's first choice of supercharger was a vane-type blower. This has a circular rotor offset within a larger circular housing, creating an open crescent through which radial vanes sweep to collect and compress the air. Using a Wittig patent, they developed long and short versions of a blower with a 200 mm housing diameter and 180 mm rotor

---

1   The first-ever supercharged racing car was an American six-cylinder Chadwick, which competed in races and hillclimbs in 1908.

Britain's Sunbeam was a successful early adopter of Roots-type supercharging drawing from a carburettor and pumping a fuel/air mixture to the inlet manifold. Although it introduced problems of cylinder-to-cylinder distribution, pumping the mixture rather than air alone was shown in tests to produce higher efficiency.

diameter. The short version was used on the 1½-litre Fiat 803 that won a 340-mile Voiturette race at Brescia on 29 June 1923, thus becoming the first supercharged car to win a race in Europe.

The first entry of a supercharged car in Grand Prix racing was the big brother of the Voiturette, the new eight-cylinder 2-litre Grand Prix Fiat of 1923. But in the French Grand Prix at Tours on 2 July the new Type 805 Fiats retired, three out of three, with blower trouble blamed on the ingestion of dirt from the circuit. Suddenly the vane-type compressor looked far less attractive. Only ten days after the race, detail drawings were being made for a Roots blower with rotors 130 mm in diameter and 140 mm in length. Like the vane-type blower it was driven through a torque-limiting multiple-disc clutch, permanently engaged, from the nose of the crank.

The change enhanced both reliability and power, increasing the latter from 130 to 150 bhp at 5,500 rpm. It also gave Fiat a victory at Monza on 9 September in the Grand Prix of Europe and Italy, making the Italian firm the first to win a Grand Prix race with a supercharged car. The flurry of interest in compressors aroused controversy as to whether they should be permitted in Grand Prix racing. Finally they were allowed for 1924, which Fiat greeted with a sophisticated sheet-metal intercooler between the front frame members. This used the onrushing air to cool the compressed air the blower was delivering to the single Memini carburettor. Ing. Memini was the new high priest of supercharged carburetion, as important to racing in the twenties as Claudel had been in the previous decade.

While Fiat was winning at Monza in 1923, Alfa Romeo was heading back to its factory with the six-cylinder unblown Grand Prix car it had decided not to race after one of its drivers was killed in a practice crash. Resolving to do better, Alfa assigned former Fiat engineer Vittorio Jano to the creation of a new eight-cylinder model for the 1924 season. Jano's Alfa Romeo P2 was running at the end of May, its Roots blower out in front of the crank, like that of the Fiat.[2] It provided pressure air through a finned aluminium manifold to a single carburettor in the 1924 version, and to two carburettors in 1925. The Roots compressor blew Alfa to victory in the 1924 French Grand Prix and many, many races more.

Strong opposition in that race had come from the British Sunbeams, freshly supercharged through the efforts of Louis Coatalen and Capt. Jack Irving. Their tests – as well as the results of British wartime aero engine trials – showed a clear advantage in output with placement of the carburettor before the Roots blower rather than after it, so they became the first in Europe to adopt this layout for a car engine. Roots-type supercharging was also preferred for France's top Grand Prix cars, such as Bugatti, Delage and Talbot.

By the mid-twenties supercharging was the *sine qua non* of Grand Prix cars. Ten years earlier only a handful of men in the engineering world knew what forced induction might mean. Few were aware of the work of the others. The intensity of a world conflict and the competitiveness of motor racing accelerated their efforts and brought many others in contact with them, creating a new technology that, by 1926, was complete in all its essential parts. What remained to be done was in the realm of application, not invention. The pioneers of supercharging had already had all the fun.

---

2   A rumour at that time was so intriguing that it's worth mentioning: that Alfa had a two-speed drive for its supercharger, under driver control. This would have allowed it to have higher boost at low engine speeds to improve acceleration. No verification of this has yet been found in the factory's excellent archives. Later, aero engines would have multi-speed supercharger drives.

Designed by Charles Planchon, a cousin of Louis Delage, the exotic Delage V-12 ran on ball and roller bearings throughout, a total of 100 carrying the crankshaft, camshafts and gears.[15] He was assisted by Albert Lory, who took over the engine's development after it failed in its too-hasty 1922 debut. By 1924 the V-12 was developing 120 bhp at 6,000 rpm, still naturally aspirated. In a new chassis built to suit the engine, this was good enough to secure second and third places for Delage in the 1924 French Grand Prix on the 14.3-mile Lyons road course.

Ever since the Fiat eight had demonstrated such speed in 1923, controversy had reigned over the use of superchargers. Bugatti swore he would never fit the demon devices, and said he could do just as well without them. Mutterings were heard from France about a possible ban. Sunbeam's Louis Coatalen spoke out against them – but added them to his cars for the 1924 season. The Pandora's box had been opened; it was too late to try to slam it shut.

For the 1924 races Fiat was back with its Tipo 805 eight, now with an intercooler between the frame dumb irons to increase the density of the compressed air being fed to the single Memini carburettor. Its power was now approaching 150 bhp. Indeed, Fiat technology triumphed in the French Grand Prix at Lyons in 1924 – but not in a Fiat. Through the intervention of Enzo Ferrari, then associated with Milan's Alfa Romeo, engineer Vittorio Jano moved from Fiat to Alfa, for whom he designed the Fiat-like straight-eight that powered the 1924 victor.

Grand Prix newcomers Alfa Romeo were well represented in the 1924 French Grand Prix at Lyons with a team of four cars designed by ex-Fiat man Vittorio Jano. Number 10 was the winner at 71.0 mph, driven by Giuseppe Campari.

---

15 According to W.F. Bradley, Delage built two versions of Planchon's engine, one with plain bearings and the other fully roller-equipped.

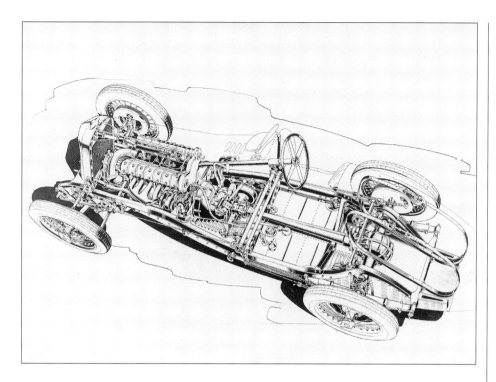

A Roots-type supercharger was fitted at the front of the six-cylinder 2-litre engine of the 1924 Grand Prix Sunbeam. Fiat-inspired like the contemporary Alfa Romeos, the Sunbeams were by far Britain's most competitive entries of the twenties.

Newcomer Alfa Romeo had built six-cylinder Grand Prix cars to race in 1923, but withdrew them after one of their drivers was killed during a test. The French race was the second outing for its new Jano-designed model, dubbed the P2, developing 145 bhp at 5,500 rpm from its Roots-blown engine, and its second victory. Although a Fiat led early, the Alfas soon dominated a fine field of twenty starters in an enthralling race.

Sunbeam's star was fading. Having decided to adopt supercharging, the British firm departed from European precedents (although not from American thinking) by having the blower downstream from the carburettor so that it sucked a mixture of air and fuel instead of air alone. Its tests had shown an advantage for this layout, which gave 138 bhp instead of 115 bhp with the blower pumping only air. Most builders later adopted Sunbeam's choice.

Faulty magnetos marred the Sunbeam team's performance at Lyons. Henry Segrave's Sunbeam won at San Sebastian in 1924; not for more than thirty years would a British car again win a Grand Prix. Sunbeam's last hurrah at this level of the sport was a third place in the 1925 French Grand Prix, still with its six-cylinder car, now developing 150 bhp.

PORSCHE'S POWERFUL MERCEDES

Another maker espousing a supercharger downstream from its carburettor was Mercedes, with a 2-litre straight-eight from the pen of its new chief designer, Ferdinand Porsche. This was only just ready in time for the Italian Grand Prix in 1924, and that because the race was delayed. In this, its only international Grand Prix appearance, one of the Mercedes eights spun off the road, killing its driver. The other two cars were withdrawn as a sign of respect.

Although installed in a chassis that did not fully do it justice, Porsche's eight-cylinder engine for Mercedes was an exceptional machine for the period. Designed

The most powerful European eight-cylinder engine of the 2-litre Grand Prix formula was this Mercedes designed by Ferdinand Porsche. It carried its crankshaft in roller bearings and had individual steel cylinders mounted on an aluminium crankcase.

The magnetos and one Roots-type blower are missing from the front of this 2-litre Grand Prix Delage V-12 in Italy's Biscaretti Museum. Each cylinder bank was fed cooling water by its own individual pump

to reach an unprecedented 8,000 rpm, it developed its peak power at 7,000 – equally unprecedented. With a boost pressure of 1 atmosphere it developed 170 bhp, more than any other eight-cylinder 2-litre engine of the time, except the centrifugally blown Miller built for Indianapolis and America's fast board tracks, which just topped 200 bhp.

Europe's horsepower champ of the 2-litre era was the V-12 Delage, newly supercharged by Albert Lory for the 1925 season – the last for 2-litre cars. In naturally aspirated form the V-12 had its inlet manifolds on the outside of the cylinder banks and the exhausts in the centre. Lory continued this arrangement with twin Roots blowers in parallel, which raised the twelve's output to a reported 190 bhp at 7,000 rpm, enough to cause its connecting rods to fail in the season's first Grand Prix at Spa. Re-rodded, the Delages placed one-two in the French Grand Prix and one-two-three at San Sebastian.

Delage decided to give the Italian Grand Prix at Monza a miss in 1925, knowing what a threat the Alfa Romeo P2s would pose on their home territory. The Alfas did win, but only after they shrugged off a remarkable threat from, of all people, Duesenberg. Three of these Indianapolis-made cars were entered, one of which set the race's fastest lap before leaving the road. Tommy Milton's Duesey placed fourth, close behind a Bugatti, after a long pit stop. Transatlantic competition was still possible.

BUGATTI ON THE RISE

Close behind a Bugatti? What was the bowler-hatted Merlin of Molsheim bringing to Grand Prix races these days after his spectacular experiments with streamlining in 1922 and 1923? Ettore Bugatti had not lost faith in the merits of aerodynamic body forms. In fact, he would win the Le Mans 24-hour race in 1937 and 1939 with envelope-bodied sports cars that were clear descendants of the Grand Prix 'Tank' of 1923. But he was a practical man. He wanted to put his racing car manufacturing on a commercial basis, and he realised that customers would not be attracted by 'freak' bodies, as aerodynamic shapes were known at the time.

The results of Bugatti's ruminations were revealed at the 1924 French Grand Prix at Lyons. Bugatti himself drove one of his new Type 35 models to the weigh-in, revelling in the sensation they caused. Here was an elegant, knife-slim racing car with a proud horseshoe-shaped radiator[16] and sparkling, eight-spoked cast-aluminium wheels. Designed to clamp the tyre beads in place and prevent them from creeping, a well-known problem at the time, the first such wheels required special Dunlop tyres – which caused grief and woes in the 1924 race. Bugatti reverted to normal tyres thereafter.

Ettore Bugatti rejected the 'freak' body designs of his previous Grand Prix cars to create the immaculate and immortal Type 35. The subsequent success of this model, both commercially and competitively, was spectacular.

16 Although 'horseshoe-shaped' is the only description that does justice to the Bugatti radiator as it evolved from its pre-war origins, it was in fact originally inspired by the natural profile of an egg.

Bugatti built an initial run of ten Type 35s and brought five of them to Lyons. The idea of a 'production' racing car that could be bought and used by private teams proved stunningly successful; Bugatti produced some 400 of this type of car. In 1925 and 1926, according to Laurence Pomeroy Jr, the Type 35 helped bring Bugatti a total of 1,045 race victories. Writing in the forties, he judged that the Type 35 'may certainly claim to be the world's most successful racing car'.

The Type 35 carried over the unsupercharged 2-litre straight-eight used in 1922 and 1923, and placed it in a chassis which was unremarkable in its general layout, except perhaps for its location of the live rear axle by leading quarter-elliptic leaf springs, trailing radius rods and a torque arm extending from the axle alongside the drive shaft to the frame, to absorb the forces imposed by braking and acceleration. What was remarkable was the detailed attention given to every aspect of its design and construction.

Pomeroy remarked that the Bugatti was able to perform on road circuits out of all proportion to its modest power and specification. 'It is thus apparent,' he wrote, 'that there was something about the Bugatti design enabling each horse-power to be utilised to far better advantage than on other racing cars of its period. The secret of this maximum realisation of power is to be found in the extraordinary controllability, road holding, and general stability of the Bugatti cars.'

In the premier events of 1925 not even a handling advantage could help the Bugattis prevail against the much more powerful Delages and Alfa Romeos. For 1926, however, the cards were re-dealt. A new Grand Prix Formula cut engine size to 1½ litres and reduced the minimum weight to 600 kg (1,323 lb). Bugatti speedily made available new blocks and crankshafts for his Type 35 to convert it to a 1½-litre Type 39 that could be run with a choice of a range of dimensions: 52 × 88, 54 × 81 or 60 × 66 mm.

More significantly, Bugatti acquiesced at last to the need to equip his engines with the hated superchargers. With the help of an Italian engineer who had been active at Sunbeam, Edmond Moglia, he evolved a precisely made three-lobe Roots blower that drew fuel/air mixture from an updraft Zenith carburettor. Output was modest at 110 bhp at 5,500 rpm, but most advantageously, Bugatti was ready to contest the new formula at its birth. Few others were.

LOW-WATER MARK FOR GRAND PRIX RACING

So unready were Bugatti's rivals for the new formula that in the first Grand Prix under the 1½-litre rules, the proud French race held at the Miramas Autodrome near Marseilles, the dozen racers that had been entered melted away to an actual grid of only three cars: all Bugattis. This was, and fortunately would remain, the lowest state to which Grand Prix racing ever subsided. Fuel problems contributed to Pierre de Vizcaya's retirement, and veteran Jules Goux won, beating Meo Costantini.

The field improved to six cars for the Grand Prix at San Sebastian, which was won by Goux's Bugatti. Six turned out again for the Italian Grand Prix, which again was won by a Bugatti, this time in the hands of a driver named Jean Charaval under a pseudonym, 'Sabipa'. It was a thin enough Grand Prix season, but where laurels were awarded, Bugattis collected them.

Two other French concerns were girding up to join Bugatti in the 1926 lists with much more ambitious and expensive designs. Louis Delage was ready with three new works cars for the San Sebastian race. These had classical straight-eight engines designed by the same Albert Lory who had assisted in the development of the predecessor V-12. Replete with roller bearings for mains, rods and twin camshafts, the exquisitely engineered eights had their cam-drive gear train at the front of the engine.

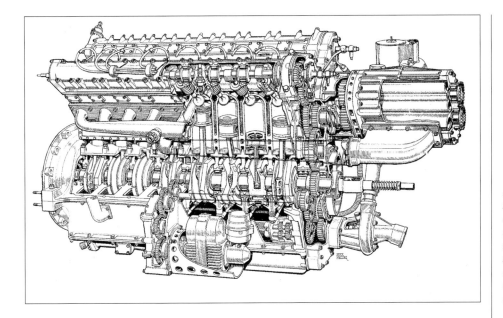

Max Millar's fine drawing of the straight-eight 1.5-litre Delage engine shows its 1927 configuration with the large front-mounted Roots-type blower supplying the right-hand side of the cylinder block. All the principal bearings for crankshaft, gears and camshafts are ball or roller.

Overheated drivers were avoided by the left-hand mounting of the exhaust pipe on the 1927 version of the Grand Prix Delage. Its creator Albert Lory had learned well from his experiences with its predecessor, the 2-litre V-12.

Now that riding mechanics no longer needed to be carried – though the rules still demanded a body width of at least 80 cm (31.5 inches) – Lory could specify a leftward offset of the engine, drive train and rear-axle gears that allowed the driver, on the right, to sit much lower in the chassis. An appreciation of the benefit to cornering of a low centre of gravity combined with a reduced aerodynamic frontal area was beginning to influence Grand Prix car design.

Not appreciated by the drivers in the 1926 version of the Delage was the nearness of the right-hand exhaust system to their feet. In their first outing at San Sebastian they were overheated by this feature and could only bring the cars to the finish by driving in relays, one Delage placing second and another setting fastest lap. In cooler conditions at Brooklands, Delage won the first British Grand Prix, although still needing two drivers to bring the winning car to the finish.

Lory radically overhauled the Delages for the 1927 season. Exhaust piping was moved to the left-hand side and the twin superchargers used in 1926 were replaced by a single Roots blower at the front of the engine. In this form the 55.8 × 76 mm engine was capable of reaching 8,000 rpm when needed and developing 170 bhp. Especially to cope with the new purpose-built track at Montlhéry near Paris, which combined a twisty road course with a speed bowl, it was the first Grand Prix car of the decade to have a five-speed transmission, top gear being an overdrive.[17] Montlhéry was first used for the French Grand Prix in 1925.

DRIVERS TO MATCH THE CARS

With its sloped-back radiator and crisp, low body lines the 1927 Delage was and looked 'the goods'. Relative newcomer Robert Benoist was the team's star driver, having signed up with Delage in 1924 after beginning racing in 1921. He and his Delage won the Grands Prix of France, Spain, Italy and Britain that year, and usually set the fastest lap as well. Delages placed one-two-three in the French and British races. Another Delage stalwart was Albert Divo, who had won the 1925 Spanish Grand Prix.

Built low to the ground with an offset driving position, the 1927 Delage was a purposeful-looking racing car. Its ground-hugging chassis and low frontal area would only be equalled late in the following decade.

17 Louis Delage was an established proponent of five-speed boxes for racing. His 1914 Grand Prix cars, like those of Nagant, had overdrive-top five-speed transmissions. He used them in earlier racers as well, to cope better with the fuel-consumption limitations.

Delage needed only the single entry of Robert Benoist to win at Monza in 1927. This fast track again attracted American entries, one Duesenberg and two 'Cooper Specials' – in fact, front-drive Millers. One Cooper-Miller survived to finish third, almost half an hour behind Benoist in a 3½-hour race. Delage withdrew from racing in 1928, when Benoist virtually retired, only to return to racing with Bugatti in the thirties, culminating in a Le Mans win with Wimille in 1937. In the Second World War, Robert Benoist was a stalwart of the French Resistance. This earned him execution at Buchenwald in 1944.

Another whose racing career began after the First World War was Antonio Ascari. A 'win or bust' racer, Ascari was both entrepreneur and driver on behalf of Alfa Romeo, for whom he won Grand Prix races in 1924 in Italy and in 1925 in Belgium. He died after crashing while leading the 1925 French Grand Prix.[18] Another Italian star of the twenties was Pietro Bordino, who enjoyed numerous successes in Fiat cars. Beginning as a riding mechanic before the war, Bordino was always at the fore for Fiat in this decade, competing with vigour both in Europe and America. At Tours in 1923, said *The Motor*, 'Bordino was amazing on corners. His dashing driving made everyone fear for his safety.' He died in a bizarre accident at Alessandria in 1928 when his Bugatti plunged into a river, drowning him.

Pietro Bordino was called 'the finest road race driver in the world' by Henry O'Neal de Hane Segrave, who was the outstanding British driver of the twenties,

In this unsupercharged 2-litre Sunbeam Briton Henry Segrave won the 1924 French Grand Prix at Lyons. The knighted Segrave was killed in 1930 just after setting a new world speed record on water.

---

18 Ascari was both the father of Alberto Ascari, who figures strongly in the fifties, and a role model for Enzo Ferrari, who admired his wheeling-and-dealing style.

although he was born in Maryland, USA, of an Irish father and American mother. His successes came at the wheels of Sunbeam and later Talbot Grand Prix cars. Segrave became engrossed with record-breaking, setting the first Land Speed Record of more than 200 mph (203.79 mph) with a twin-engined Sunbeam in 1927.

For Bugatti, fine results were achieved by Venetian Meo Costantini, who became team manager for Bugatti after retiring from racing after 1926. Towards the end of the twenties, Bugatti successes were scored by newcomers to racing Louis Chiron,

Tazio Nuvolari and René Dreyfus. Racing simply as 'Williams', William Grover-Williams was an Englishman born and raised in France. He was also an excellent Bugatti driver, earning a place in history as the first winner of a Monaco Grand Prix and scoring a French Grand Prix victory in the same year, 1929.

TALBOT FROM STD MOTORS

Although 1927 was Europe's last year to adhere to a 1½-litre formula, with the minimum weight raised to 700 kg (1,544 lb), racing in America kept that engine limit through 1929. This brought further advances in cams, bearings, supercharging and intercooling for the American Millers and Duesenbergs which, according to Griff Borgeson, allowed the best Miller engines to develop a stunning 285 bhp and rev as high as 8,500 rpm. Nevertheless, in 1929 Delage chanced an entry of one of its Grand Prix cars in the 500. Driven by Louis Chiron, it performed creditably with a seventh-place finish at an average of 87.7 mph against the winning Miller's 97.6 mph.

At least as ambitious as the Delage was another French-made Grand Prix entry in 1926. In the convoluted company that was STD Motors Limited – the

The low build of the Delages was matched by the sleek design of the 1926–27 Grand Prix Talbot, although it required its driver to have one elbow in the breeze. Henry Segrave sits in the Talbot in which he won an event at Brooklands in 1926.

Franco-Britannic enterprise that produced Sunbeam, Talbot and Darracq cars – engineering chief Louis Coatalen decided to assign to Vincenzo Bertarione and Water Becchia the design of a new 1½-litre Grand Prix car which this time would be a French-built Talbot, not a British-built Sunbeam.

At their Suresnes works in the Paris outskirts the ex-Fiat engineers created a new straight-eight racer using the same welded-steel cylinders they had brought to Sunbeam from Fiat. With dimensions of 56 × 75.5 mm, the Roots-blown Talbot eight developed 145 bhp at 6,500 rpm in 1926 and was uprated to 160 bhp at 7,000 rpm for 1927. Set low in the chassis, the engine rested behind a steeply sloped radiator.

The Talbot designers placed their driver as low as Lory did in the Delage, although without the benefit of an offset drive line. This required the right side of the body to be cut away to give the driver much-needed elbow room. The Talbot's frame rails were exceptionally deep and perforated for lightness to serve as a primitive space frame; the solid front and rear axles extended through gaps in the frame. Although lightness was a goal of this design, the cars were well over the minimum weight at 1,765 lb.

Here was a formidable-looking racing car on which huge sums had been lavished from the STD coffers. Still driving for STD, Henry Segrave was among the Talbot pilots for their baptismal outing in the British Grand Prix of 1926. Although suffering from front-axle judder under braking, they led the early laps only to retire with various maladies. The team returned to Brooklands later in the year for the Junior Car Club's 200-mile race, where Segrave led a Talbot one-two victory.

Against the all-conquering Delages the Talbots had little luck in the only major race they contested in 1927. Always a wizard starter, Albert Divo led the early laps of the French Grand Prix, but retired. One Talbot finished a distant fourth. STD couldn't afford to send its cars to San Sebastian, Monza or Brooklands. As a last howl, in 1927 one of the cars set a new international record for 1½-litre cars at 129 mph on the Arpajon road. Thereafter Vincenzo Bertarione brokered the sale of the three French cars to Italian racing driver Emilio Materassi.

SWAN SONGS OF THE VOLUME CAR MAKERS

The sale of the Talbots symbolised the end of an era of Grand Prix racing of the twenties – the era in which such car-making firms as STD, Delage, Mercedes, Fiat, Ballot and Voisin would build and enter racing cars in the major Grand Prix events. Outbursts of major activity by auto makers would characterise the period 1934–39 and again 1950–55, but otherwise Grand Prix racing would become the playground of such specialist racing car builders as Bugatti and, soon, Maserati.

An enigmatic swan song for Fiat in Grand Prix racing was heard at Monza in September 1927. For Pietro Bordino, the Turin firm's Giulio Cesare Cappa had engineered the Tipo 806, the only twelve-cylinder racing car to appear on the track under the 1½-litre formula. Cappa placed two six-cylinder engines side-by-side on a common crankcase, geared together, and opened the inboard inlet valves of both 'engines' with a single central camshaft. Fiat's classical fabricated-steel cylinders were retained.

Rated at 187 bhp at 8,500 rpm, the Roots-supercharged Fiat twelve was installed in a conventional, albeit low-profiled, chassis. The ambitious car's only race was the rainy Milan Grand Prix of 1927, which was combined with other events at Monza. Others led at first in the final Free Formula race, wrote Paul Sheldon, but 'the magnificent Bordino came steaming past into a lead which he held to the end, winning by no less than half-a-minute after just twenty minutes of racing against the cream of Italy's Formule Libre cars'.

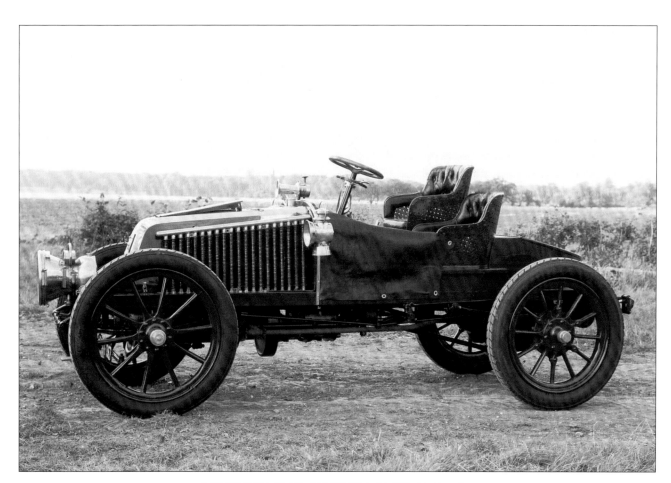

Exemplifying the style and spirit of the earliest racing cars is this impeccable replica of the Renault that was driven by Marcel Renault to win the race from Paris to Vienna held on 26-29 June 1902. Although competing in the light-car class, the 5.4-litre four-cylinder Renault defeated the heavy Panhards and Mercedes. Renault, wrote Gerald Rose, 'was presented with a laurel wreath almost as large as his car'.

The Star Motor Company in England's Wolverhampton produced a Mercedes-inspired racing car for the British eliminating trials for the 1905 Gordon Bennett races. Its four-cylinder engine, featuring mechanically operated overhead inlet valves, measured 140 x 165 mm for 10,160 cc. The brothers Harry and Fred Goodwin were not quick enough in their Stars to win a place on the British team.

The inventive genius of Wilhelm Maybach that had advanced the state of the automotive art with the first Mercedes of 1901 was not always appreciated by his employer. For the 1906-07 season he created a new six-cylinder overhead-cam racer of 11.1 litres that introduced high-tension coil ignition – which Daimler considered too risky. Its rejection coincided with Maybach's departure from the firm. Nevertheless it was the first of many overhead-cam racing cars from Mercedes and later Mercedes-Benz.

The 1907 Grand Prix Fiat raced under rules that allowed no more than 30 litres of fuel to be consumed for every 100 kilometres. In the hands of Felice Nazzaro it was successful in a race of 769 miles over a circuit at Dieppe organised by the French Automobile Club. With its vee-inclined overhead valves the four-cylinder Fiat developed 130 bhp at 1,600 rpm from its 16,286 cc.

Although one of the three team cars entered was as high as fifth during the ten laps of the 1908 French Grand Prix, the 12.8-litre Panhards did not figure strongly in the event. The success of winner Mercedes followed by Benz pushed the best Panhard, driven by George Heath, back to ninth place. This was Panhard's final Grand Prix entry.

In the eyes of all Benz loyalists, Victor Hémery was the moral victor in the 1908 French Grand Prix driving a Benz with this four-cylinder engine. He battled for the lead against the winning Mercedes but was delayed by damage to an eye from shattered goggles, finishing second. Designed by Louis Groulart, the engine had pushrod-operated overhead valves and produced a nominal 120 bhp at 1,500 rpm from 12,076 cc.

Elegant bonnet styling was a feature of the 1913 Th. Schneider Grand Prix car, equipped here with wings for use on the road. Four Schneiders of 5,501 cc started the 1913 French Grand Prix. Their cornering power impressed but their speed was inadequate; three finished in seventh, ninth and tenth places. The fourth Schneider retired with reported carburettor trouble.

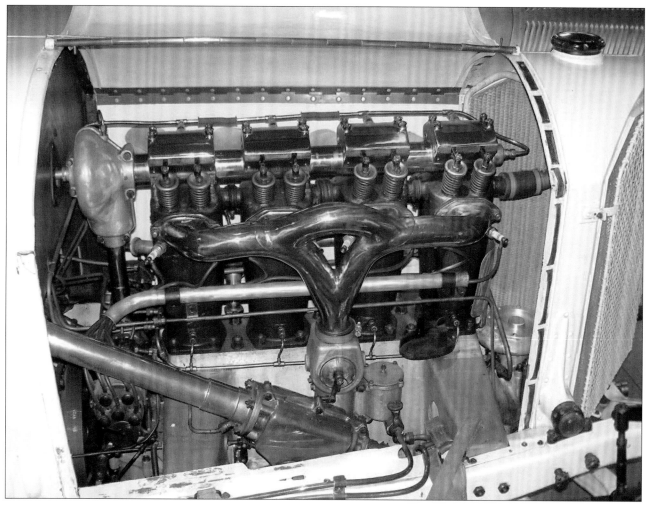

Under the direction of Paul Daimler, son of the founder, the Daimler Motoren Gesellschaft produced a fleet of cars from scratch for the 1914 French Grand Prix. Their four-cylinder engines had a single shaft-driven overhead camshaft operating four valves per cylinder through rocker arms. Powering the Model 18/100, which placed one-two-three, they developed 106 bhp at 3,100 rpm from 4,483 cc.

With Swiss engineer Ernest Henry at the drawing board, France's Peugeot set new standards for racing engines with gear-driven twin overhead camshafts operating four vee-inclined valves per cylinders. The first such four-cylinder models appeared in 1912, a 7.6-litre Peugeot for Grand Prix racing and a 3.0-litre car for Voiturette racing. Shown is a version of the smaller engine produced after the Great War.

Having set his sights on the creation of a marketable car with his Type 35 of 1924, Ettore Bugatti was eminently successful. His 2.0-litre straight-eight racing car was blessed with lines both stylish and aggressive. Its cast aluminium wheels, with their integral brake drums, were a spectacular innovation and a major money-spinner for Bugatti.

At first dubious about supercharging, in 1927 Bugatti created his Type 35C with a three-lobe Roots-type blower which brought its output to 135 bhp at 5,300 rpm. Such models enjoyed 14 victories in major events in the seasons from 1928 through 1930 when Grand Prix racing was run without specific displacement limits.

A mechanic manipulates the throttle on the front-mounted carburettor of a 1927 straight-eight Delage. Its supercharged 1½-litre engine was capable of development that kept one such car competitive for a decade. This car was fitted during the 1930s with an independent front suspension designed by the Delage's creator, Albert Lory.

Right: The driver of a 1927 Delage 15-S-8 faced a compact dash panel dominated by a huge tachometer. Although its engine could rev safely to 8,000, such speeds were only used in racing when necessary. Lory provided a high-geared fifth ratio that allowed Delage drivers to rest their engines on long straights.

Overleaf: Making a comeback to Grand Prix racing in the early 1930s, Alfa Romeo introduced its immortal Type B model in 1932. Also known as the P3, it was a pure single-seater with its driver perched above a unique drive line that had separate shafts from the gearbox to each rear wheel. Capable of 140 mph, the Type B Alfa was the outstanding GP car of the 1932 and '33 seasons. Between its 1932 debut and mid-1934 it took part in 26 races, of which it won 22.

The straight-eight engine of Alfa Romeo's Type B followed the pattern of that Milan company's 8C 2300 of 1931 – also a creation of Vittorio Jano – in having two blocks of four cylinders separated by a central gear drive to its overhead camshafts and superchargers, each set of cylinders having its own Roots-type blower. Displacing 2,655 cc, the eight developed 215 bhp at 5,600 rpm.

Britain's contribution to single-seater racing in the 1930s was the ERA, with a Riley-derived supercharged six-cylinder engine and chassis designed by Reid Railton. Engine sizes of 1.1, 1.5 and 2.0 litres were offered to allow competitors to choose their category. Among the ERAs competing in post-war Grand Prix racing was R.5.B., shown, dubbed 'Remus' by its first owner, Prince Bira.

Both Mercedes-Benz and Auto Union produced revolutionary cars for the new 750-kilogram Grand Prix formula in 1934. The W25 from Mercedes stunned with its clean lines and fully enclosed all-independent suspension, parallel wishbones in front and swing axles at the rear. Powered by a Roots-supercharged straight-eight, it competed through 1935 and occasionally in 1936.

In their Bologna workshops the Maserati brothers produced an ambitious GP car for the 750-kilogram formula. Their V8RI was introduced late in 1935 with a supercharged 4,244 cc V8, the first V8 engine built expressly for Grand Prix racing. Enlarged to 4,785 cc in 1936, the all-independently-sprung V8RI was a race-winner at Pau but otherwise outpaced by the silver German cars.

Blending a new 5,560 cc straight-eight engine with chassis ideas brought forward from a planned future model, Mercedes-Benz produced its W125 for the 1937 season after struggling against Auto Union in 1936. Motivated by up to 575 bhp at 5,500 rpm, the W125 was developed under the supervision of new racing-department chief Rudolf Uhlenhaut. The car above has unique bodywork, with a seam curving up to its cowl while (left) pre-war star Hermann Lang demonstrated a W125 at Monaco.

Opposite: Apotheosis of the pre-war front-engined Grand Prix car was the Mercedes-Benz W154 in its 1939 form. Powered by a V12 of 2,962 cc, its drive line was angled across the chassis to allow a low seating position for its driver. Output of 480 bhp at 7,500 rpm gave it a top speed of 185 mph. The W154 shown was one of the three prepared to race in Argentina in 1951, with a narrower grille inlet.

For the French Grand Prix at Reims in 1939 Auto Union introduced this two-stage Roots-type supercharger for its 3.0-litre V12 engine. Thus equipped, the D-Type Auto Union produced 485 bhp at 7,000 rpm and could attain 500 bhp at 7,500, although this wasn't always used in racing. In spite of the success enjoyed by the Auto Unions, their mid-engined initiative was followed up by few immediately after the war.

Italy's red Maseratis were stalwarts of the racing scene before and after World War II. On the right is an 8C 3000, the first Maserati to win a major Grand Prix – the French race in 1933, in the hands of Giuseppe Campari. On the left is a 4CL, introduced as a Voiturette in 1939. With 16 valves, its Roots-supercharged four-cylinder engine suited Maserati's 4CL perfectly to post-war 1½-litre Grand Prix racing.

In May 1948 Tony Lago introduced his proper Grand Prix Talbot-Lago, the Type 26, one of the handsomest cars of this or any era. With its unsupercharged 4½-litre six-cylinder engine it was successful at Montlhéry (in both 1948 and 1949) and in 1949 at Chimay and in the French and Belgian Grands Prix. Right, Louis Rosier is driving his Talbot-Lago to third in the 1949 British Grand Prix.

Poised in later years next to a Vanwall transporter, the BRM V-16 looks every inch the ultimate racing car, as indeed it was conceived in the late forties. It appears here in its 1952 configuration for entry in Formule Libre races and for a Formula 1 race at Albi in 1953 in which it won its heat but shed a rear-tyre treads in the final. The 1$\frac{1}{2}$-litre 135-degree V16 was angled in the chassis so that the drive line could pass to the left of the driver on its way to the rear-mounted transaxle.

Here was a car capable of competing with the Delages. Bordino's fastest lap was 96.5 mph, against Benoist's 94.3 mph earlier in the day in the Delage. But it was destined to be the Tipo 806's only outing. The great car was broken up when Fiat announced a definitive withdrawal from racing. Neither Delage nor Talbot would be continuing in 1928. For all these firms the cost of building and maintaining such exotic and specialised cars had become excessive in relation to the promotional benefits that the races provided. Haemorrhaging money, the 1½-litre formula had expired. What would follow it?

In Paris the AIACR threw up its well-manicured hands and offered what amounted to Free Formula rules for 1928. Eligible cars would have to weigh 550–750 kg (1,213–1,654 lb) and races would have to be over at least 600 km (373 miles). In fact, only one race, the European Grand Prix at Monza, was run to these rules. Ironically, it suffered the greatest tragedy that Grand Prix racing has ever experienced when the Talbot of the skilled and much-liked Emilio Materassi left the track at speed and careered into a spectator area, killing 22 and injuring 20. The driver also died.

Materassi was much missed. With the Talbots he had formed the first private racing team, or *scuderia*. Enzo Ferrari would later follow his example. Materassi had won with the French cars at Mugello and Montenero, and they would win again in 1929 at Tripoli and Mugello in the hands of Gastone Brilli-Peri. Indeed, in modified form one of the cars would compete in the 1949 Swiss Grand Prix.

For the 2-litre formula of 1924 Daimler built this ambitious straight-eight Mercedes racing car from the pen of Ferdinand Porsche. After only one Grand Prix appearance the cars were consigned to sports-car races and sprints. Not until 1934 would Daimler's successor, Daimler-Benz, again produce a purpose-built Grand Prix racer.

Alfieri Maserati, at the wheel, drove his 1.5-litre Tipo 26 to a first in class in the 1927 Targa Florio. Its unsupercharged straight-eight would be the progenitor of a family of successful racing engines.

The AIACR's new rules played into the hands of the company that was now France's leading racing car producer, Bugatti. Simply lengthening the stroke of his Type 35 allowed him to produce the supercharged 35B of 2,262 cc (60 × 100 mm), giving 135 bhp and an useful torque increase. Here was a fast, reliable and serviceable (if you paid Ettore's high parts prices) racing car weighing just under the Grand Prix maximum. The 35B and its sister, the supercharged 2-litre 35C, became the staple Grand Prix cars of the end of the twenties.

A genial Frenchman, Louis Chiron, was the winner of the tragic race at Monza in his 35B. He was also successful at Rome, Reims and San Sebastian. A former motorcycle racer from Mantua who first competed in cars in 1927, Tazio Nuvolari, was another Bugatti exponent. He won the first race of 1928 at Tripoli in his Type 35C. Other Bugatti chauffeurs from whom more would be heard in the future were Achille Varzi and René Dreyfus.

INTRODUCING THE MASERATI BROTHERS

In the meantime another specialist racing car producer had been heard from. Deciding that they could do better on their own account than with the Diattos they had been racing, the Bologna-based Maserati brothers built straight-eight 1½-litre racing cars under their own name. Two Tipo 26 Maseratis retired early in the 1926 Italian Grand Prix, one euphoniously piloted by Emilio Materassi. Lacking in lightness, the Maseratis figured only secondarily in the 1927 races, although the first victories for the marque were scored in minor events.

There was no gainsaying the practical elegance of the racing engine designs of the Maserati brothers. Their supercharged 2.5-litre 26M was one of the most successful Grand Prix cars of the 1930 season.

Enlarged to 2 litres as the Tipo 26B, a Maserati scored a welcome win at Catania in Sicily in 1928 in the hands of Baconin Borzacchini. The cars from Modena were fifth and sixth in the European Grand Prix at Monza, the latter driven by Ernesto Maserati. Still in its swaddling clothes, the young Maserati marque was not yet able to attract the quicker-driving customers.

In spite of the onset of the Depression, open-wheeled-car racing prospered in 1929 and 1930 under anarchic conditions that allowed organisers to frame their events as they saw fit. The only rule promulgated by the AIACR for those years was a minimum weight of 900 kg, with a suggestion of a limit on the allowable consumption of fuel and oil.

Seizing the day, Alfa Romeo dusted off its three 1924 P2 racing cars and began entering them on behalf of drivers such as Achille Varzi. The old cars were updated in their suspension and body shape to resemble the more current 6C 1750 Gran Sport model, and their supercharging systems were modified to bring their power to 175 bhp at 5,500 rpm from their 2 litres. By 1930 Tazio Nuvolari was driving the resuscitated P2 Alfas for the newly formed Scuderia Ferrari.

The year 1929 was notable for the first race held on the roads and hills of Monte Carlo. This audacious idea, for which many had forecast disaster, was crowned with success. A Bugatti victory was foreseeable, but the race's sensation was the third place scored by young German Rudolf Caracciola in his fenderless Mercedes-Benz SSK, by comparison a mammoth, stripped touring car with a supercharged 6.8-litre six-cylinder engine. Rudy actually led the race at one point, but had to stop to refuel his behemoth.

Both races run that year to the Grand Prix rules, the French and Spanish Grands Prix, were won by works-entered Type 35B Bugattis. Only one Grand Prix entirely to the rules was raced in 1930, the European Grand Prix at Spa. Louis Chiron's Bugatti won after Molsheim's team orders obliged Guy Bouriat to stop before the finishing line and let Chiron pass so that he could win the European Championship, for which points were awarded to drivers for success in designated races.

Intervening in the largely Bugatti entry for the 246-mile 1930 French Grand Prix was a big green British car: Sir Henry 'Tim' Birkin's supercharged 4½-litre Bentley. The fast course on the outskirts of Pau suited the 240 hp four-cylinder Bentley, which finished an astonishing second behind Philippe Etancelin's Type 35C Bugatti. The same year saw René Dreyfus win at Monte Carlo and Reims for Bugatti.

Maserati was now shifting into high gear. In 1930 its new 2½-litre 26M won at Rome (Arcangeli), Montenero (Fagioli) and Pescara, Monza and San Sebastian (Varzi), marking a new presence at the top of Grand Prix racing. To be confident of having a car for any occasion, the Maserati brothers also built a 4-litre V-16 named the 'V4', based on a pair of their 2-litre straight-eights. The eponymous Ernesto drove it to victory in the third heat of the Monza races in 1930.

A SURPRISINGLY HEALTHY SPORT

Although conducted without much reference to the international authorities in Paris, increasingly controlled by circuit owners and managers, Grand Prix racing was surprisingly healthy at the end of the twenties. Alfa Romeo among the bigger firms was still active, and Bugatti and Maserati were well established as capable purveyors of first-class racing cars to teams and drivers.

Not until 1934 would a rigorous Grand Prix formula again be widely enforced, a 750 kg maximum weight to which some of the most spectacular cars of the inter-war racing era would be produced. In the meantime Grand Prix racing had survived the nadir of the 1926 French Grand Prix to sustain the position as the premier road-racing category that it still enjoyed at the end of the twentieth century.

PRACTISING FOR THE GRAND PRIX.

Trial Runs on the Course Indicate that the Great Race at Lyons on August 3rd will be a Test to Destruction. By W. F. Bradley, " The Autocar" Special Representative on the Course.

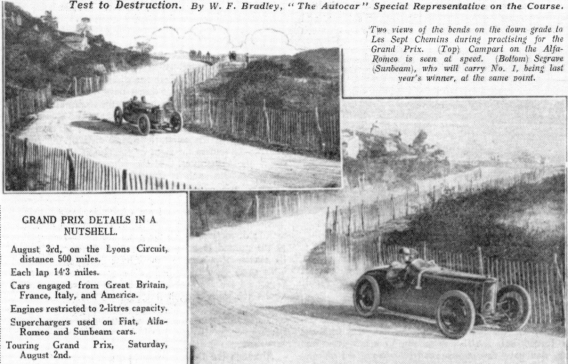

Two views of the bends on the down grade to Les Sept Chemins during practising for the Grand Prix. (Top) Campari on the Alfa-Romeo is seen at speed. (Bottom) Segrave (Sunbeam), who will carry No. 1, being last year's winner, at the same point.

GRAND PRIX DETAILS IN A NUTSHELL.

August 3rd, on the Lyons Circuit, distance 500 miles.

Each lap 14·3 miles.

Cars engaged from Great Britain, France, Italy, and America.

Engines restricted to 2-litres capacity.

Superchargers used on Fiat, Alfa-Romeo and Sunbeam cars.

Touring Grand Prix, Saturday, August 2nd.

AT daybreak, last Friday morning, the competitors in the European Grand Prix made their first appearance in public for official practice on the Lyons circuit. The advanced state of preparations and the form which the machines showed in practice only served to confirm the impression that this year the race will be more keenly disputed than any previous event of this kind held in France. Of the twenty-two cars entered, nineteen were ready for the first day's practice, which is a result rarely seen more than a fortnight before the day of the race. The only absentees were the two cuff-valve Schmids, which, however, were reported to be on their way from Annecy, and Salamano's Fiat.

The Cars Show Their Paces.

The road was thrown open at 4.30 a.m., but, as the light was poor at that time, it was not until 5 o'clock that the first starts were made, and the machines were allowed to run until 8.30 o'clock, thus giving more than three hours' full practice. M. Bugatti had the five cars entered for the Grand Prix on the course, in addition to a sixth practice car, his drivers being Chassagne, Vizcaya, Constantini, Friedrich, and Garnier. M. Delage brought out only two cars, with which Divo and Benoist put in a number of practice laps, Thomas finally taking over Divo's car for a few rounds of the course. The Alfa-Romeo straight-eights were in full force with Ascari, Campari, Ferrari, and Wagner at the wheel. Bordino, Nazzaro, and Pastore represented the Fiat team; the three Sunbeams, driven by Segrave, K. Lee Guinness, and Resta were the first to start away, while Count Zborowski's all-white Miller, held up with plug trouble, was half-an-hour late in getting into action.

It was soon evident that the circuit is a particularly difficult one, from the standpoint of both drivers and machines. On the first round Bordino failed to reappear, and all sorts of rumours were rife, for a short time, concerning his fate. After Givors there is a winding climb over a narrow road with a number of very difficult turns, conditions being such that, in the opinion of all the drivers, it would be folly to attempt to pass on this stretch. Bordino appears to have gone into one of these turns at too high a speed, and, unable to get round, crashed through the outer pallisading, and was brought to a stop by a stout fencing made of railway sleepers, just on the edge of a sheer drop. The front end of the car was completely wrecked, but fortunately the driver escaped with nothing more serious than a little skin scraped from his chin, while his mechanic suffered a slight scalp wound. The car was sent by lorry to the factory at Turin the same morning, and is expected to be ready for the race on August 3rd.

Hazards of the Course.

Although this was the only accident of any importance, there were numerous incidents which proved the difficult nature of the course. In Givors one of the drivers took down a lamp-post as he skidded on the right-angle turn, but rushed off with such rapidity that nobody knows who was responsible for this little incident. At half-a-dozen points around the course the light pallisading was torn down, luckily with no injury to the cars.

In practice work it is not possible to get more than an approximation of the speed ability of the respective cars, for the spectators never know whether a driver is travelling " all-out " or not, and there are no means of

Practising for the Grand Prix.

ascertaining whether a car has covered a complete lap at speed. Judging from their performance along the grand stand stretch, the Sunbeams had a remarkably fine turn of speed and wonderful acceleration. Segrave is credited with a round of the circuit at 74 miles an hour, but this must be accepted with a certain amount of reserve, and even the driver of the car was not inclined to attach much

An impression of one of the straight-eight Bugattis at speed at a bend. The driver in this case is Garnier.

importance to the time with which he was credited. It seems doubtful if the average of 65.5 miles an hour of 1914 can be equalled this year.

The Bugattis created a most favourable impression for speed, acceleration, and road-holding ability, and undoubtedly are the best racing productions this firm has ever turned out. Alfa-Romeo put in some very fast work, and gave the impression of having a set of cars which will very seriously have to be reckoned with on August 3rd. Owing to Bordino's accident, there were only two Fiats on the course on the second day of practice, and, as they were frequently stopped for experiments with various pressures in the tyres, there was not much opportunity of estimating their speed. Compared with the others, the Delages seemed slow, but this was probably due largely to their silence compared with such cars as the Bugattis and Alfa-Romeos.

A Very Open Race.

Never, in any Grand Prix race, has it been more difficult to forecast a winner, or even to pick out the winning firm. Personally, I should bracket Sunbeam, Fiat, and Bugatti together, any one of these three being capable of providing the winner, with Delage, Alfa-Romeo, Schmid, and the privately owned Miller in the second grouping. It is quite safe to predict such a fast pace at the outset that, together with the difficult nature of the course, the percentage of withdrawals during the first two hours will be extremely high. On this hilly, winding set of roads, with one portion already strewn with stones, and the fastest stretch having a modern dressing of concrete, tyres are going to play a most important *rôle*.

Only three makes of cars will start with a supercharging device. These are Fiat, Sunbeam, and Alfa-Romeo. So far as Fiat is concerned, the same general type of supercharger will be used as last year, with the addition of a very big capacity air cooler mounted between the front dumb irons, through which all the air is aspired by the blower on the forward end of the crankshaft. This assures air being aspired at a lower temperature than when going in direct, as on last year's car, and assures more complete filling of the cylinders

C 4

Alfa-Romeo was announced to have a two-gear blower with a clutch, but, although experiments in this direction were carried out, it is with a single gear blower, mounted on the front end of the crankshaft, the air being drawn in around the base of the radiator, that the race will be run, the general design being similar to that of last year's Fiats. From the blower the air is led through a cast aluminium conduit filling up the space between the right-hand side of the engine and the frame member, the carburetter being bolted on the top of this conduit and the base being ribbed for cooling.

While the two Italian firms have the blower before the carburetter—in other words, the compressor blows into the carburetter—the Sunbeams have the blower after the carburetter. A very big single Solex is used, and is mounted at the front right-hand side of the engine, just behind and to the right of the blower. The air first enters the carburetter, and the mixture then passes into the compressor, and is distributed to the six cylinders.

Superchargers; Pros and Cons.

To obviate any danger from a backfire, there is a relief valve on the main pipe between the blower and the intake manifold, through which the gases are discharged directly to the ground if an artificially high pressure is created by reason of a charge blown back from the cylinders. This same general method of using a supercharger was found on the Duesenberg which won the recent Indianapolis 500 miles race, and appears to have in its favour a greater simplicity, for the carburetter has not to be balanced, and the advantage of setting up a high degree of turbulence. That it is advantageous is proved by the increased power at all engine speeds.

Although the Delages were designed to be used with a supercharger, they will start in the race without this device, the twelve-cylinder engine being fitted with a couple of Zenith carburetters. Bugatti pronounces himself opposed to the supercharger, and in an animated conversation with Mr. Coatalen maintained that he could get the same results with his atmospheric pressure engines

The new aluminium wheel on the Bugatti Grand Prix racers. The brake drum is cast integral with the wheel and has a steel liner. The whole weighs four pounds less than the more usual racing wire wheel.

as any of the others were obtaining with a compressor. The new straight-eight Bugattis have a couple of Solex carburetters, and can, it is claimed, spurt up to 7,000 revolutions a minute.

Much interest was aroused during practice in the aluminium wheels with which the Bugattis are fitted. These are an aluminium alloy casting, made in the Bugatti factory, with the drums forming an integral part of the wheel. There are two rows of eight flat spokes, about 3 millimetres thick, and for the purpose of braking a steel liner is let into the drums. It is stated that the weight of the wheel is 4 lb. less than that of a commonly used racing suspension type wire wheel of equal size, but

Albert Divo on the 12-cylinder Delage Grand Prix car on the Lyons circuit, which, it will be observed, is already barricaded.

this, of course, includes the brake drum on the Bugatti, whereas on any other wheel the drum is separate.

Another feature which attracted attention on the Bugattis is the hand-forged tubular axle which, although in one piece, has a 30 mm. hole through the centre, and is only bored out 6 mm. in the two end parts. There was much speculation as to how this apparently impossible mechanical task was accomplished, for the axle is not an assembled or a welded job. The explanation is that the axle is first bored out to a uniform diameter, and is then reforged until the two end portions, outside the spring seats, are practically solid. Enough metal is left to allow of this closing up, and the entire axle is machined externally. Instead of using spring clips, the short, perfectly flat front springs pass through a rectangular slot formed in the axle.

Cushion Tyres for Racing.

Probably the Grand Prix will witness the first use of balloon tyres for racing, for the Alfa-Romeos came up for practice with 31 × 5in. straight sides on their rear wheels, while the Fiats had the same section, but a much smaller diameter on both front and rear wheels, giving them an appearance quite foreign to racing cars. It was ascertained that the Fiats were carrying out experiments with 6in. tyres, and, as this corresponds to 152 mm., and the usual size for a car of this weight is 105 mm., it will be seen that the increase is really considerable. These, however, are not " soft " tyres, for all the Italian cars were running with a pressure of 56 lb. to the square inch, only the Bugattis, which were on Dunlop cords, having the comparatively low pressure of 42 lb. at the rear, and 31 lb. in the front tyres. The Sunbeams have definitely decided to run on Rapsons, which, incidentally, were in wonderful condition after three and a-half hours' running in practice, and Delage is also negotiating for the same make of tyre. Pirellis are to be found on the French Schmids and the Italian Alfa-Romeos and Fiat cars. As the course is only about

14½ miles round, it is quite likely that some of the cars will start without a spare wheel, but the final decision on this point will depend, to a certain extent, on the results obtained by the various drivers in practice.

Although great improvements have been made in road-holding ability, it is certain that drivers are in for a really strenuous time on August 3rd. Guinness, after three hours' speed work, said he felt like a pea on a hot plate; while Mr. Louis Coatalen, after acting as mechanic for a round, declared that every organ in his body seemed to have been shaken out of place—and this on cars which, in the opinion of all the drivers, hold the road in a wonderful manner.

Protection from Shocks.

Segrave had an interesting fitment in the shape of a steel box bolted to his steering column, with motor cycle knee grips attached to the two sides of the box, thus enabling him to grip with his thighs. Nazzaro had fitted up the seats of his car with rounded-off upholstery, thus avoiding all sharp or hard edges in the division between himself and the mechanic or on the sides and back of the seats. In addition, the Fiats had pneumatic cushions and back-rests to ease the drivers' lots.

Sixteen days before the race, preparations were very advanced. The very handsome and elaborate grand stands, which are in the same position as those of 1914, were finished, with the exception of a little upholstery. The replenishment pits, directly opposite the grand stands, do not belie their name, for they are sunk well below the level of the road, and there are three of four steps from them to the counter over which goods must be passed to the racing cars. The view across country

Felice Nazzaro on the Straight-Eight Fiat negotiating one of the many bends.

to the winding descent from Les Esses to Les Sept Chemins hairpin appears to be more unobstructed than ever, thus making it possible to follow the movements of the cars for a long time before they flash past the grand stand. The only criticism which can be raised against this portion of the course is that the road is none too wide in front of the replenishment pits, in view of the possibility of two or three cars pulling out together while others are going by at speed.

Practising for the Grand Prix.

Since 1914 the road from Les Sept Chemins to Givors has been laid with a hard, modern dressing, which is unaffected by the most terrific accelerations. The bends here are long, easy, and treacherous, and the course is rendered all the more dangerous by the fact that it is not the road but the tyre which receives punishment when skidding on such a surface. Towards the end of the practice there was a slight shower—just sufficient to show that things are going to be lively if any rain falls on the race day. On the winding hill section, from Givors to the switchback straightaway, conditions are going to be much worse, after two hours' racing, than on the stoniest section of the Tours circuit. It will be a wonderful car and a master driver who wins this year's Grand Prix.

THE ALFA-ROMEO CARS.

An Eight-cylinder Italian Competitor which has Already Given Promise of Great Speed.

EIGHT-CYLINDER engines are found on the Alfa-Romeo cars entered in the European Grand Prix. The cylinders, which have a bore and stroke of 61 × 85 mm., are separate steel forgings, with a water-jacket for each pair, and are mounted in line on an aluminium base chamber. There are two valves per cylinder, inclined in the head and driven by a couple of overhead camshafts from a vertical shaft at the rear. A single magneto is used, and there is one plug per cylinder, placed centrally in the combustion chamber.

One of the Alfa-Romeo cars which will   run in the race.

The rotary blower is at the front end of the engine, driven directly off the crankshaft and always in engagement. The air, which is aspired through openings around the base of the radiator, is delivered under pressure to the Memini carburetter through a separate cast aluminium conduit on the right-hand side of, and bolted to, the engine base chamber. It is stated that the engine runs at 5,000 to 5,500 revolutions, and that the power output is from 130 to 140. Roller bearings are used for the crankshaft and for the big ends, and lubrication is of the dry sump type, with the supply of oil maintained in a tank under the cowl.

The engine forms a unit with the clutch and gear box, the former being of the multiple disc type, and the latter providing four speeds and reverse. In common with all the Grand Prix cars, four-wheel brakes are fitted. These are of the mechanical type, with, however, a hydraulic servo mechanism mounted in the bottom of the gear box, and making use of the gear box oil. Wheelbase is 8ft. 6in., with a track of 53in. in front and 49in. at the rear. Pirelli tyres are used on Rudge-Whitworth wire wheels. Three of the cars have profiled tails, with the spare wheel carried on the side; while the fourth machine, to be driven by Ascari, has the tail cut short and the wheel carried behind. This driver is of the opinion that, as the average speed cannot be high on the Lyons circuit, the convenience of the wheel behind outweighs any advantage which might be gained by better streamlining. The cars are said to be very fast, and to have averaged over 90 m.p.h. in a race in Italy.

THE SUPERCHARGED FIATS.

Straight-eight Engines and Cars, Based on Last Year's Experience, to be Used at Lyons.

CONTRARY to all the reports which have been circulated, no unusual type of two-stroke supercharged engine will be used by Fiat in the coming Grand Prix, nor has there been any really serious intention of racing with such a type of engine. The leading Italian firm will come to the start with four cars which are very similar in all their general features to those of a year ago; indeed, two of the machines are practically last year's racers rebuilt, with detail modifications, while two others are new, but do not differ in any way from the older models.

The features are eight steel cylinders in line, of 60 × 87 mm. bore and stroke, a sheet steel water jacket for each group of four cylinders, two valves per cylinder, with a couple of overhead camshafts driven from a vertical shaft at the rear, roller bearings in practically every part of the engine with the exception of the gudgeon pins, and, of course, a supercharger device. While there are no radical changes a considerable amount of detail work has been carried out, with the result that 150 b.h.p. has been obtained from these small engines.

Lubrication is of the dry sump type, with a scavenger and a feed pump, the oil tank being under the scuttle, but isolated from it so as to allow a cooling draught of air to play around it. A single Bosch magneto is used, and there is one plug per cylinder placed centrally.

Many detail refinements have been carried out in the supercharging device, among these being a redesigning which makes it impossible for dust or road grit to injure the compressor, and the fitting of a cooler between the front dumb irons which assures really cold air being drawn into the compressor. The carburetter is of Fiat design and construction.

The racing Fiats have unit construction of engine, clutch and gear box, with drive and torque transmitted through the propeller-shaft housing. Brakes are on the four wheels, but instead of the hydraulic servo of a year ago, a mechanical servo mechanism is now used.

CHAPTER FOUR

THE THIRTIES

We drove, naturally, from race to race; and whenever we found a better way to go, or a nicer hotel to stay at along the way, or a better restaurant, we would tell each other about it. We had quite a grapevine. After a race, our first thought always was, where do we eat? We all were gourmets, we all loved to dine well and tell stories and unwind. Only with Scuderia Ferrari, perhaps, was this different, only when working with Enzo Ferrari did a race driver feel a little bit like a businessman. Otherwise he certainly did not.

René Dreyfus

The thirties, which to many represent a glowing Golden Age of Grand Prix racing, are paradoxical, almost schizophrenic in retrospect. Tremendous technical progress was made during the decade. The supercharged 3-litre Mercedes-Benz and Auto Union Grand Prix cars of 1939 achieved a standard in the integration and utilisation of available human and mechanical means that has only been approached since – never surpassed.

No modern examples can provide meaningful parallels to the way the Germans went Grand Prix racing from 1934 to 1939. Their dominance, especially in the last three years, was total. As one example of many, both Mercedes and Auto Union brought five cars each to the starting line of the German Grand Prix at the Nürburgring in 1937; several spare cars remained in the pits. During the race Bernd Rosemeyer in an Auto Union set a lap time which was not bettered in competition until 1956. And back at their factories both firms had duplicate teams of cars being prepared for the next event, plus two engines for each car!

So lofty in conception and cost was this scale of operation that it rendered completely irrelevant the technical consequences of the Grand Prix formulae that preceded it. Put another way, the physical means brought to bear on the design problem were now far more important to the results obtained than the mere conditions imposed by the various formulae. Not until 1951, the last year of mechanically driven superchargers in Grand Prix racing, were any manufacturers able to deploy effectively even a few of the design elements that had made the German machines so overwhelming in 1938–39. The means to implement them on the German scale had simply not been available.

THE DECADE AND ITS COMPETITORS

The first four years of the thirties contrasted sharply with the extravagant final six years. Technically retrograde, these early years plumbed a nadir of Grand Prix racing car quality, if not quantity, which was since reached only in 1952–53, 1961–62 and in the 'Ford Formula' years of the Cosworth V-8's dominance. The reason was simple: the Great Depression, which affected Europe as well as

America. It was remarkable enough that racing continued at all during those first years of the decade. It did so without the strong financial backing of the car manufacturers, mainly French, whose participation had been dominant in the last significant formula, the 1½-litre years of 1926–27.

Great credit must go to Italy, and especially to Count Vincenzo Florio, for providing enough major events in the early thirties to make Grand Prix racing financially survivable by the private teams that then made up most of the entries. But in the first two years of the decade the machinery remained French – that is to say, Bugatti.

The beginning of the decade saw the last great year of the Bugatti Type 35. It scored six major wins in 1930 before being replaced the following year by the twin-overhead-camshaft Type 51, a very impressive 2,262 cc straight-eight of 160 bhp which helped Bugattis record eleven wins that season.[1] A new and strong competitor, however, was the 2,495 cc Maserati straight-eight, which won seven events in 1930, including a one-two-three finish at Monza, but won only two races in 1931.

Fascist support for Italian automotive projects went not to the minuscule Maserati firm, but to Alfa Romeo, which in the early thirties was assuming major truck and aircraft engine production responsibilities for Mussolini's government, and in 1933 was taken over by IRI, the government-owned industrial holding company. Alfa's role in racing in the first two years of the decade had been modest but effective. It scored two 1930 wins with its updated P2, and seven 1931 victories with engineer Vittorio Jano's new 8C 2300 Monza, a 2.3-litre eight which also doubled as a sports car in this economy minded era.

For the 1932–33 seasons Jano produced the Tipo B, a serious single-seater racing car which, together with the Monzas still racing, recorded nine wins for Alfa Romeo in 1932 and six in 1933. Between its 1932 debut and mid-1934 the Tipo B took part in 26 races, of which it won 22. In seven of these races the Tipo B filled the first three places. It achieved a 92 per cent finishing record from 62 race starts in these years – an impressive achievement.

Bugatti, which began the thirties as one of the dominant Grand Prix racing cars, was eclipsed by the end of the decade when this beautiful single-seater was competing. Advanced technology had conquered intuitive brilliance.

---

1 Influential in their design was the knowledge gained by Bugatti from the two front-drive 1½-litre Miller racing cars that the French firm acquired from American racing driver Leon Duray after the 1929 European season.

TAZIO NUVOLARI

If ever a man lived to drive racing cars it was Tazio Nuvolari. When he made the transition from motorcycles to cars in 1927–28, driving for Bugattis, he was an immediate winner.

For sheer driving skill and panache, the outstanding personality of the thirties was Tazio Nuvolari. It took the achievements of Stirling Moss and Juan Fangio to make other men than the great Tazio bywords for racing flair and determination. In spite of the German cars – and in 1938–39, in concert with Auto Union – Nuvolari enjoyed remarkable success throughout the thirties. In both Alfa Romeo and Maserati Grand Prix cars, he was the dominant figure of the decade's early years.

Like so many drivers of this era, Nuvolari began with Bugattis. Born in 1892 near Mantua into a motorcycle-racing family, he began to take car racing seriously at the end of the twenties. He was taken up by that talent-spotter Enzo Ferrari for his stable of Alfa Romeos, with which he began winning regularly at the age of thirty. Dissatisfaction with their reliability occasioned defections to Maserati and Bugatti in 1933 and 1934 respectively, but for the rest of the thirties Nuvolari drove the blood-red Alfas until he joined Auto Union in 1938.

Tazio Nuvolari was one of the sport's greatest personalities, both in his achievements and in his way of achieving them. Wrote Peter Hull of Tazio:

His yellow shirt bore the monogram 'TN' and the little tortoise emblem given to him by Gabriele d'Annunzio, the soldier-airman-poet, as the symbol of prudence and slowness. He gave an impression of immense vitality in the cockpit, almost dancing from side to side, pulling faces, and jiggling the wheel. He liked to sit rather high up, and well back from the steering wheel. He took his corners like a slalom skier, flinging the car into a slide and going around in a four-wheel drift with little or no use of the brakes, yet with the car perfectly placed for a straight line exit, accelerating hard.

In the ease and precision with which he executed these manoeuvres Nuvolari had much in common with a later ace, Juan Fangio. In his memoirs a passenger, Enzo Ferrari, gave us an eyewitness glimpse of Tazio's technique at the wheel of a 1931 Monza Alfa Romeo:

At the first bend I had the clear sensation that Tazio had taken it badly and that we would end up in the ditch; I felt myself stiffen as I waited for the crunch. Instead, we found ourselves on the next straight with the car in a perfect position. I looked at him. His rugged face was calm, just as it always was, and certainly not the face of someone who had just escaped a hair-raising spin. In the meantime, I had noticed that through the entire bend Tazio did not lift his foot from the accelerator and that, in fact, it was flat on the floor.

As bend followed bend, I discovered his secret. Nuvolari went into the bend rather sooner than would have been suggested to me by my own driving instinct. But he went into it in an unusual way, that is to say, suddenly pointing the nose of the car at the inner verge, just where the bend started. With the throttle wide open ... he put the car into a controlled four-wheel skid, utilising the centrifugal force and keeping the machine on the road by the driving force of its rear wheels. Right round the whole of the bend the car's nose shaved the inner verge and, when the bend came to an end, the machine was pointing down the straight without any need to correct its trajectory.

Nuvolari modified his style to cope with the more powerful and softer-sprung cars of the late thirties, but as Ferrari said, 'his technique remained a supreme demonstration of skill carried to the very bounds of human achievement and the laws of balance and momentum'.

The handsome Tipo B Alfa Romeo was one of the many mounts of Tazio Nuvolari. He is joined by Rudi Caracciola, left, and Giuseppe Campari, right.

'We all tried to emulate him a little,' said Bugatti team-mate René Dreyfus, 'but it didn't work. Only Tazio could drive like Tazio. He was so instinctive, his reflexes were so uncanny, and he seemed to do everything right, even when it appeared he wasn't. There were times when we all thought he was driving badly, but still he was going faster than any of us, so we must have been wrong.'

Tazio Nuvolari won most of the classic races at least once, including Le Mans (1933), the Mille Miglia (1930 and 1933), the Tourist Trophy (1933) and the Targa Florio (1931 and 1932). Happily for his fanatical home-country fans, he won the Italian Grand Prix in 1931, 1932 and 1938. He won many fans in America as well with a victory in the Vanderbilt Cup race on a very twisty circuit on Long Island, New York, in October 1936.[1]

In spite of the advanced technology unleashed on the German cars Nuvolari was able to score some successes against them with Ferrari's Alfas. Most celebrated was his victory in the 1935 German Grand Prix. Under damp conditions he succeeded in wresting the lead from the Germans by mid-race, only to fall far behind with a botched refuelling stop. Piling on the speed thereafter, he was still trailing the von Brauchitsch Mercedes on the last lap when Brauchitsch – not without good reason known as the team's *Pechvogel* ('unlucky bird') – burst a tyre and watched Nuvolari race by to win.

Much like Stirling Moss later, Tazio Nuvolari relished just such a fight from behind against heavy odds. One of his biggest battles was with his own health after the war, for he contracted an illness that made him vulnerable to exhaust and fuel fumes. He still had speed, but no longer durability. Still racing in his fifties, however briefly, Nuvolari met a new arrival from Argentina in 1948. Disliking the way Nuvolari was being exploited then by team owners and race promoters, Juan Manuel Fangio resolved to retire before he reached such a pass.

The 'Flying Mantuan' – as he was known to several generations of racing fans throughout the world – died at home in 1953. In his honour the route of the Mille Miglia was changed so that the racers could roar through Mantua on their way back to Brescia.

---

1 The artificial track had been made tortuous by the Americans, who reckoned thereby to put much of the action in front of the grandstands. Their success was such that the wining average speed of 65.99 mph was the slowest of any Grand Prix race of the year, with the exception of Monaco (51.69 mph).

Many of the Tipo B's successes were also those of Tazio Nuvolari, the wiry Mantuan who was startling the racing world with his skill and determination. In 1933 they were also victories for the Scuderia Ferrari, which had been racing Alfas since its founding in Modena by Enzo Ferrari in December 1929. Ferrari represented Alfa almost exclusively in racing from 1933 until the *scuderia* was bought out by Alfa Romeo in March 1938 so that the company could set up its own racing unit.

The only threat to Alfa's superiority came late in 1933 when Nuvolari switched to Maseratis, which were still leading in displacement with a 2,991 cc straight-eight. Maserati ended 1933 with three wins and six fastest laps.

A Bugatti (left) and Alfa Romeo led from the starting line in the Monaco Grand Prix in 1933. This was the last season in the thirties in which the beautiful blue and red cars were to have it all their own way.

In 1932 Alfa Romeo introduced its Tipo B, powered by a supercharged straight-eight of 2,655 cc; this was later enlarged to 2,905 cc. Chris Staniland is seen racing this ex-Sommer car at Donington in 1936.

Enter Mercedes-Benz and Auto Union

Appropriately, the central two years of the thirties were mixed, years of confused and hesitant transition between the old order and the new. In 1934 the new W25 Mercedes-Benz eights and Type A Auto Union V-16s shared the laurels. They scored three wins apiece after their initial teething troubles allowed the Tipo B Alfa Romeo to win four races. With new suspension and an enlarged engine, Alfas were able to win three more races in 1935, including Nuvolari's great victory in the German Grand Prix, but the Germans otherwise dominated the season with 11 wins, 7 by Mercedes-Benz.

Late in 1933 Bugatti introduced his new Type 59, designed for the new weight-limit formula of 1934. It scored only one major win, at Spa in 1934 (which the German teams boycotted because the Belgians wanted them to pay too much duty to bring in their special racing fuel), and two minor victories in 1935.

In fact, France had placed her hopes for the 750 kg formula on the SEFAC, a completely new car produced with a degree of national backing. Engineered by Emile Petit, author of successful Salmson racing cars, its power unit was a pair of twin-cam four-cylinder engines placed side-by-side and geared together, adding up to 2,970 cc. The right-hand engine's crankshaft drove the supercharger, while power was taken to the clutch and the offset drive line from the left-hand crank. Although the SEFAC appeared in several practice sessions it was usually a non-starter. In the 1938 French Grand Prix, for which its displacement qualified it, the SEFAC did complete one race lap.

By virtue of their 1933 successes Maseratis were in great demand among private owners during these two years, but they failed to return any important wins. Late in 1935 Maserati produced a new 4,244 cc V-8 which was enlarged to 4,785 cc in 1936 to win a single race, at Pau. This was the first V-8 engine built expressly for Grand Prix racing. In 1936–37 Maserati concentrated on the concurrent 1½-litre Voiturette category, while its privately owned cars made up the numbers at the major races. For example, seven Maseratis started in the 1937 German Grand Prix – but filling the last three rows of the grid.

Auto Union was consistent with its Type C V-16 in 1936–37, scoring five wins each year with the great Bernd Rosemeyer at the wheel. A convert from motorcycle racing, Rosemeyer was instantly at home in the unusual rear-engined car. The first of those two years was disastrous for Mercedes-Benz with only two wins by Rudy Caracciola, allowing Nuvolari five victories in Alfa Romeos. But in 1937 Mercedes came back in a big way with 5,660 cc, and by the end of the year, 580 hp, winning five races backed by second and third places. Alfa won only a few minor Grand Prix races with its new 4,064 cc V-twelve, against occasional Auto Union entries, at Milan, Turin and Genoa.

By 1935, for its Tipo 308C, Alfa Romeo had expanded its straight-eight to 3,823 cc, supercharged to develop 330 hp. As on the Tipo B and its predecessor the 8C 'Monza', the gear drive to the twin overhead camshafts was at the centre of the engine.

In front of the pits at Monte Carlo in 1937 Mercedes-Benz marshalled four of its new W125 models, designed to meet the requirements of the team's new racing engineer Rudy Uhlenhaut. They won five Grand Prix races that season.

In the last two years of the thirties, under a new formula, Mercedes-Benz was decisively on top with five major wins each year. After the tragic loss of Rosemeyer in a speed record attempt at the end of 1937, Auto Union started slowly in 1938. Nuvolari joined the team and scored two wins late in the year. This inspired Mercedes-Benz to make extensive improvements for 1939, and it again held off the Auto Unions to two wins in major races.

Terminating its relationship with Ferrari's team and racing on its own as 'Alfa Corse' in 1938–39, Alfa Romeo found itself in general disarray without Nuvolari and with a choice of engines of eight, twelve and sixteen cylinders to install in two different chassis. It scored no wins. Neither did Maserati, which, however, made a comeback with a superb new straight-eight, the 8CTF, which was at least able to lead a Grand Prix briefly each year and win the Indianapolis 500 in 1939 and 1940.

The French were represented not by Bugatti, whose new car was entered only fitfully, but by Delahaye, which built a new, unsupercharged V-12 that was able to win the first two races of 1938 while the Mercedes W154s were still being sorted out. The decade closed with a victory by Auto Union, a firm which had not even existed in 1930.[2]

---

2 Auto Union was literally that: a union of four German auto companies, DKW, Wanderer, Horch and Audi, effectuated in 1932 to give them the ability to survive the Depression. The 'Auto Union' racing cars thus bore the name of the company, not any single marque, as a means of publicising the new firm and, indirectly, its products.

Maserati was capable of producing a very fast 3-litre Grand Prix car for the 1938 season, the 8CTF, but neither the small firm nor its customers had the resources to mount a serious challenge to the German teams in 1938 and '39.

FORCES BEHIND THE FORMULAE

In the early years of the thirties Grand Prix racing was still recovering from the complexity and cost of the 1½-litre formula of 1926–27. Race organisers steadfastly rejected the various peculiar formula suggestions that the AIACR had been putting forward, as we saw in Chapter Three. Thus racing through 1933 was essentially unrestricted, although some attention was paid to the long race durations of five to ten hours that were called for by the AIACR as a means of emphasising reliability.

In this permissive atmosphere private owners raced big SSK Mercedes-Benz sports cars, stripped of their wings, in Grand Prix events. One of them, lightened in 'SSKL' form and driven by Rudy Caracciola, defeated two Type 51 Bugattis in the rainy 1931 German Grand Prix. This race saw the introduction of the quick-lift racing jack, an innovation by Caracciola's factory backed private team.

The Italians and Italian-born also took advantage of these *laissez-faire* years to indulge their passion for the elaborate, extravagant and excessive in engine design. In 1930–31 Bugatti produced his Type 45, powered by two Type 39 straight-eight cylinder blocks side-by-side and geared together to create a sixteen-cylinder power unit.[3] Built along similar lines were the Maserati Type V4 of 1929, a twin-crankshaft V-16 of 3,961 cc, and its 1932 successor, the Type V5 with a twin-crankshaft 3,800 cc sixteen-cylinder engine. In 1931 Alfa Romeo produced its Tipo A. This had two complete and separate six-cylinder engines placed side-by-side, giving a total displacement of 3,504 cc.

These multi-cylinder supercharged machines, some of which were not entirely unsuccessful in spite of the heavy burdens they placed on their tyres, were thought of as 'freak cars' and 'monsters' in their day.[4] The same was true of two

---

3   Bugatti had first done this with an aero engine developed during the First World War. His Type 45 was credited with record-breaking fastest times at the Bernina and Klausen hillclimbs in 1930. Another important twin-crankshaft racing car was the U-12 Type 406 Grand Prix Fiat of 1½ litres which raced once – and won – in 1927.

4   The Alfa Romeo Tipo A won the Coppa Acerbo at Pescara in 1931.

WHY AND HOW THE NAZIS BACKED GRAND PRIX RACING

In the Germany of 1932, the economic crisis was acute. Employment at Daimler-Benz was reduced to half its 1928 level, and millions of skilled men were out of work all over the nation. In mid-year four motor firms sought safety in numbers with the formation of a new company called Auto Union. Pinched in the pocketbook, crushed in ego, the nation was of a mood to vote in the rule of the National Socialists and their leader, the new Chancellor, Adolf Hitler.

In the depths of the Depression, on 12 October 1932 the AIACR announced its new formula for Grand Prix racing from 1934 to 1936. No one in the land was more interested in seeing German firms gear up for this than the new Chancellor, who was keen on cars and racing. Born in Braunau, Austria, Hitler was forty-four years old in the spring of 1933 when he put in motion the rumbling wheels of his benighted regime. Born virtually at the same time as the automobile, Hitler carried an infatuation with it, and with other forms of technology that he associated with his youth, throughout his life.[1]

Motorisation was a major goal of the administration that began with Hitler's appointment as Germany's Chancellor on Monday 30 January 1933. Only a few days later, in his speech at the opening of the Auto Show in Berlin on a Saturday 11 February, he set out his guidelines for a car-filled future: tax abatements for car buyers, the building of the Autobahns, repeal of obligatory driving tuition, and encouragement of motor sports.

A month later Daimler-Benz took the decision to go back into top-level racing, primarily for its publicity benefits. It did so on the first wave of enthusiasm that accompanied Hitler's rise to power. After they realised that the more radical National Socialists weren't actually going to take over their companies, Germany's industrialists welcomed Hitler's banning of labour unions, his acceleration of armament production and the credit-expanding schemes of his economists.

Racing, however, would be costly at the top level. Daimler chairman Wilhelm Kissel confided to Ewald Kroth, a chemical tycoon, that it wouldn't be possible to launch a racing effort properly with less than 1 million Reichsmarks (then the equivalent of about £65,000 or $250,000). Government backing would be virtually essential for a company still grappling with the Depression. Was Hitler's Third Reich willing to walk its talk?

Contact with the Third Reich was maintained by Jakob Werlin, manager of the important Daimler-Benz branch in Munich, the home of the National Socialist German Workers (Nazi) Party. Werlin's personal acquaintance with the new Chancellor was pivotal in gaining approval for the Transport Ministry to pay 450,000 Reichsmarks annually to the maker of a Grand Prix racing car, with bonus payments of 20,000, 10,000 and 5,000 Reichsmarks for finishes in first, second and third place.

This largesse was, of course, to go to Daimler-Benz. But a young upstart with good social connections also staked a claim, backed by a strong sales pitch by Ferdinand Porsche.[2] Auto Union wanted its place in the sun too. 'Each wanted it all for himself,' Daimler's Alfred Neubauer recalled.

Finally, Transport Ministry Director Brandenburg decided as had King Solomon of yore: each firm would receive half. It was less than a quarter of Kissel's absolute minimum, and about one-tenth of what Daimler-Benz would spend on racing every year. But it was encouragement, and that was what they needed.

Briton George Monkhouse, a close personal observer of racing during the Hitler era, felt that the Führer deliberately pitted Mercedes-Benz against Auto Union. Wrote Monkhouse:

> Hitler was wise enough to realise that if these cars turned out to be as successful as his advisers told him, the only way to maintain world-wide interest would be for Germany to produce two rival Grand Prix teams of cars. Without this foresight, Mercedes-Benz would have swept the board with no real competition, instead of which the Mercedes-Benz/Auto Union battles produced the fastest and most exciting motor racing ever seen.

---

1   Passing the time of night of 24 January 1942 with some of his confidants, Adolf Hitler remarked: 'In former times I used to read regularly the publications devoted to the motorcar, but I no longer have the time.' He assured them that he nevertheless continued to keep up with new developments in the automotive field.

2   A meeting was held with Hitler in Berlin on 1 March 1933, attended by Porsche, racing driver Hans Stuck and a deputy board member of Auto Union, Baron Klaus von Oertzen. Hitler drew Porsche away from the others to a table by the window, where they talked privately for twenty minutes. 'They were both from Austria and spoke the same language – I think Hitler took a liking to him,' recalled Ghislaine Kaes, Porsche's nephew and secretary.

No effort was spared to ensure that the German public were well aware of the achievements of the national racing cars that were supported, in part, by their government. An impressive panorama of Mercedes-Benz and Auto Union racing and record-breaking cars greeted all visitors to the 1939 Motor Show in Berlin.

In the author's view, this interpretation requires us to put too much faith in Hitler's ability to judge racing car designs and to envision the shape of the future. According to Porsche's nephew, Ghislaine Kaes, as quoted by Chris Nixon, in putting his argument to Hitler in their Berlin meeting Prof. Porsche had pointed out 'that it would surely be better to have two irons in the fire, as the German cars would be up against Alfa Romeo, Bugatti, etc.'. With two teams and two design concepts there would be safety in numbers.

Such a decision was highly consistent with one of Hitler's favourite managerial techniques. As Albert Speer explained it, Hitler 'did not like establishing clear lines of jurisdiction. Sometimes he deliberately assigned bureaus or individuals the same or similar tasks. "That way," he used to say, "the stronger one does the job."' Splitting the responsibility between Mercedes-Benz and Auto Union to keep both on their toes and ensure that they achieved victory – that is a method we can associate with Adolf Hitler.

other Bugattis, the nose-heavy 4.9-litre Type 54, built in just thirteen days for the 1931 Italian Grand Prix, and the four-wheel-drive Type 53 of 1932 which was powered by the same 300 bhp engine.

During 1932, while it was giving thought to the next Grand Prix formula for the 1934–36 period, the AIACR had been alarmed by the high speeds reached by these big-engined cars. It wanted some way to rule them out, not necessarily by curtailing their displacement. A weight comparison showed that these cars scaled 900 kg or more, while the 'normal' single-seaters were in the 700–800 kg bracket. To the AIACR committee, a constraint on weight looked like the logical answer. It proved to be one of their less valid conclusions.

Tipo V4 - 16 cilindri

Gruppo Motore

With their 4-litre sixteen-cylinder Tipo V4 of 1929, the Maserati brothers raised alarm among Grand Prix racing's rule-makers. To exclude such powerful and heavy 'freak' racers they established a new 1934 Grand Prix formula that limited car weight to 750 kg.

Thus was promulgated in October 1932 a new Grand Prix formula. It imposed a maximum weight of 750 kg (1,653 lb) for the car, dry and without tyres. The new weight limit was in fact a throwback to a formula that the AIACR had first proposed in 1928, and the accompanying new minimum-body width rule was similar to a 1929 suggestion. The minimum race distance of 500 km was carried over from the 1933 rules.

The new regulations were greeted by the customary grumbles from car manufacturers. The Italians said that the Germans had suggested it, and vice versa, while the British said that it would produce cars like MG Midgets which would go all of a hair-raising 120 mph. In fact, the formula seemed doomed to the same apathetic reception that the previous ones had received. Had conditions remained unchanged it might have been an equal failure as an inspiration to more advanced engineering. But conditions did change. Major German motor companies, encouraged by their government, took a sudden interest in a dramatic return to motor racing.[5]

THE GERMANS CHANGE THE RULES

Germany's new Chancellor, Adolf Hitler, had a strong personal interest in motor sport, as well as a desire to promote Germany's motorisation. Thus it was taken for granted that Daimler-Benz, with its long albeit erratic history of Grand Prix participation, would engineer and build a new car for 1934. Auto Union, however, was an utter outsider. Formed in Saxony in June 1932 from four foundering auto firms – Audi, Horch, DKW and Wanderer – the new group symbolised by its four linked rings seemed to have its hands full trying to achieve mere survival. But it obtained a design by the engineering consultancy recently set up by Ferdinand Porsche and enough of a share of a government subsidy to encourage it to go racing. By early 1933 both firms were hard at work on their respective vehicles.

Staying within the weight limit required not only ingenuity but also sheer hard work on the part of the Germans. With its conventional front-engined layout requiring a long propeller shaft from the engine to the rear-mounted transaxle, the W25 Mercedes presented special problems. In its final form it was a textbook for lightness-drillers. Lacy and filigreed hole patterns penetrated both stressed and unstressed components.

---

5   Proof was once again provided for one of Ludvigsen's Laws of Motor Racing: It matters not how absurd the Formula is; if a major motor company wants to go racing at a given time it will do so, whatever the obstacles. Statements indicating anything to the contrary are to be taken with multiple grains of salt.

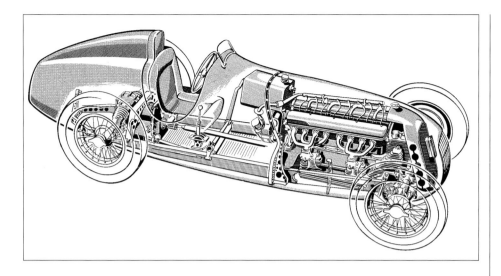

Advanced features of the Mercedes-Benz W25 Grand Prix car of 1934 included a rear-mounted transaxle and independent suspension of all four wheels. An oil reservoir for the straight-eight engine's dry-sump system was cowl-mounted.

The cost, of course, was tremendous. The direct Mercedes racing outlay in 1934 was $1 million (equal to £200,000). This did not necessarily include machine work done by the main Daimler-Benz shops on behalf of their racing arm. Auto Union spent similar sums, but had to use them to support a self-contained racing operation that manufactured all its own parts. The engines were made at the Horch plant at Zwickau, and the cars were put together and tested at the Wanderer plant in Chemnitz.

The unprecedented and awesome scale of the German effort posed problems for the AIACR framers of the follow-on Grand Prix formula for the three years 1937–39. It's likely they failed to realise that nothing they could do would restore international competition to Grand Prix racing in the face of the German onslaught. They were late in reaching a conclusion, and not until February 1936 did they provisionally announce a new formula which matched 4.5-litre unsupercharged engines against 3.46-litre supercharged engines, each set against minimum weights.

The evolution of the Mercedes-Benz Grand Prix car from 1934 to 1939 was rapid and spectacular, in the latter year producing this superbly low-built W154. In both technology and appearance it set a new high standard for the Grand Prix racer.

Mercedes immediately began making modifications to its unsuccessful 1936 cars along the lines of the planned 1937 rules. But in September the AIACR had a change of mind and extended the 750 kg formula for one more year, 1937, and moved the next formula to the 1938–40 period. It retained the mooted 4.5-litre unblown limit, but lowered the boom further on blown engines to 3 litres, both with an 850 kg minimum weight.

Moreover, a sliding scale of minimum weights was set up, all the way down to a 400 kg minimum for engines that could be 1,000 cc unblown and 666 cc blown, which Britain's S.C.H. Davis pungently dismissed as 'a manifest absurdity'. It was apparently thought by the rule-makers that such cars would be able to compete with the bigger-engined models. ERA did give some thought to building a 2.2-litre version of its E-Type car, but realised that this would never be in the running, even if it could be built down to the applicable 696 kg minimum.

These last two formulae witnessed a spectacular increase in the maximum speed of the Grand Prix car. During the first four years of the thirties top speeds remained around 140 mph. The 1934 German cars could reach 170, however, and by 1937 they could attain 195 mph in racing trim. In spite of their reduced engine capacity and power the 1939 cars were just about as fast, thanks to their improved aerodynamics. But otherwise, aerodynamic advances played no part in this dramatic speed increase of the Grand Prix car, which with its exposed wheels is fundamentally a high-drag object.

A RACE FOR POWER

Did a reduction in frontal area help raise the speeds? The area that a car exposes to the air it rushes through has a direct bearing on its total drag. No, in fact the racing cars of the thirties all had frontal areas of 10–12 square feet, a significant increase over the very low 9½ square foot frontal areas (a little more than a square yard) of the low and compact 1½-litre cars of 1927. As we learned in Chapter Three, these had reached a high degree of (costly) perfection.

Sheer power was the source of the skyrocketing velocities of the German cars. They gained a huge jump on their Italian adversaries in 1934 and kept the margin during 1937, when both German cars had 5.5-plus litres, 500-plus hp and 190-plus mph. In contrast, the best that Alfa Romeo had been able to do was 4.5 litres, 430 hp and, with a favourable wind, 180 mph.

The Italians were and are rightly renowned as builders of fine racing engines. In fact, they had begun the thirties with a dilly of an engine. Towards the end of the twenties Alfa Romeo had enjoyed success in Grand Prix racing simply by dusting off and updating its P2 model of 1924. For the new decade, however, something better was needed. Vittorio Jano produced it in the 1931 8C racing car, nicknamed the 'Monza' after its victory in the Italian Grand Prix there in that year.

As its name indicated, the 8C was powered by an in-line eight-cylinder engine, but one with a significant difference. Jano divided the engine into two steel-lined light-alloy blocks of four cylinders resting on a common aluminium crankcase. Each block had its own cylinder head of aluminium, with two valves per cylinder. The crankshaft was also made as two separate four-cylinder parts united at the centre by a pair of helical gears. One of these drove the camshafts (which were also made as fours) through a gear train, while the other drove the supercharger and the oil and water pumps.

Jano's design overcame one of the major disadvantages of the in-line eight: the length of both the camshafts and crankshaft, which introduced torsional vibrations that harmed both valve timing and reliability.[6] Instead, this was composed of two four-cylinder engines back to

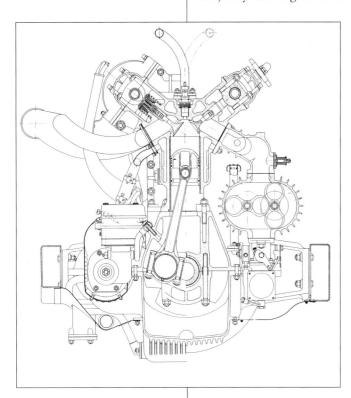

Visible on the right side of this front view of the engine of the Alfa Romeo Tipo B in 1932 form are the intermeshing lobes of its Roots-type supercharger. Unlike the exotic German cars, the Tipo B carried its crank and rods in plain bearings.

6   A direct precedent for Jano's division of an eight into two fours with a central camshaft drive was an 1,100 cc eight, of which three were designed and built for Salmson by Emile Petit in 1928. Petit also used the central gear train to drive two superchargers and the magneto or distributor; both were provided for in the design. Jano may have been aware of the elegant little Salmson engine. Another feature of the Salmson was desmodromic retraction of its tappets.

back – each with short cams and cranks. With an eye on cost and practicality, Jano made the major parts symmetrical so that one four-cylinder block casting, for example, would serve both ends of the engine. Manufacturing scrappage due to foundry imperfections and machining errors was greatly reduced. Simplicity also characterised the bottom end, which used plain bearings instead of rollers.[7]

The design of the 8C served as the launching pad for the engine of the Tipo B Alfa Romeo Grand Prix car of 1932. Instead of detachable cylinder heads, it unified each of the four-cylinder heads and blocks in a single 'monobloc' aluminium casting with dry steel cylinder liners. The valves were symmetrically inclined at the broad included angle of 102°. Only two valves per cylinder sufficed; Vittorio Jano was a member of the Fiat school which taught from the early twenties that two valves in a hemispherical combustion chamber were superior to the four-valve chamber that Peugeot and others had used so successfully. The Delages had also relied on two-valve chambers.

Here was an excellent racing engine, now equipped with twin Roots superchargers. It was built to match Maserati, which in 1930 had introduced its 8C3000 straight-eight racing car developing 230 bhp from 2,991 cc. By 1933 this had been developed into the 8CM with 260 hp from the same displacement. The Italians clearly knew something about building racing engines. How, then, did the silver machines get such a decisive power lead over the red ones after 1934?

There were two main reasons. The first was the 'size syndrome'. Prior to 1934 neither Alfa Romeo nor Maserati had ever built a modern single-crankshaft racing engine of more than 3 litres capacity. Their bigger twin-crankshaft engines were, as mentioned earlier, regarded as specialised 'freaks' suitable only for very fast tracks like Monza and Berlin's Avus, a motorway with turns at both ends. Bugatti had the imagination to use a big engine in 1931 for his Type 54, but lacked the know-how to get its power onto the road or to make the car light enough to compete under the 750 kg formula.

Large engines were antithetical to Latin concepts of 'rightness'; Latin auto makers retain much the same attitude today. For the Germans, however, the problem was to make their engines small enough to fit them into those little single-seater cars. Throughout the early thirties a 'normal' racing engine to Mercedes-Benz was the 7-litre SSK six, which had been developed to produce 300 hp in sprint racing trim. The designer of this aluminium-block engine had been Ferdinand Porsche, during a spell of employment by Daimler and, as it became during his tenure in the twenties, Daimler-Benz. The Germans, then, were already in a frame of mind to 'think big'. They thought and built their engines accordingly – Auto Union even more than Daimler-Benz.

KEEPING THEIR SECRETS

The second decisive factor in the Grand Prix power race was secrecy. Today we possess most details of the pre-war German racing cars, but during the thirties they were kept very much under wraps, far more than would be possible today. Not until the first weigh-in to check the maximum weights would observers actually be able to see that the new cars had independent suspension, for example. Mercedes-Benz kept its suspensions well covered by the bodywork. And horsepower! That was entirely a matter for rumour and guesswork, and the estimates were well short of the reality.

---

7   This is one of the reasons why Alfa engines of this type are so easy to rebuild and indeed remanufacture. They are very simple in spite of their complexity.

'The Mercedes-Benz jobs have a straight-eight engine of about 185 cu. in. piston displacement,' wrote W.F. Bradley after their first appearance in the 1934 French Grand Prix, 'although the exact figure is kept secret.' Bradley's knowledgeable estimate was equivalent to 3,032 cc. The actual displacement was 3,360 cc, from which the supercharged engine developed 314 bhp. Its primary rival at the time was the Alfa Romeo Tipo B, also known as the P3, which produced only 215 bhp from 2,905 cc.

There was much more to come. In 1934 the Mercedes engineers increased the power of their W25 racing car to 348 bhp (3,710 cc) and 370 bhp (3,990 cc). They enlarged the eight to 4,310 cc to produce 402 bhp for the very successful 1935 season. Expanded to 4,740 cc for 1936, the eight gave typically 453 bhp, and in the best instance 473 bhp. When, in late 1934, Alfa Romeo planned a new V-12 with an eventual potential of 4½ litres and 400 bhp, it could have been excused for thinking it was designing a more than adequately competitive engine.

How could Alfa's Vittorio Jano have conceived that by 1936 Auto Union would have 6-litre engines or that by 1937 the Mercedes-Benz racing car would produce more than 350 bhp at only 3,000 rpm and carry its power curve to 580 bhp at 5,800 rpm? Nothing that was publicly known then could ever have hinted that such heights could or would be scaled.

Yet there was nothing secret or spectacular about the means used to obtain this power. In their structural design the Mercedes straight-eights harked back to Porsche's 2-litre eight of 1924, which had four valves per cylinder, welded-up steel monobloc cylinders and a full roller-bearing crankshaft. The design of ten years later was obviously all-new and much larger, but remained unfashionably loyal to the four-valve concept that had served Mercedes well since 1914.

Both for aerodynamic reasons and for the sake of secrecy the Mercedes-Benz W25 had enclosures over its front and rear suspensions. This first such car, completed in February 1934, had an antiquated-looking external hand-brake lever.

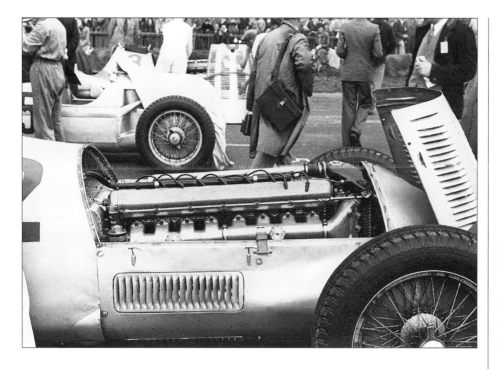

Special techniques were used to ensure equal distribution of fuel/air mixture to all cylinders of the long straight-eight engine of the 1937 Mercedes-Benz W125. The induction system seen here, in which the blower pumped both air and fuel to the cylinders, was adopted in mid-1937.

The new engine seemed retrograde in having its single (Roots) supercharger pump through two carburettors instead of sucking through a single one, as on the 1924 eight. This was a conservative carry-over from the known technology of the SSK engine that also took into account the fact that the throttle response of the 1924 engine had been dismal. Not until the mid-1937 versions of the 5,660 cc engine did Mercedes-Benz adopt suction carburetion after rigorous testing had confirmed its superiority.

What was most remarkable, of course, was that an engine as big as the Mercedes eight could be built to weigh only 491 lb, as it did in 1937. Had it been appropriately focused, Italian technology could have achieved this, however, especially with the use of magnesium, as pioneered by Maserati.

HIGH-TORQUE AUTO UNIONS

Auto Union achieved the maximum of results with a minimum of apparent effort through the very fine structural design by the Porsche team of the cars and their engines. Porsche's staff had conceived a big high-torque 45° V-16 engine which would run so slowly – never over 5,500 rpm – that it could get by with a single central camshaft which operated the inlet valves through finger followers, and from which pushrods operated the outboard exhaust valves. The engine had two valves per cylinder.

In its final 1936–37 form the Auto Union V-16 measured 366 cubic inches (6,005 cc), weighed 540 lb, developed 520 bhp at 5,000 rpm and reached its peak torque at 2,900 rpm.[8] With the exception of the torque speed, which would

---

8 A bigger-bore engine of 6,330 cc was produced, for use only in record-breaking in and after 1937. Its output was 545 bhp.

A top view of the Auto Union's V-16 engine reveals the single central camshaft which drove its inlet valves directly and the exhaust valves through pushrods and rocker arms. Porsche's design of this engine was a masterpiece of logic and simplicity.

For its 8CTF straight-eight of 1938–39, Maserati fitted two Roots-type superchargers (at right) which delivered fuel/air mixture to a common inlet manifold. Designers considered that two small Roots blowers offered higher efficiency and greater compactness than a single large unit of the same capacity.

be too low, these could have been the vital statistics of the big, tuned American V-8s that powered the Can-Am sports cars of the sixties.

All the Auto Unions were designed to have broad power curves. Unlike Daimler-Benz, Auto Union did not undertake exhaustive recording of data about the characteristics of the various racing circuits. The team had only four final-drive ratios from which to choose; one of them would usually be good enough for the job. In 1937 both German cars had so much sheer power and torque that they drove the entire Monte Carlo circuit, reaching speeds of 120 mph, without shifting gear. Caracciola's Mercedes lap record set during the race stood until 1955.[9]

Linked with the new emphasis on supercharging, the 3-litre cars of l938 were notable for their use of twin Roots blowers working in parallel. The use of twin Roots blowers was a feature of the eights of Alfa and Maserati, the V-12s of Mercedes, Alfa and Auto Union, and the twin-crankshaft Alfa Romeo V-16 of 1939.

Prior to 1939 Mercedes-Benz realised that internal mechanical losses could be lowered, and output raised, by making one blower bigger than the other and connecting them in series instead of in parallel. This idea was initially explored for Mercedes by the Porsche office, which ceased working for Auto Union after the 1937 season and began consulting for Daimler-Benz. Porsche built a two-stage supercharger that showed that the concept was right. Mercedes designed its own superchargers for its 1939 cars. Auto Union also adopted such 'two-stage' supercharging later in 1939.

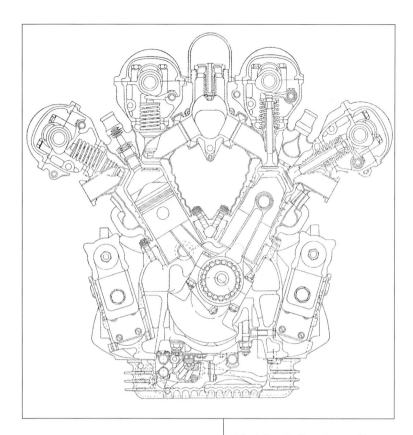

The 3-litre V-12 engine used by Mercedes-Benz in 1938–39 set its cylinder banks at an included angle of 60 degrees. Visible at the sides of the block are the two Bosch pumps for direct fuel injection, which was experimented with for this engine but not used in competition.

REFINEMENTS TO BRAKING

Throughout the thirties Grand Prix car designers emphasised increases in power output because most of them believed that every other avenue toward faster circuit lap times had been exploited to its ultimate. In 1939 Auto Union designer Robert Eberan von Eberhorst wrote: 'You can rule out of the discussion the braking power as well as the roadholding, the determining factor for cornering speed, because it is no longer thinkable that either one can be significantly improved.'

From his viewpoint at the time Eberan was correct in his statement because tyres, whose grip on the road was and is vital to both braking and cornering, had offered little improvement in either department for a decade, and showed only slight promise of doing so in the future.

Brakes themselves had improved significantly. Hydraulic actuation, reintroduced to Grand Prix racing by Maserati in 1933, was not without its risks. The design had to be clever to avoid brake fading caused by boiling of the hydraulic fluid; most brakes had special cooling ducts in the backing plates for the wheel cylinders. The new German entrants used hydraulics in 1934, as did Alfa Romeo from 1935.

Hydraulic systems, with their more flexible connection from chassis to wheels, were especially needed to allow the use of the independent suspensions that were being adopted then. In 1938, freed of the maximum-weight restriction, Mercedes introduced a further refinement to its brakes in the form of twin master cylinders, one operating the front circuit and the other the rear brakes. In addition to adding a safety factor in the event of a failure of one circuit, this introduced for the first time the now-common ability to adjust the balance of

---

9   It was broken by a Mercedes-Benz W196 Grand Prix car driven by Juan Manuel Fangio.

Wide and finely finned, the drum brakes of the 1938–39 Auto Union were among the best of its era. Also visible in this Type D model are its triple-camshaft V-12 engine and tubular de Dion rear axle.

braking effort between the front and rear wheel pairs by shifting the balance-bar proportion between the two master cylinders.

Brakes were also made wider and equipped with deeper and finer cooling fins. From the mid-thirties as well, their mechanisms were what is known as two-leading-shoe. This meant that for both of the brake's two shoes the rotation of the drum was from the actuated end of the shoe toward its pivoted end. Two wheel cylinders instead of one were needed to achieve this, but the advantage was that both shoes had a self-wrapping or 'servo' effect that increased the braking effect for a given pedal pressure. At the end of the decade Auto Union went one better than its rivals by giving each wheel four leading shoes.[10]

With four shoes instead of two, the Auto Union's brakes were better able to adapt to the changing shape of the brake drum as it heated up. For the same reason Auto Union used relatively flexible brake shoes fabricated of sheet steel. Mercedes concentrated more on cooling the brake. In 1939 it introduced a new drum which had shrouded diagonal finning at its periphery to draw cooling air across the outside of the braking surface by means of a turbine effect. British investigator Cameron Earl wrote that a Mercedes engineer 'stated that before the adoption of the cooling fan, temperatures had risen sufficiently high upon occasion to cause the light alloy drums to melt'.

MAKING BEST USE OF THE TYRES

In the meantime, racing tyres had changed remarkably little. In 1932 the Tipo B Alfa Romeo wore 5.50×18-inch tyres front and rear, changing later to 6.00×19 and then to 6.50×18 or 19 in 1935. The 1934 W25 Mercedes wore 5.25×17 or 19 tyres at all four corners. From then until 1939 front tyres remained at 5.25×17 on almost all Grand Prix cars while 1935 brought the first use of larger rear tyres. The rears were invariably of 7-inch section, with rim diameter varying between 19 and 22 inches, depending on the circuit speed.

10 The French racing car, the SEFAC, was introduced in 1934 'with about six self-wrapping shoes per drum', wrote Chris Draper, 'with the result that the car could really stop, but each corner wanted to stop at a different time'.

Racing tyre research during the thirties was directed almost exclusively toward resolving the conflict between gradually increasing the tread thickness to get more racing mileage while at the same time preventing the tread from becoming separated from the carcass at the extremely high speeds being reached. The thicker the tread the more likely it was to be flung off the carcass by the immutable law of centrifugal force. Achieving this meant keeping tyre temperature at or below 85°C (185°F). Large-diameter tyres run at high pressures were needed to reduce heat absorption and increase its dissipation.

German tyre maker Continental deserved credit for keeping its tyre sizes more or less the same, in spite of the 35 per cent increase in car speeds, during the thirties. But in terms of sheer traction and grip in all directions, the racing-car designer in 1939 had very little more to work with than he had in 1929. The focus of tyre research in later years – the effort to increase adhesion to the road – was ignored in the thirties. Only in the fifties would it begin to play a role.

Under these conditions the factor that was important, indeed decisive, was what the designer did with his tyres. In making maximum use of a racing car's tyres the designer had to engineer a recovery from the astonishingly backward conditions that existed in the early thirties. Car-handling theory had admittedly been in its infancy then, but it was nevertheless becoming appreciated that a low centre of gravity was vital to the attainment of high cornering power because, for a given cornering speed, a low centre of gravity reduced the amount of the car's weight that was transferred from the inner to the outer tyres. And when the outer tyres reached their limit of grip, to put it simply, breakaway occurred. Accordingly a low centre of gravity helps delay the onset of breakaway until a higher cornering speed has been reached. It also aids braking by reducing the amount of weight that is transferred to the front wheels when the brakes are applied. That means that the braking effort can be deployed more efficiently among all four wheels. Thus the lower the centre of gravity, the better the car's braking and grip on the road – all other factors being equal.

The designers of the 1926–27 Grand Prix cars had the right idea. The cowls of the Delage and the Fiat 806 were only 35 inches high. The Talbot was even lower at 33½ inches. These cars, like the equally low contemporary Indianapolis Duesenbergs, had differentials offset on their rear axles and angled drive lines which permitted the driver to sit very low, alongside the drive shaft, thus lowering the whole profile of the car.

Grand Prix cars roaring away from the start at Pescara in 1938 were transmitting 450 hp through relatively narrow rear wheels and tyres. Designers and drivers alike had to exercise great care to preserve their durability.

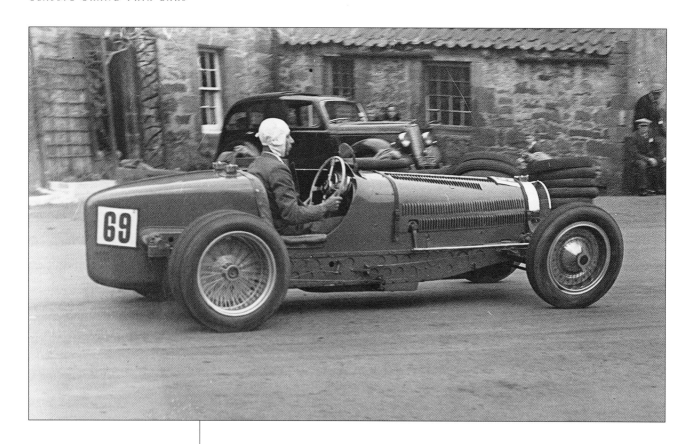

Although not capable of challenging the German cars, the Type 59 Bugatti was a capable racer in the hands of private teams. This one is fitted with twin rear wheels for use in a British sprint event.

In the first years of the thirties this excellent configuration was abandoned for several reasons. The economic exigencies of the times called for the development of versatile racing cars that were equally suitable for Grand Prix events or the mountainous Targa Florio and, in sports trim, the Mille Miglia. Such a car was the 1931 8C 2300 Monza Alfa, essentially a two-seater with high ground clearance and a high profile. In the same category was the Type 35 Bugatti, a multi-purpose machine with a 42-inch cowl height, a typical value for the year 1924 in which it was first built.

REFINING THE SINGLE-SEATER

Because it was successful in the tasks that it was built to perform, the Monza Alfa became a trend-setter. It also formed the point of departure for the next Alfa Romeo Grand Prix car design: Alfa's first true single-seater or *monoposto*.[11] Bugatti had built narrow, single-seat cars for Indianapolis during the twenties and a single-seat 1,100 cc car in 1926. Maserati built an 1,100 cc monoposto in 1931, attracting adverse comment about its gear lever protruding between the driver's legs – a feature that was to be typical of single-seater Maseratis for twenty more years.

Laid out during 1931, Jano's monoposto Tipo B Alfa first appeared at Monza in June, 1932. In order to be positioned centrally, the driver had to sit high above

---

11 This is so with the exception of the two-off Tipo A of 1931, the model with two six-cylinder engines placed side-by-side.

the Alfa's rear-axle shafts, which, of course, had to have adequate clearance above them to permit vertical suspension movement. As a direct result the Tipo B had a cowl height of 42½ inches and the top of the driver's head was 54 inches above the ground, much as it had been in a Ballot or Fiat a decade earlier.

From this awkward starting point the designers of the thirties had a very difficult time solving the design problem posed by the central-seated configuration of the front-engined racing cars that all but one of them were building. They had to get the propeller shaft past the driver somehow, yet they didn't want to return to the offset layouts of the twenties. These were regarded as old-fashioned. Moreover, some drivers had not been happy about sitting so low, feeling that they had better control of the car if they were seated higher.[12]

Although the driver of the 1934–35 Mercedes-Benz W25 sat directly over its propeller shaft, this was lowered enough to reduce the car's frontal area from that of the older-style cars that surrounded it. Enclosing the suspension offered an useful reduction in drag.

This did not concern Bugatti, however, when he designed his Type 59 of 1933. In this new 2.8-litre car[13] the driver was offset to the right, in the sports-car manner, and a low profile and centre of gravity were achieved. The Type 59 was a good roadholder, but was not favourably regarded by old-line Bugatti drivers because it was a 'gripper' rather than a 'slider', responding less lightly to its controls. With its unique 'piano wire' wheels it was also exceedingly handsome,

Rudy Caracciola demonstrates the lowered driving position of the 1938 W154 Grand Prix Mercedes-Benz. At last racers were again approaching the wind-cheating lowness that had been engineered into the best cars of the late twenties.

12 Tazio Nuvolari was a good example of such a driver. In the fifties a high seating position was also preferred by another master of the powerslide, Fangio.
13 In 1934 its displacement was increased to 3,257 cc by means of a bore enlargement, and the cars were generally known as the '3.3-litre' Bugattis.

Auto Union did not bother with suspension enclosure for its mid-engined cars of 1934–37; the Porsche trailing-link front suspension was out in the open, unless the circuit was judged to be especially fast. Warm air from the radiator was exhausted through vents at the sides just ahead of the cockpit.

so much so that Laurence Pomeroy Jr wrote that it 'may well be thought, hundreds of years from now, the best-proportioned motor car ever made'.[14]

Further problems were posed for the single-seater designer by rear-mounted transmissions. These were combined with the final drive or axle gears, leading to their being called 'transaxles'. Moving the transmission to the rear usefully shifted more weight to the driving wheels but – depending on the design – took up even more room under the driver's seat. Also, independent rear suspensions, by their layout, tended to force the propeller shaft to run along the centre line of the car.

Both a transaxle and independent rear suspension were features of the 1934 W25 Mercedes-Benz, which had a cowl at about the same height as the Tipo B Alfa: 42 inches. By offsetting the drive line downward, however, and reducing the ground clearance, the Stuttgart engineers lowered the driver 6 inches from the Tipo B's height. No useful driver depression could be achieved in the 1937 W125, which retained a cowl level of 41 inches.

Mercedes made its most dramatic improvement in height reduction in its 1938–39 Grand Prix cars. These reinterpreted the techniques of the twenties by angling the engine and offsetting the propeller shaft to the left so the driver could be placed alongside it. The driver was lowered 5 inches more, with his head at the 42½-inch level, and the cowl in 1939 was 34½ inches from the ground. It had taken more than ten years to get the cowl height back down to the level of the 1927 cars.

The Mercedes-Benz solution, with an angled drive shaft connecting to an offset transmission input, was the best way to lower the driver in a front-engined racing car. The only other solution – tried by ERA and others – was to place step-down gears at the engine and the transaxle to lower the drive line beneath the driver's seat. This imposed obvious penalties in weight and efficiency. Thus the angled drive line was used in the forties and fifties in the BRM V-16, Maserati 250F (especially in one low-chassis model), Lotus Type 16, Lancia D50 and Ferrari Dino 246.

Auto Union neatly ducked the entire issue in 1934 with its rear-mounted engine, which successfully lowered both profile and centre-of-gravity. Its cowl height was only 35 inches and its driver sat only a little higher than in the 1939 Mercedes-Benz. This was a major advantage of the rear-engined layout.

Advantageous too was the car's starkly simple concept. This helped Auto Union meet the 750 kg weight limit with far less effort than Mercedes had to expend. In fact, in spite of the criticism that has been directed at Porsche's Auto Union over the years, it may fairly be said that its cars were ideally suited to their manufacturer's relatively limited resources. If Auto Union had tried to fight Mercedes with a front-engined car it is likely that it would never have matched them in any season.

---

14 Pomeroy also commented as follows: 'The Type 59 Bugattis, of 1934, were probably the last Grand Prix cars which could profitably carry a registration number, be used on the road, and driven to a race under their own power, if necessary. Since then all the cars, and a host of impedimenta, have had to be moved around Europe on lorries.' Pomeroy did not live to experience the era in which Grand Prix cars covered far more miles in 747 cargo jets than they ever did on the road.

FIRST STEPS TO INDEPENDENCE

The high centres of gravity that prevailed in the racing cars of the first half of the thirties prevented their designers deriving the fullest advantage from the new independent suspension systems that they had developed. At the rear these were swing axles, so-called because each individual axle shaft swings in an arc from a simple universal joint adjacent to the frame-mounted differential. Mercedes-Benz and Auto Union used them from 1934, and Alfa Romeo and Maserati adopted them in 1936.

The main merit of these early swing axles was that they freed the driving wheels of the torque reaction that lifts the right rear wheel of a live-axle car. This greatly aided the drive traction of these more powerful cars. Such suspensions had a high roll centre, this being the geometric centre around which the car rolls in a turn. In this respect swing axles were similar to live-axle suspensions, so they did not alter roll behaviour much. Also, they could be used with relatively soft springs – another aid to drive traction on the rough surfaces some tracks still offered then.

A different problem was posed at the front. The parallel-wishbone Mercedes-Benz suspension, with its nearly equal-length wishbones, and the Porsche-patent parallel trailing arms of Auto Union and, later, Alfa Romeo provided roll centres that were down at ground level. Especially in combination with the high centres of gravity of the 1934–35 cars, this tended to promote cornering roll and degrade the grip of the front suspension and tyres.

To restore roll resistance and transient cornering stability, designers were forced to use very high spring rates at the front – just as high as they had used in their old solid-axle cars. Not yet part of the racing-car designer's lexicon was the torsion anti-roll bar, which is able to provide stiffness in roll without adding to the stiffness of a single wheel in jounce. None was used on the racing cars of the thirties, although they were well-known to Daimler-Benz and were fitted to American passenger cars as early as 1934 (Cadillac).

Initial impressions of the results achieved by the German designers were positive. Referring to the Auto Unions at the 1934 French Grand Prix, W.F. Bradley wrote: 'These cars proved remarkably steady both on the straightaway and on bends, being appreciably better in this respect than the Alfa Romeos, which are the most successful racing cars Europe has yet produced.' However, British engineer Alec Issigonis watched the 1935 Grand Prix cars through the turns at the Nürburgring and concluded that their still-stiff springs prevented the German all-independent cars from enjoying a significant cornering margin over their cart-sprung contemporaries.

As originally raced in 1934 the Auto Unions were outrageously radical by the standards of the day. The exhaust manifolding that was initially used gave way later to individual pipes for each of the sixteen cylinders.

The masterful design of the de Dion tube connecting the rear wheels of the 1938–39 Mercedes-Benz included a coupling at the centre of the tube that allowed relative rotation between its two ends. This kept the axle from acting like an anti-roll bar when the car rolled in a corner. A slot in the back of the transaxle guided the axle tube laterally.

In addition, stiff springs in front and soft springs at the back were the diametric opposite of the arrangement that is best for a flat, stable ride. This was a feature of the Auto Unions in their versions through 1937, which had spring rates of 344 lb per inch in front and 249 lb per inch in the rear. Although this would have acted to offset the car's natural oversteering tendency, the spring-rate disparity made them especially prone to pitching on bumps, which, together with the rear swing axles, did little to help their rear-wheel adhesion.

Softer spring rates became feasible with the lowered centres of gravity mentioned earlier. They were also facilitated by the adoption of de Dion rear suspension by Mercedes-Benz in 1936 and by Auto Union in 1938, connecting the wheels by an axle tube but keeping the transaxle frame-mounted.[15] Auto Union showed particular sophistication and gained more balanced handling by using a low-placed Panhard rod to locate its de Dion tube laterally, thereby lowering the rear roll centre and levelling the car's roll axis. Mercedes located its axle laterally by a bronze block sliding in a vertical groove in the back of the transaxle.

DAMPING THE ACTION

Mercedes-Benz showed the way to more consistent spring damping. The hydraulic dampers used by Renault in the first Grand Prix winner had long been forgotten. The friction-type dampers or shock absorbers used universally in racing cars during 1936 were responsive in their effect only to movement. They paid no attention to the speed of that movement. Thus if a friction-type damper were already busy damping the movement of a wheel on a bumpy surface it would have no ability to sense the additional movement, say, of the car leaning over in a corner.

A hydraulic damper, in contrast, can be made responsive to the speed of movement. In the example given above it can simultaneously suppress both motions because it simply adds their velocities together and damps accordingly. Based on these premises, and several others,[16] a young engineer named Rudolf Uhlenhaut threw out all friction dampers when he came into the Mercedes-Benz racing department in 1936.[17] As his team manager, Alfred Neubauer, said of

---

15 Both companies also used de Dion axles for some of their road cars during the same period.

16 Hydraulic dampers are much more consistent in their operation, less affected by road conditions and can be tuned in their operation much more closely to the overall needs of the suspension system.

17 Uhlenhaut had to do it gradually because the drivers were suspicious of these new-fangled dampers. Initially he equipped cars with both types at the same time, and then, after a successful test, pointed out to the driver that the friction dampers had been doused in oil and were having no effect.

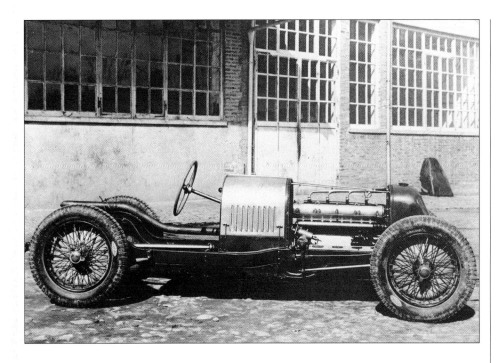

Although fully up to the standards of the twenties, the solid front and rear axles of the Maserati 8CM were unequal to the demands of racing in the thirties. Only hesitantly did Maserati, with its limited means, adopt more advanced suspension solutions.

Uhlenhaut: 'He showed the way to an entirely new era in racing car design. He sprung softly – and damped strongly.'

A private owner-driver, Briton T.P. Cholmondeley Tapper, had an excellent opportunity to observe this new era at close range as the pilot of a 1934 Maserati in the 1936 German Grand Prix. While Tapper's own car 'jumped about on its own suspension like a cat on hot bricks', he reported that 'it was a revelation to see the new German cars glide by as if on air when they passed me. The bodies of the cars continued along a smooth track while the wheels rode up and down over a distance of what appeared to be two feet, transmitting little shock to the chassis.'

Tapper's 8CM Maserati had a reputation for poor roadholding which was owed only partially to its suspension. Like many other cars of the early thirties – and perhaps worse than most – the Maserati had a chassis frame which was far too flexible, rendering its handling almost entirely unpredictable. Flexibility was also a serious fault of the W25 Mercedes-Benz frame, which had box-section side members so heavily drilled to meet the weight limit that their torsional stiffness was extremely low. This was especially damaging on a car with all-independent suspension, which needs high frame rigidity for precise control.

In 1937 Mercedes followed Auto Union's lead (and Rudy Uhlenhaut's own earlier work on a tubular frame for its 170V passenger car) and adopted an oval-tube ladder-type frame with four round-tube crossmembers. It was three times as stiff in torsion than the stand-alone W25 frame, and half again as stiff when the engine – which contributed to frame stiffness with its solid mountings – was bolted in. Much stronger while still light, the new frame allowed Uhlenhaut and the chassis designers under Max Wagner to concentrate on suspension improvements with some confidence that their changes would actually have an effect on the handling.

In the same year Alfa Romeo had the misfortune to introduce a new frame of very narrow box-type design which was as flexible as the new Mercedes frame

ALFRED NEUBAUER

Robust in stature, Alfred Neubauer was also a big man in his total dedication to motor sports and to the success in that field of his adopted company, Daimler-Benz. Neubauer was the heart and the soul of the commitment of Daimler to racing. Would it have persevered so successfully in racing in the fifties as well as the thirties without him? The likelihood is that it would not.

Two of the very great men of the Classic Grand Prix era at Monza: Alfred Neubauer, left, and Enzo Ferrari. Neubauer was capable of making himself misunderstood in many languages, Italian better than most.

Neubauer came to Daimler in the early twenties as a protégé of its then engineering director, Ferdinand Porsche. Porsche had met Neubauer when the latter, then a soldier, was a liaison man between the Austrian Army and Austro-Daimler, where Porsche was managing director. First a car tester there after the war, Neubauer raced one of Porsche's creations in the 1922 Targa Florio at the mature age of thirty-one. When Porsche moved to Daimler in Stuttgart in 1923, the Bohemian-born Neubauer came along.

Neubauer continued racing as well as testing, placing fifteenth overall and third in class in the 1924 Targa Florio. But driving Porsche's new eight-cylinder supercharged Grand Prix car at Monza late that year was more of a challenge, especially on a damp and oily track. Coming out of the Lesmo corner, Neubauer wrote, 'We're already on the straight when the car starts to slide at the back. To the right, to the left, more and more violently . . . Before I can do anything the car spins right around.' Neubauer and his mechanic Hemminger were unhurt when their car hit an earth bank, but the driver's confidence was irreparably dented.[1] He did not race again.

Alfred Neubauer assisted in Berlin in 1926 when Rudy Caracciola won the Grand Prix on the Avus with a sports version of that same eight-cylinder Mercedes. Neubauer was aware that Caracciola had little idea of how well or poorly he had been doing, and realised that 'the man at the wheel of a racing car is the world's loneliest human being'. Neubauer considered how he might be able to convey useful information to this isolated man who needed to know so much.

This had not yet been done in a formal way by either Mercedes or Benz. After their race at Indianapolis in 1923, one Daimler man had reported that 'the management of the Americans was decidedly superior to ours. They didn't leave it to the individual drivers to come into the pit when they felt it was right to do so, but rather the drivers were called to the pits by signals, when their management considered it proper, evidently according to a plan worked out earlier, naturally excepting defects that required immediate attention.' By contrast, priorities in the Mercedes pits were established by the driver's prestige, personality and power of elocution.

A new racing era was dawning, with new drivers. Neubauer sat down with them to try out some of his ideas for systems to tell drivers how far ahead or behind they were, how fast they were going and how far they had to go. Devoting himself also to the detailed arrangements of the pits and the assignments of the crews, Neubauer reached

---

1   Cooling his heels in the pits during practice for the 1924 Italian Grand Prix was a young reserve driver thought to have promise, Rudy Caracciola. 'There were so many things wrong with the cars that even the first-string drivers hardly had time for practice,' said the Berliner. Caracciola and Neubauer would develop a close and sympathetic relationship.

a conclusion that was pivotal in the history of racing: 'I discovered that my real talent lay not in driving but in organising, planning and managing races.'

At the Solitude circuit north of Stuttgart on 12 September 1926 the racing world first saw the figure of Alfred Neubauer in front of the Mercedes-Benz pits with his flags and signals, 'for the first time', as he put it, 'guiding the drivers through the race with invisible strings'. The cars, drivers and Neubauer's strategies were successful at Solitude. In a race of 275 miles, Otto Merz placed first among racing cars with a Mercedes. Neubauer had found his true vocation.

No shrinking violet, Neubauer took care to develop a close, confidential and reliable relationship with each Daimler-Benz management board chairman. This endowed him with the ability to speak authoritatively on behalf of the company and also to ensure that his management was well informed with all the latest news and gossip in the racing world. His office became fully responsible for the planning of each racing season, for all the team's contractual arrangements, and for the movement of men and machines to tracks in all parts of the world.

A racing driver since 1922 and a team manager since 1926, Alfred Neubauer had seen more than many of the triumphs and tragedies that racing had to offer. If a driver needed comforting he was the man for the job.

When Mercedes-Benz cars began competing in Grands Prix in 1934 the arrangements were simple: the engineers designed and built the cars and gave them to Neubauer to race. During a duff 1936 season, however, a new system was put in place. A separate engineering department dedicated to racing, the *Rennabteilung* ('racing department'), was set up under Rudy Uhlenhaut to act as a technical intermediary between the track and the company's engineering resources. This unlocked the company's full potential and helped the racers, under Neubauer, take command of the 1937–39 seasons.

After the war the relentless enthusiasm of Neubauer ensured that Daimler-Benz returned to racing, first in 1951 with pre-war cars, in 1952 with the 300SL and in 1954 – when Neubauer was sixty-three – with the W196 Grand Prix car. He famously told Stirling Moss's manager that the youngster wasn't ready for the big time in 1954, then signed Moss to backstop Fangio so successfully in 1955. 'He was an amazing character,' said Stirling, 'who could have anybody snapping to attention if necessary, but would also show great thought and understanding. In relaxed moments he could have us all rolling about with laughter. The only thing I disliked about him was that he made me get up too damned early.'

Neubauer's most poignant driver choice was Frenchman Pierre Bouillon, who raced under the name 'Levegh'. In 1952 Mercedes-Benz won Le Mans because Levegh's Talbot-Lago, which was being driven without relief, retired just before the finish. As a gesture to the French in those sensitive years after the war, Neubauer included Levegh in his 1955 Le Mans team. Levegh was at the wheel 2½ hours into that race when his 300SLR bounced off another car and scythed into the crowd in the worst accident in the history of motor racing. Neubauer was persuaded to withdraw his other two cars, still healthy, as a sign of respect.

After the 1955 season Daimler-Benz withdrew from major-league racing and Alfred Neubauer stepped down from the *Sportabteilung*, as his domain was known, in favour of Karl Kling. Neubauer remained active at Daimler-Benz, dealing with historical matters and continuing his extensive correspondence with all parts of the world. He died in 1980.

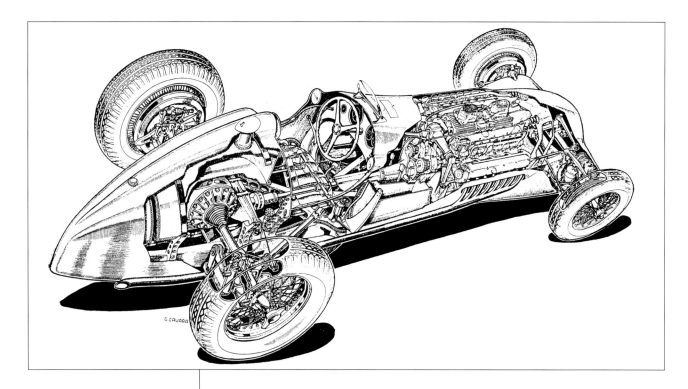

By 1939 Alfa Romeo had produced a supercharged V-16 Grand Prix car that in technological terms was capable of mounting a challenge to the silver cars from the north. It made only rare race appearances, however, and was never perfected at that time.

was rigid. It was susceptible to improvement, however, and the same frame was used for the V-12 and V-16 Alfas of 1938–39. But Mercedes-Benz and Auto Union remained the only firms to make successful use of tubular frames for Grand Prix cars in the thirties. The others retained closed-channel, box-type frames inherited from the beam-axle era.

MEN TO MATCH THE CARS

Considering their narrow tyres, stiff springs and/or low centres of gravity, combined with their excess power, the racing cars of the thirties were driven with amazing abandon for their size and weight. Only a few photographs of the cars in action capture the opposite-lock slides and four-wheel drifts that were freely indulged in by the expert drivers of the day. These alone allow us to answer the oft-repeated question: 'Were the drivers of those days as good as today's?' Beyond peradventure they were.

One driver that Alfred Neubauer confidently expected to join his 1934 team was the Austrian Hans Stuck. Making his mark in the twenties as a hillclimb specialist with his native Austro-Daimlers, the tall Stuck had been racing Mercedes SSK sports cars in 1931 and 1932, with works support in the second year and a string of successes. But Hans Stuck was snapped up by the new Auto Union team, a coup for them. His skill at tail-sliding was just what was needed to master the mid-engined Porsche design.

Hans Stuck was single-handedly responsible for Auto Union's three Grand Prix victories in 1934, including the all-important German Grand Prix on the awesome Nürburgring. In 1935 he was joined in the four-ringed team by Achille Varzi, considered the only Italian driver then to rival Nuvolari. Both men continued to drive for Auto Union throughout the rest of the decade, Stuck continuing into the 1938–39 formula, but Varzi withdrawing before then.

Auto Union's reputation was defended by Bernd Rosemeyer, a blond ex-motorcyclist who first drove an Auto Union in 1935 and who single-handedly won the company's total of ten victories in the 1936–37 seasons. A phenomenal driver, Rosemeyer was the only man who ever exploited to the full the capabilities of the V-16 Auto Union. Without him the cars from Chemnitz would have been far less successful. He was killed attempting to break a speed record on the Frankfurt–Darmstadt Autobahn on 28 January 1938 – a grievous loss to German motor sports. In 1938 his role as team leader was taken over by Tazio Nuvolari, who was responsible for three of the four wins scored by Auto Union in 1938–39.

As an exponent of balanced design, Daimler-Benz was also able to field the best-balanced team of drivers for its Grand Prix cars. From 1934 to 1939 it employed the incomparable stylist Rudy Caracciola – a particular 'pet' of Alfred Neubauer, and not without good reason – and the inveterate power-slider Manfred von Brauchitsch, nephew of the field-marshal of the same name. Others who drove for Mercedes were Frenchman Louis Chiron, Italian Luigi Fagioli and Englishman Richard Seaman, who took risks behind the wheel that had friends fearing for his life. He lost it after crashing at Spa while leading in 1939.

The year 1937 saw the rise of a former Mercedes mechanic, Hermann Lang, to a full-fledged position on the team. Like Rosemeyer a graduate from motorcycles, the Swabian Lang had first driven the cars in the 1935 and 1936 seasons. He was responsible for most of the Mercedes-Benz wins in 1939. Perhaps best of all the team's drivers, Lang knew how to put the big W154 Mercedes into a true four-wheel drift at the very high speeds reached at Spa or at Reims, where he set lap records which were not bettered until 1951. His mechanical skills also allowed him to give the team valuable technical feedback. Hermann Lang would continue racing successfully to 1954, including a Le Mans win in 1952.

Such was the domination of the silver cars that few other drivers had a chance to make a mark in the latter years of the thirties. Driving Maseratis and Delahayes, René Dreyfus was among those who did. Luigi 'Gigi' Villoresi and Giuseppe 'Nino' Farina best showed the paces of the cars from Maserati and Alfa Romeo respectively; their careers would blossom with the Italian supremacy through much of the forties and fifties.

The increase in performance of the Grand Prix car during the thirties was spectacular, but its metamorphosis as a mechanism was far less dramatic than the change that occurred at the end of the fifties. Pre-war propaganda pressure did, however, lift the Grand Prix car from its Depression doldrums and raise it to a new peak of speed and technical refinement. And the war itself generated many of the new technologies of rubber, fuels, structures and materials that made possible the much more versatile and efficient racing cars of the coming decades.

15. 7. 1934.

MERCEDES-BENZ-Turm-Nürburgring

Einlaßkarte für eine Person

✳

Betreten und Aufenthalt auf eigene Gefahr

A special yellow card granted admission for VIP visitors to the Mercedes-Benz tower at the Nürburgring for the German Grand Prix on 15 July 1934.

Justly celebrated for his exploits during the thirties, Tazio Nuvolari is seen on his way to second place in the 1936 Italian Grand Prix at Monza driving a twelve-cylinder Tipo 12C-36 Alfa Romeo. The talented Mantuan moved to Auto Union in 1938.

NÜRBURGRING 1936

ROSEMEYER WINS AGAIN

Auto-Unions take four out of first six places: Me at 150 m.p.h.: Tremendous cro Telephone report by "Gra

RESULT

1. **Rosemeyer** (Auto-Union), 3 hrs. 48 mins. 39.3 secs., 81.807 m.p.h.
2. **Stuck** (Auto-Union), 3 hrs. 52 mins. 36.2 secs.
3. **Brivio** (Alfa-Romeo), 3 hrs. 57 mins. 5 secs.
4. **Hasse** (Auto-Union), 3 hrs. 59 mins. 13.1 secs.
5. **Fagioli and Caracciola** (Mercedes), one lap behind.
6. **von Delius** (Auto-Union), one lap behind.
7. **von Brauchitsch and Lang** (Mercedes), one lap behind.
8. **R. Seaman and Count Trossi** (Maserati), one lap behind.

NOT PLACED

Sommer (Alfa-Romeo), three laps behind.
Cholmondeley Tapper (3-litre Maserati), four laps behind.
Won by 3 mins. 57 secs., with 4 mins. 29 secs. between second and third and 2 mins. 8 secs. between third and fourth.
Last year's speed (Nuvolari) was 75.25 m.p.h.—over 20 minutes slower than this year's race.
Record lap: Rosemeyer, 85.54 m.p.h. Previous record: von Brauchitsch, 80.75 m.p.h.; that is, 9 mins. 56 secs. compared with 10 mins. 22 secs.

Adenau, Sunday Night.

AN enormous crowd, estimated at nearly 400,000 people, flocked to the Nurburgring Race Track last Sunday, despite dull and overcast weather, to watch the 1936 German Grand Prix.

Bernard Rosemeyer, who won the recent Eifel Race at Nurburg, again drove his Auto-Union to a magnificent victory, followed 3 mins. 57 secs. later by Hans Stuck (Auto-Union), with Antonio Brivio (eight-cylinder Alfa) third—over 4 minutes behind Stuck.

Once again the Mercedes team ran into trouble, and Louis Chiron crashed half-way through the race, after working his way into fourth place. Nuvolari and Dreyfus, in the 12-cylinder Alfas, both retired. After the first lap there was no one to challenge Rosemeyer.

The first quarter of the race was wildly exciting, with the drivers in full cry after Rosemeyer; but one by one they retired and the last stages of the race provided a runaway win. He took the lead after the first lap and, except for a tyre stop, held it right through.

Auto-Unions were first, second, fourth and sixth; Alfas were third; Mercedes could do no better than fifth and seventh; Seaman and Trossi were eighth, a performance with a 2½-litre car which was one of the outstanding features of the day.

c14

Tremendous excitement ran throughout Germany during the week of practising before the German Grand Prix. The papers waxed almost hysterical over the importance of the race. One journal went so far as to call it "The Race of the Century." Excitement rose to fever heat after the practising on the Thursday, when Caracciola, Rosemeyer and von Brauchitsch all lapped well under the old record. Caracciola went round in 10 mins. 3 secs.

So far this season Mercedes have been off form. The new short-chassis model has coil springing at the rear, with extra universal joints at the extremities of the rear axle. The engine is a straight eight with twin overhead camshafts, and a capacity of 4.9 litres. The Auto-Unions are all well over 5 litres with 16-cylinder push-rod engines at the rear, and a torsion-bar, independent suspension front and back. The two newest Alfas have 4.1-litre V-type 12-cylinder units, with twin o.h.c., independent suspension all round and at the rear a five-leaf transverse spring. The other Alfas are the older 3.8-litre eight-cylinder, with independently sprung chassis.

Seaman's 4-litre eight-cylinder Maserati is the car that Farina drove at Donington last year and is independently sprung. This car was heavily handicapped by a too-low back-axle ratio, and the speed of the car was not

over 135 m.p.h. Trossi's Maserati had an old-pattern 2½-litre four-cylinder engine in the same light 1,500 c.c. chassis with which he won the recent 1½-litre Eifel race.

Some of the Independents

Wimille arrived and put in two practice laps only with the 3.3 Bugatti—his Deauville car. Cholmondeley Tapper had the 3-litre Maserati from Deauville. Raymond Sommer, independent driver, had his old 2.9 monoposto Alfa with normal suspension. He broke a back axle in practice and only received a spare on the day before the race. Rens, the Dutchman, had entered one of the old 2.3 Bugattis.

(Left) Victorious B. Rosemeyer, whose time for the race was faster than all previous records. Stuck, the second man home, likewise third and fourth, excelled last year's winning speed. Rosemeyer led all through but for one very brief period.

AUTO-UNION VICTORY IN GERMAN G.P.

rcedes debacle: Chiron crashes
wd of spectators.
nde Vitesse"

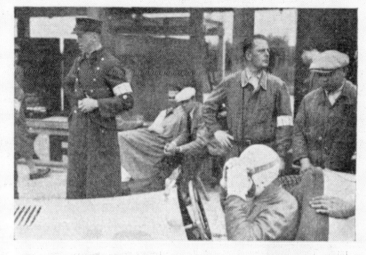

The only accident in the race, befell Louis Chiron (here just about to set off on a practice lap): his car overturned and Chiron was taken to hospital with slight head and shoulder injuries; internal injuries are also feared. In the background, R. Caracciola can be seen sitting in front of the pits.

A colossal crowd, estimated at nearly 400,000, swarmed to the Nurburgring, 2,000 ft. up in the Eifel Mountains, the most picturesque circuit in Europe; 10,000 crowded in one corner, and there were 20,000 people on the Karussell alone.

The starting order at Nurburg is determined by drawing lots. The order of the first three of the eight rows:—
1st rank, Nuvolari, Stuck, Wimille; 2nd rank, Caracciola, von Brauchitsch; 3rd rank, Dreyfus (Alfa), Trossi (Maserati) and Rosemeyer (Auto-Union).

The fourth Auto-Union was being driven by the cadet driver Hasse in place of Varzi; the third by von Delius. The third Mercedes driver was Fagioli and the fourth the cadet Hermann Lang.

Ten minutes to go! The air was

(Below) The Karussell corner, with Sevari (Alfa - Romeo) photographed during practice. This corner is remarkable in that it is almost a complete circle, steeply banked for a few yards on the inside (the banking used to be a ditch) and almost flat on the outside.

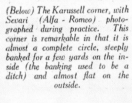

Richard Seaman, one of England's most outstanding drivers to whom signal honour was paid, in that he was invited to drive one of the official Maseratis. He is seen here, calm as ever, at the wheel during a fast practice lap.

electric with excitement. A company of helmeted Storm Troopers marched to the starting point with band playing, while the crowd stood at the Nazi salute, and a huge Nazi flag was unfurled. Then the 20 racing cars burst into life one by one, until the air shook with the thunder of the exhausts.

As the gun banged and the flag fell the whole field shot forward like bullets. Instantly, Brauchitsch (Mercedes) streaked through from the second rank and shot into the lead. Behind him came Stuck (Auto-Union), Rosemeyer (Auto-Union), Brivio (Alfa),

Dreyfus (Alfa V-12), Lang (Mercedes) and Caracciola (Mercedes).

On the return, past the pits into the slightly banked Nordkurve, Lang flashed past Stuck and Rosemeyer into second place. All round the course the enormous crowd leapt to its feet, as the cars streaked through the bends, twisting and turning, driving headlong downhill and rushing uphill through the innumerable corners of the Ring, while the mountains roared back the flying echoes.

As they plunged down Fuchsrohr and took the far curve by the Adenau

c15

THE GERMAN GRAND PRIX . . . . Contd.

Gate, Brauchitsch led Lang and Stuck. Nuvolari was biding his time in fifth place, driving with his usual icy calm and cornering with his usual precision. At the Karussell, with its saucer-like banking, Rosemeyer shot up into second place, wrenching his car through the bend, with one wheel throwing up clouds of dust from the gutter, and scarcely a second behind came Caracciola.

Through the maze of bends and hills towards the Brunnchen, Caracciola passed Rosemeyer into second place, but on the three-kilometre stretch with its hump-backed bridges. Rosemeyer and Lang roared past him. At the stands, where the cars cut off at 170 m.p.h. for the distant Sudkurve, the order was: Brauchitsch, Rosemeyer Lang, Caracciola, Stuck and Nuvolari, all lapping at over 81 m.p.h.—a colossal speed for a standing lap.

On the second round, the first three all broke the lap record, setting thus early the tempo of this astounding race. Then Rosemeyer took the lead at the Adenau curve, while Brauchitsch suddenly slowed up and let Lang pass into second place. On that lap the order was: Rosemeyer (Auto-Union), Lang (Mercedes)—the cadet driver winning his spurs—Caracciola, Nuvolari, Stuck, Chiron and Fagioli. Brauchitsch came in to adjust the front suspension, losing 5 minutes. Dreyfus, with the second V-12 Alfa, lost 2 minutes changing five plugs.

A Third Lap Record

Stuck passed Nuvolari into the Nordkurve, only to be repassed coming through the forest at Hocheichen. On the third lap, while Rosemeyer led with a record of 9 mins. 56 secs. (83.54 m.p.h.), came the first retirements: Zanelli's Maserati with fuel feed, Seaman (Maserati) with no brakes, and Wimille with a broken gearbox.

On the fourth lap Rosemeyer led by nearly half a minute, with the amazing Lang—feet hard down—behind him, leaving Caracciola and Nuvolari. Caracciola stopped at the pits with a scream of tyres, losing a minute and a half tuning the carburetter, and amidst tremendous excitement Nuvolari went by into third place.

Lang, the Cadet, Drives Well

Rosemeyer still kept his lead at about half a minute, and Lang, driving like a demon in second place, broke his little finger in a too vigorous gearchange, thereafter driving in great pain. Stuck, steady as a rock, was fourth behind Nuvolari; then came von Delius (Auto-Union); then Chiron; so that after five laps the car order was: Auto-Union, Mercedes, 12-cylinder Alfa, two more Auto-Unions, Mercedes, eight-cylinder Alfa and Fagioli's Mercedes.

On the sixth lap Dreyfus was in again for more plugs, and the 12-cylinder Alfa was not feeling at all well. It got away 2 minutes later.

c16

The Race Progress

SECOND LAP
(1) Rosemeyer (Auto-Union), 20m. 31.1s., 82.77 m.p.h., leading by 9.1s.
(2) Lang (Mercedes), 20m. 40.2s.
(3) Caracciola (Mercedes), 20m. 48.4s.
(4) Nuvolari (Alfa), 21m. 8.1s.

FOURTH LAP
(1) Rosemeyer, 40m. 35s., 83.63 m.p.h., leading by 29s.
(2) Lang, 41m. 4s.
(3) Caracciola, 41m. 18.4s.
(4) Nuvolari, 41m. 41.4s.

SIXTH LAP
(1) Rosemeyer, 1h. 0m. 57.1s., 83.57 m.p.h., leading by 29.3s.
(2) Lang, 1h. 1m. 26.4s.
(3) Nuvolari, 1h. 2m. 13.1s.
(4) Stuck (Auto-Union), 1h. 2m. 55.1s.

EIGHTH LAP
(1) Lang, 1h. 21m. 52s., 82.89 m.p.h., leading by 21m. 3s.
(2) Rosemeyer, 1h. 22m. 13.3s.
(3) Nuvolari, 1h. 23m. 1.2s.
(4) Stuck, 1h. 23m. 26.2s.

TENTH LAP
(1) Rosemeyer, 1h. 42m. 39.1s., 82.7 m.p.h., leading by 1m. 54s.
(2) Stuck, 1h. 44m. 33.1s.
(3) Nuvolari, 1h. 44m. 59.4s.
(4) Chiron (Mercedes), 1h. 45m. 8.2s.

TWELFTH LAP
(1) Rosemeyer, 2h. 3m. 13.4s., 82.5 m.p.h., leading by 2m. 27s.
(2) Nuvolari, 2h. 5m. 40.4s.
(3) Lang and Caracciola, 2h. 6m. 2.2s.
(4) Stuck, 2h. 6m. 33s.

FOURTEENTH LAP
(1) Rosemeyer, 2h. 23m. 48.1s., 82.64 m.p.h., 2m. 32s. lead.
(2) Nuvolari, 2h. 26m. 20.1s.
(3) Stuck, 2h. 27m. 43.4s.
(4) Brivio (Alfa), 2h. 30m. 1s.

SIXTEENTH LAP
(1) Rosemeyer, 2h. 45m. 45.1s., 81.96 m.p.h., leading by 3m.
(2) Stuck, 2h. 48m. 45.4s.
(3) Brivio, 2h. 51m. 9.3s.
(4) Hasse, 2h. 53m. 30.4s.
This above order continued until the finish. Rosemeyer's lap speeds:—Lap 18.—81.84 m.p.h. (leading by 3m. 21s.). Lap 19.—81.84 m.p.h. (leading by 3m. 27s.). Lap 20.—81.87 m.p.h. (leading by 3m. 30s.). Lap 21.—81.76 m.p.h. (leading by 3m. 42s.).

A lap later came the first tyre change, after 98 miles, Rosemeyer dashing in and out in 41 seconds, a wonderful display of pit work. One mechanic jumped clean over the car to save running round it. Then came more sensations. Caracciola walked in, leaving his car out on the circuit with carburation trouble. Temporarily Lang went into the lead, while Rosemeyer was at rest.

On the eighth lap several cars came in for tyre changes, and the pits were a marvellous scene of frenzied activity. Mechanics ripping wheels off and on, as if not only their job but their very lives depended on it. Nuvolari took 1 min. 2 secs.; Delius, whose hands were simply raw flesh, took 51 secs.; Brivio, 45 secs.; and then Trossi stopped to change wheels and hand over to Dick Seaman, dropping 1 min. 10 secs. in the process. Dreyfus came slowly in and gave up the race.

During the first 11 laps (half distance) Rosemeyer had broken the old lap record eight times, and put up a new record of his own on the third circuit at 83.54 m.p.h., lapping in 9 mins. 56 secs.—a speed not catered for by the lap speed table in the programme. He steadily increased his lead lap by lap from 9 secs. on the second lap to 2 mins. 12 secs. on the 11th, including his pit stop.

The race speed fell very slowly from this staggering velocity, which was breaking all records, coming down gradually as the distance increased from 83.63 m.p.h. to 82.64 m.p.h. During the remaining 11 laps it fell slightly to a shade under 82 m.p.h., and Rosemeyer, easing up greatly, put his lead up to over 3 minutes; no one could get near him.

On the 9th lap Lang stopped for tyres, while the crowd cheered itself hoarse. Although the youngest driver of the Mercedes team, he had brought the car up into second place. The cheers of the crowd suddenly changed to hisses and whistles—hisses and whistles of execration. Caracciola was getting into the car and Lang, nursing his injured hand, walked away to have it put in splints.

Tyre Stop in 40 Seconds

At half distance (11 laps) Stuck made his first tyre stop in the record time of 40 seconds, and Sevari handed over his eight-cylinder Alfa to Dreyfus. Fagioli had a longish stop to tune the front suspension, and Hasse, the cadet Auto-Union driver, lost 1 min. 7 secs. changing wheels. Dreyfus retired after 18 laps.

The terrific speed wrought havoc among the Mercedes team, leaving the Auto-Unions unscathed. Throughout the race no work was done under the bonnets of these cars. Caracciola had retired with one Merc. after seven laps, and, taking on Lang's machine, boiling hard with a split radiator hose, retired with that one also after another six laps. Brauchitsch's car, now driven by Lang, was likewise not going properly, and was too far behind to be dangerous. Fagioli was having trouble with the front of the car.

Chiron's Crash

On the 12th lap Chiron touched the grass at the 150-m.p.h. curve after the three-kilometre straight, slid backwards and turned upside down.

On the 15th lap came more sensation in this extraordinary race. Nuvolari, pacing the flying Rosemeyer 2½ minutes ahead, broke his back axle just off the Karussell, and the most feared driver in the race became a spectator.

So the race drew to its close. With the disappearance of Caracciola as a threatening driver, Nuvolari, Chiron and Brauchitsch, much of the interest departed, and the race simply became a struggle in which the Auto-Unions strove to displace Brivio's remaining Alfa and lead the race in one, two, three order. Brivio, however, was motoring too rapidly.

All this time Cholmondeley Tapper, in his 3-litre Maserati, was going round and round with complete steadiness, despite hardly any practice, comparatively slow no doubt, but with clockwork regularity, in the tail of the race. Seaman was losing no time with the Maserati, and kept his car in 8th place —a fine show.

CHAPTER FIVE
THE FORTIES

The coming season bids fair (to coin a phrase) to be memorable. It may be said that the Type 158 Alfa Romeo, dominant vehicle of 1946–1948, is no longer in that satisfactory niche. We saw at Turin that this design had more or less met its match at last, as all designs must sooner or later, which is a good if inevitable thing. The Alfa Romeo concern will not be the last to rejoice, although apparently they do not think it is yet time to reach up and pull down from its shelf the legendary Type 512, with 12-cylinder engine and more superchargers than a busy journalist can count at a single glance.

Rodney Walkerley, *The Motor*, forecasting the 1949 season

I t was not one of those race meetings that technicians love to analyse or that enthusiasts recall with awe and wonder. Many histories of motor racing don't even bother to mention it. However, for the 90,000 people who swarmed to the thickly wooded park to see it, it was unforgettable – even epochal, a liberating catharsis. The three races on 9 September 1945 in Paris's park, the Bois de Boulogne, were the first held after the end of the Second World War. To many it seemed incredible that thoughts could turn so quickly to something so frivolous and wasteful of scarce resources as auto racing. They were the Philistines whose senses are immune to the shriek of an open exhaust and the pungent scent of castor oil.

In temporary stands around the 1¾-mile circuit on the roads of the Bois de Boulogne, these faithful saw the first races held in Europe in more than five years. They were organised by the Independent Drivers' Association and its spark plug president, Maurice Mestivier, who had raced Amilcars in the thirties. They had the backing of a prominent Resistance organisation. Racing drivers had been disproportionately represented in the wartime anti-occupation underground.

The first race, the Robert Benoist Cup, honoured the great French driver who had been executed as a member of the Resistance. For 1,500 cc cars, it was won by an Italian-born builder whose blue cars would be prominent after the war, Amédée Gordini. Henri Louveau's Maserati collected the Liberation Cup in the race for 2-litre cars. The main event, the Prisoners' Cup, was won by a car that was on the way out of the racing world, a Bugatti, and by a driver who was very much on the way in: France's own Jean-Pierre Wimille.

A hint of the excitement and drama of the final years of the 1½/4½-litre Formula 1 is provided by the sight of the Ferrari team preparing for battle at Barcelona. Checking out their 4½-litre V-12s are Alberto Ascari (in number 2), Piero Taruffi (number 4) and Dorino Serafini (number 6). They sound as good as they look.

THE SPORT'S REBIRTH

The French led the way in organising races while other nations gradually joined the motor sports revival. In Italy a hillclimb was staged at Naples in December 1945, and in 1946 racing reawakened in England, Switzerland, Belgium and even in Germany. The international association of motoring clubs, the pre-war AIACR, was reconstituted as the FIA (Fédération Internationale de l'Automobile), based in Paris. Its sporting commission the CSI (Commission Sportive Internationale) was convened for the first time on 28 February 1946. It elected a new president, Augustin Pérouse, and settled on a new formula for Grand Prix racing to take effect in 1948 and continue through 1951.

Some of the debate necessary to resolve a new formula had already taken place seven years earlier. We recall that the last Grand Prix formula, effective from 1938 through 1940, was the first to attempt a balance between supercharged and unsupercharged engines, imposing respective maximum displacements of 3 and 4½ litres in association with minimum weights. In Europe it hadn't taken long to discover that the supercharged 3-litre cars were overpoweringly superior (in American racing the pairing worked out better; the pre-war formula was retained in the forties and fifties, when unblown engines dominated).

Conceived before the war for Grand Prix Racing, this 4.5-litre six-cylinder Talbot was ready and waiting to serve in the new postwar Formula 1, which was created specifically to accommodate it and other cars built to the pre-war 4½-litre limit.

By 1939, sentiment in European circles strongly favoured the establishment of a future formula that would carry over the 4½-litre unblown category and pit it against supercharged 1½-litre racing cars. The latter had always been a popular engine size in Europe. It had been used since 1935 for the Voiturette racing category in parallel with the main Grand Prix formula – what we'd think of later as Formula 2.

Italy, fed up with being defeated by the Germans on their own territory, switched her major races to the Voiturette class in 1939.[1] All the companies involved in racing were working on new 1½-litre cars because it seemed likely that a change to a 1½ blown/4½ unblown Grand Prix formula could come as early as 1940. The only formula-car road races held that year, two in Italy, were for 1,500 cc cars.

Not many 4½-litre unblown cars had competed before the war, but those few – French Talbots, Delahayes and Delages – had somehow survived. So had almost all the supercharged 1½-litre machines. On the other hand, the 3-litre blown Grand Prix cars of the thirties, most of them German, were not immediately available, and none, felt the CSI members, was likely to be made for some time.

---

1   This resulted in the building by Mercedes-Benz, on short notice, of a pair of V-8 1½-litre cars to race at Italian-held Tripoli. They deeply embarrassed their Italian hosts by scoring a one-two victory. Auto Union was also well advanced on its plans to build a V-12 1½-litre car.

A formula was needed, as Alfred Neubauer of Daimler-Benz observed, 'to bridge the gap between the difficult war years and the time when firms building racing cars would once more have settled down'. The choice of the CSI was indeed a formula for Grand Prix cars of 1½ litres supercharged and 4½ normally aspirated. Although it wasn't officially in effect until 1948, the new formula was adopted earlier by the organisers of major Grand Prix events.

At the same time consideration was given to a new secondary or Voiturette formula. This was eventually settled at 2 litres unblown. Initially, the two categories were distinguished as Formulas A and B, but the usage of Formulas 1 and 2 was soon adopted. Thus by the end of the forties the term 'Formula 1' for Grand Prix racing was both established and accepted.

PROTECTING THE ITALIAN PATRIMONY

'The end of the war did not find me altogether unprepared.' Thus spake Enzo Ferrari, who had taken his first tentative steps towards building cars in his own right in 1940 after a decade of running his Scuderia Ferrari, the official Alfa Romeo racing team. Ferrari, like his contemporaries, had not let the hostilities pass without thinking about motor racing. After Italy entered the war on 10 June 1940 he produced small aero engines for training planes before starting to manufacture fine grinding machines, copied from German originals, that were unique in Italy and very much in demand.

Supercharged 1.5-litre 4CL Maseratis were the weapons of choice for many private teams after the Second World War. The semi-works cars of the newly formed Scuderia Milan dominated the front row of the grid at Nice in 1946. Villoresi (number 10) was the eventual winner.

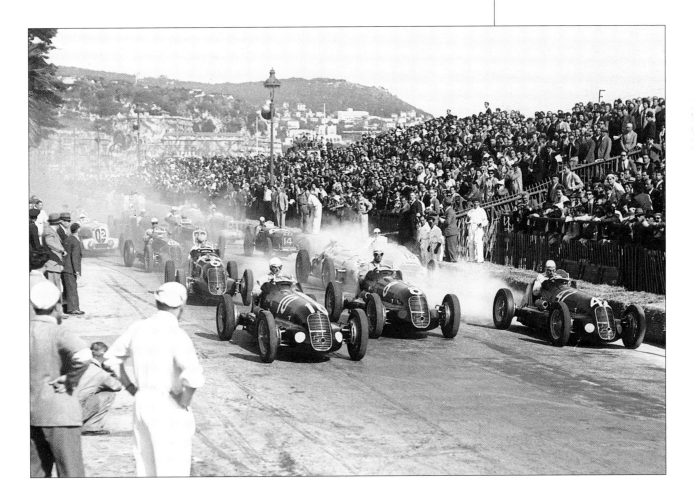

ENZO FERRARI

In the sixties there was quite a to-do when racing drivers began setting up businesses to produce their own cars. Among them were Jack Brabham, Dan Gurney and Bruce McLaren. This was seen as quite a new idea at the time. Overlooked was the much earlier decision of another racing driver to do just that. Before exploding on the scene in the forties as a car maker, Enzo Ferrari had enjoyed a respectable career behind the wheel.

Enzo Ferrari broke off a conversation with Argentine driver Froilán González, right, to admonish photographer Rodolfo Mailander. In the fifties Ferrari frequently visited both tests and races but in his later years he was more likely to stay at home and rely on colleagues to relay information – not always impartially.

Born in Modena on 18 February 1898, Enzo Ferrari was the son of a structural engineer who produced railway gangways and sheds – appropriate enough for a family whose name in Italian is the equivalent of 'Smith'. With both his father and his brother dying in 1916, young Ferrari was forced into the world of work, first of all in the workshop of the Modena Fire Brigade. He also had to survive the war, which he ended in poor health after succumbing to the flu epidemic of 1918.

Demobbed and turned down for a job with Fiat, Ferrari found work in Turin as a tester for a company converting old vans into sports cars. He then moved to CMN (Costruzioni Meccaniche Nazionali) in Milan to work as a test driver. He also raced for CMN in the 1919 Parma–Berceto hillclimb and the Targa Florio, in which he finished ninth.

In 1920, with the assistance of his friend Ugo Sivocci, Ferrari moved to Alfa Romeo. This began a relationship with the Milan firm that lasted two decades. Ferrari's career with Alfa Romeo took him from test driver to race driver to sales assistant, and finally to the post of director of the Alfa's racing division, Alfa Corse, which he left in November 1939 after differing with the company over its racing and technical policies.

Driving an Alfa, Enzo Ferrari placed second in the 1920 Targa Florio only 12 minutes behind the winner after 8½ hours of racing. In 1921 he was fifth in the Targa and second in the 1921 Circuit of Mugello.[1] In 1923, after retiring in the Targa and at Mugello, he won the Circuito del Savio at Ravenna.[2] Among those impressed by his form, which included the fastest lap as well, were the parents of Francesco Baracca, an Italian flying ace who had lost his life in the war. They asked Ferrari to carry the heraldry that had marked out Baracca's fighter: a prancing horse on a yellow shield.

Ferrari won again at Ravenna in May 1924, followed to the finish by none other than Tazio Nuvolari. In July, still driving an older Alfa Romeo RL, Ferrari scored a victory in the Coppa Acerbo held on the roads at Pescara. Ferrari had been warned not to hold up team-mate Giuseppe Campari, who was driving the latest P2 at Pescara, but Campari retired with shifting troubles. To keep the pressure on Ferrari's rivals, however, Campari cleverly concealed his car down a side street. Ferrari came through the winner.

These successes led to the appointment by Alfa Romeo of Enzo Ferrari to its official team for the 1924 Grand Prix de l'ACF at Lyons. Driving a P2, he was to join Louis Wagner, Giuseppe Campari and his role model, Antonio Ascari, at the wheel of one of these first-line cars. The new straight-eight P2 was the work of Vittorio Jano, whom Ferrari had enticed away from Fiat to join Alfa. Thus this race was of great significance to Ferrari. This may have accounted for his sudden pre-race decision not to drive – described by some as 'a nervous breakdown'.

---

1   Ferrari had raced an Isotta-Fraschini at Mugello in 1920. Much later, Ferrari's company would buy a circuit built at Mugello and develop it for both testing and racing. Mugello certainly held positive memories for Enzo Ferrari.

2   Following Ferrari over the line was Edoardo Weber, driving a Fiat 501. Weber would later become a celebrated manufacturer of racing carburettors.

In 1952 Ferrari, right, showed one of his 4½-litre V-12 engines to Gerry Grant, whose piston-ring company was to help sponsor their entry at Indianapolis that year. Throughout Ferrari's life he viewed the engine as the essential element of the Grand Prix racing car.

Competing only occasionally thereafter, Ferrari concentrated on his responsibilities at Alfa, where he acted as the right arm of Giorgio Rimini, aide to company chief Nicola Romeo. An Alfa Romeo distributorship in Modena was an additional reward. But Ferrari, in his own words an 'agitator of men', had another idea. Backed by textile-making brothers from Ferrara, Augusto and Alfredo Caniano, he set up the Scuderia Ferrari in 1929, *scuderia* simply meaning 'team'. The Baracca shield became its emblem.[3] At the young age of thirty-one, Enzo Ferrari was ready to put wheels under other drivers.

Although the Scuderia Ferrari's backbone was its stable of wealthy amateurs – fifty (!) in its first year, 1930 – Ferrari was also able to attract such first-line talent as Campari, Nuvolari and, in 1935, René Dreyfus. Wrote Dreyfus:

> With Ferrari I learned the business of racing, for there was no doubt he was a businessman. Enzo Ferrari loved racing, of that there was no question. Still, it was more than an enthusiast's love, but one tempered by the practical realisation that this was a good way to build a nice, profitable empire. I knew he was going to be a big man one day, even then when the cars he raced carried somebody else's name. I felt sure that eventually they would carry his.

By the mid-thirties the scuderia had been transformed into an engineering-racing division of Alfa Romeo, having taken over the racing function entirely in 1933. With this more businesslike orientation, the interests of the founding Canianos were bought out by Count Carlo Felice Trossi, himself a driver of considerable merit.

True to the forecast of René Dreyfus, after the war Ferrari commenced building and racing his own cars. His Grand Prix cars are a major leitmotif for the forties and fifties in this history of the classic Grand Prix cars. In 1960 his business was turned into a joint stock company. Fiat became a fifty-fifty partner in 1969, and later, in 1988, the majority shareholder, thus securing the future of the Ferrari enterprise.

Enzo Ferrari was given the Italian award of Cavaliere for sporting merit in 1924, and went on to receive further honours from the nation: Commendatore in 1927 and Cavaliere del Lavoro in 1952. In 1960 he received an honorary degree in mechanical engineering from Bologna University. Under his leadership Ferrari cars won more than 5,000 races in all parts of the world and earned twenty-five major world titles. Enzo Ferrari died in Modena on 14 August 1988 at the age of ninety.

---

3   The shield did not actually appear on the cars until 1932, when it adorned the bonnets of two Alfas entered by the scuderia in the Spa 24-hour race on 9 July.

In 1943, to meet the requirements of an industrial decentralisation edict, Ferrari moved his plant from Modena to a nearby town where he had some land and a summer house: Maranello. There he established a superb small factory which he immediately converted to racing car manufacture at the end of the war, making good the damage that had been caused by air raids in November 1944 and February 1945.

Ferrari's former associate, Alfa Romeo of Milan, accomplished even more during the early war years. During 1940 and 1941 Alfa continued developing its Type 158 1½-litre car, built in 1938 under Ferrari's direction and in his workshops as a Voiturette racer. Alfa designed a two-stage supercharger for it and tried out a de Dion rear axle, and even built and tested a new rear-engined flat-twelve 1,500 cc racer, the Type 512.

In 1942 seven of Alfa Romeo's 1½-litre racing cars were stored in the paddock garages at Monza. When the Germans occupied northern Italy in September 1943 the cars were spirited away to a hiding place near Orta Lake to the north, between Turin and Milan, where the Alfa Romeo engineers had also relocated for the duration.

Other fine racing cars remained in Milan in the loving care of real enthusiasts. The last and best 1,500 cc cars from the shops of the Maserati brothers were placed in the hands of the Ruggieri brothers, who hid them in Milan and prepared them for the eventual return of racing. Succumbing to a financial crisis, the Maserati brothers had sold their company to Adolfo Orsi in 1937, and had moved their base from Bologna to Modena in 1940 to suit Orsi's operations. There they worked on spark plugs, electric trucks and a new six-cylinder sports car that they began testing on the road in 1941, a car that was destined to be the first of a new generation of Maserati automobiles.

These were not the only Italians who worked during the war to keep the nation's great racing patrimony intact. Racing driver Piero Dusio was planting the seeds that would bloom as Cisitalia after VE Day. As Briton John Lloyd wrote: 'The Italians . . . had of course one less year of war than the other contestants and do not take war seriously enough to exhaust their total wealth and manpower in its following as it was necessary for us to do to secure victory.'

With its low build, de Dion rear suspension and Zoller-blown 1½-litre engine, the late thirties E-type ERA seemed just the job for postwar racing. Conspicuously lacking, however, were the resources needed to make it raceworthy.

EUROPE'S OTHER NATIONS

The British weren't able to build new racing cars during the conflict, but they lost few of those they had. After Britain declared war on 3 September 1939, Geoffrey Taylor turned his small Alta shop over to aircraft components. But he did find time during the first few months of the conflict to finish something he'd been working on: a new 1,500 cc blown Alta with torsion-bar springing. Altas had been respected but not feared Voiturettes before the war.

ERAs, which were among the fastest Voiturettes, were carefully salted away in England. Their supercharged six-cylinder engines were derived from a Riley design. The two newest ERAs, the handsome low-chassis E-types, were stored in Derby, where the ERA chief mechanic could look after them while not working for Rolls-Royce. And two former members of the ERA *équipe*, promoter/driver Raymond Mays and engineer Peter Berthon, were

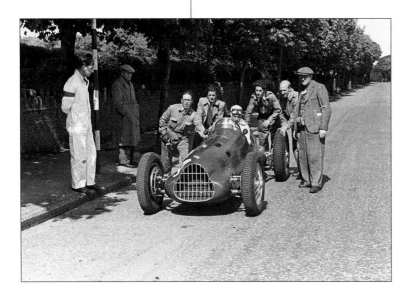

Upright and purposeful, the pre-war ERA was much in demand among racing Britons after the war. ERA moving spirit Raymond Mays drove his in the Swiss Grand Prix at Bern in 1947, placing an excellent third in his heat but retiring in the final.

already dreaming of the creation of a magnificent new car that could carry Britain's colours in Grand Prix racing.

The preservation of racing cars was more difficult in wartime Germany. The main Mercedes-Benz stable was shipped to a hiding place in Dresden. The two W165 1½-litre cars, built as Voiturette racers in 1939, had been improved well into 1940. They were later smuggled to Switzerland. The Daimler-Benz designers remained in Stuttgart while the Porsche design team was relocated to the east to Gmünd, a country town on the border between Austria and Czechoslovakia. The great cars Porsche had helped build, the Auto Unions, were sequestered where they were made in the eastern part of Germany – whence they were slow to emerge after the postwar occupation by the Soviets.

Ferdinand Porsche, his son Ferry and his great chief engineer Karl Rabe, with their other associates, found themselves occupied after the war ended: fixing Volkswagens. Conditions in most European countries were anything but ideal for building Grand Prix cars and finding places to race them. The materials required, high-quality steels especially, were almost impossible to get. Fuel of any kind was scarce, let alone racing brews. High-performance spark plugs scarcely existed. As for racing tyres, they existed only in jealously hoarded pre-war caches. Alfred Neubauer was guilty of uncharacteristic understatement when he wrote: 'The early resumption of racing in 1946 was perhaps less due to industrial interests than to the great enthusiasm shown in the sport itself.'

This enthusiasm was highest by far in France and Italy. 'It is clear that they are up against the same difficulties as ourselves,' reported John Dugdale from Italy to his fellow Britons, 'but the looseness of government control gives them more scope.' While enthusiasts in England were still trying to get clearance to use airport perimeter roads for racing, round-the-houses road races were being promoted on the Continent.

There were good reasons why so many races were held between the kerbs and buildings of cities like Turin, Nice, Paris, Pau, Brussels, Angoulême, Marseilles, San Remo and Bari during the forties. Rodney Walkerley of *The Motor* commented on it: 'Promoting clubs are faced with the fact that as in Britain there is no basic [petrol] ration for the family car which tends to keep the family in the nearest cafe on a Sunday instead of driving out into the nearby landscape to watch a race.' The only way for a club to try to break even was to run its races where the people were: in town.

'Thus we can look forward to a series of round-the-houses races again,' continued Walkerley in 1948, 'with short twisty circuits, low average speeds and a premium on low axle ratios and big acceleration and braking – races in which, to date, the 1,500 cc supercharged car has had the legs of the heavier 4- and 4½-litre unsupercharged brigade.'

ALFA IN THE ASCENDANT

Walkerley could have put it even more simply. He could have said that when it chose to race, the Alfa Romeo Type 158 was invincible. From the Grand Prix des Nations at Geneva in 1946 through the French Grand Prix at Reims in 1951 the Alfa Romeo team entered and won 26 races. The Alfas raced in 44 completed events for cars of their engine size from 1938 to 1951, and were beaten on only 5 occasions when one of the 158s was still running.

Those defeats were delivered before the war by Maserati and Mercedes-Benz, one each, and after it by Ferrari – three in the 1951 season. (That year is included in the forties to make up for the racing years lost during the war, and also to complete the first postwar Grand Prix formula.) The Ferraris that beat the Alfas were unsupercharged cars that ended the virtual domination of Grand Prix racing by supercharged engines since the early twenties. As the forties closed, so did the age of the blown Grand Prix car – until the turbocharged revival during the eighties.

The Type 158 Alfa traced its beginnings to 1937, a season in which the red cars from Milan were shut out of success in front-line Grand Prix events by Mercedes-Benz and Auto Union. Enzo Ferrari, who was responsible for the racing of the cars assigned to his scuderia by Alfa, decided to build a 1½-litre machine to run in the Voiturette events that were becoming more and more popular. Alfa loaned Ferrari a designer, Gioachino Colombo, who had worked under the great Vittorio Jano, and a draftsman, Giovanni Nasi. Assisting Colombo was Ferrari's own Luigi Bazzi. Hired in to work on the transmission and rear suspension design was the versatile Alberto Massimino.

Early in 1938 the first Type 158 cars were being completed in Ferrari's shops in Modena. Before they were raced, Alfa Romeo took over Ferrari's complete organisation and hired him to run its own new racing department, Alfa Corse. Their new Voiturette was the first eight-cylinder model to be built specifically for that class, its in-line engine having a gear train up the front to twin overhead cams operating two valves per cylinder.[2]

The 158's engine and its rear-mounted four-speed transaxle were carried by an oval-tube frame, suspended by Porsche-type trailing arms at the front and swing

Seen before one of its pre-war racing appearances, the type 158 Alfa Romeo 'Alfetta' was a slim and elegant automobile, built largely in the workshops of Enzo Ferrari. Its trailing-arm front suspension was designed in accord with Porsche patents.

---

2   Jano's concept of a gear train to the camshafts at the centre of the block was not pursued in the 158. A probable reason for this is that the same monobloc cylinder units were doubled up to make a twin-crankshaft U-16 engine for Grand Prix racing; a central gear train would have been daunting to organise. Interestingly, the U-16 had its drive to the cams at the flywheel end of the crankshaft instead of at the front.

Not the most elegant of racing cars, Alfa Romeo's mid-engined Type 512 was completed just before the outbreak of the Second World War. Designers and managers already believed that the next Grand Prix Formula would include a category for 1½-litre supercharged cars.

axles at the back, and sprung at both ends by transverse leaf springs. It was a spare, trim car, ambitious in its basic conception and very simply executed by people obviously aware that they would have to service it as well as build and race it.

These Alfas first raced on 7 August 1938 at Livorno, winning. Apart from the usual teething troubles they showed their superiority in other races and victories up to a one-two-three finish at Tripoli in 1940. Cooling troubles that had plagued them at Tripoli a year earlier left the way clear for a victory by the new V-8 W165s built specifically by Mercedes-Benz for the 1939 Tripoli race. This defeat was considered an ill omen by Wifredo Ricart, the creative Spaniard who had become Alfa's technical director, so he decided to start work on another new 1½-litre racing car.

Ricart's Voiturette was extravagant in concept, a rear-engined flat-twelve. Its fuel tank was at the centre of the chassis and its driver was a rather lonely passenger at the front. This Type 512 was ingenious in many details but unsatisfactory as a complete car, with a scrawny frame and treacherous handling. 'I sent first a verbal and then a written communication to the Board [of Alfa],' wrote Enzo Ferrari, 'in which I said that the car was outdated and good only for scrapping or exhibition in a museum. The 512 was never made fit to compete in any race. And a cruel fate decreed that the great mechanic and test driver [Attilio] Marinoni was to be killed in it on the Milan-Varese autostrada.'

As late as 1943 the two 512 Alfas were being tested both on the autostrada and at Monza, with the results mentioned by Ferrari. The world knew that such a car existed, but it wasn't aware that it was so unsatisfactory. During the late forties the press often speculated about the possible entry of the 512 by Alfa Romeo when and if the 158 was no longer able to hold off the opposition. Thus kept secret, it had a certain value as a deterrent to would-be Grand Prix competitors – except to Ferrari, who knew all about it.

In 1947, with two-stage supercharging and 254 hp, the Type 158 won the four major races it entered. It entered four and won four in 1948 also, usually

Piloting an Alfa 158 to victory in the 1948 French Grand Prix, Frenchman Jean-Pierre Wimille was acknowledged as one of the finest drivers of his day. His skill was the ideal match for this stylish and well-prepared racing car.

finishing one-two in these years, and often one-two-three. At the end of 1948 a 158/47 model was first raced with bigger blowers for 310 hp, to counter the challenge from a new supercharged Ferrari.

The tall, dour Frenchman, Jean-Pierre Wimille, led the Alfa team during those years, and was acknowledged to be the finest driver of his day. Wimille was killed in a racing accident in a Gordini early in 1949, however, and by April it became known that Alfa Romeo would not race that year. Instead it developed the engine further to 350 hp, matched a stronger gearbox to it, designed bigger brakes and made enough other improvements to warrant changing the designation to Type 159. Cars of this type were phased in during 1950, when Alfa returned to Grand Prix racing.

The Drivers' World Championship

The year 1950 saw the first world championship for drivers. It was won by the proud and crash-prone Dr Giuseppe 'Nino' Farina, astride an Alfa. The team from Milan entered ten races that year and won them all, monopolising the major Grand Prix races as few have dreamed of doing before or since. Four new Type 159s were made for the 1951 season, fated to be the last under the 1½/4½-litre formula. That year they were dealt three defeats by Ferrari but nevertheless achieved enough victories for Juan Manuel Fangio to win the first of his five world championships at the wheel of an Alfa Romeo.

Fangio had joined the team at the beginning of the 1950 season, delighted to receive an invitation to drive the 158, 'spoken of by every European driver with extreme admiration', as he wrote. 'A few minutes after the signing with Alfa,' continued Fangio, 'the heads of the firm took me to see a 158 model covered with a tarpaulin. When I laid eyes on her I saw what a gem she was. Immediately I wanted to get behind the wheel, to take it in my hands. It was a new sensation, one that I had again each time I made the acquaintance of a new model. Seated behind the wheel, I got to know that machine a little, as if, on meeting a man for the first time, I shook hands with him.'

Rivals though they were, Farina and Fangio both performed outstandingly well for the Alfa Romeo team, which was controlled rigidly from the pits by Battista Guidotti, who had passengered Tazio Nuvolari in his 1930 Mille Miglia victory. They also raced with the knowledge that a substantial organisation backed them up. It was not unusual for Alfa Romeo to arrive at a major race with two spare cars, more than two dozen mechanics, eight five-ton vans and a mobile workshop with its own generator set. At the height of their success the cars were maintained in the same unstinting style: transmission and axle gears replaced after every race, cylinder liners, pistons and roller bearings after four races, connecting rods after six races and crankshafts and superchargers after every season.

It was possible to step into a Type 158 or 159 Alfa Romeo with every assurance not only of seeing the chequered flag, but also of seeing it first. Exceptional power accounted for much of the race-winning speed of the Alfa; in

1950 Fangio's car was timed at 192.84 mph over 1 km on the Pescara circuit. But another 'speed secret' was no less important. At that time the Type 159s were estimated to weigh more than 1,750 lb. However, the actual dry weight of the 1951 car was only 1,560 lb. Weights were rarely divulged in those first years when engine capacities were limited, just as horsepower figures were seldom revealed before the war, when all cars were held to similar weights. Lightness was an unpublicised but very real advantage for the Grand Prix Alfa Romeos.

In 1951 Alfa's former ally, Enzo Ferrari, showed conclusively for the first time that the Alfa Romeo dominance of Grand Prix racing could be broken. In so doing, Ferrari, just feeling his way in his first years as an independent car constructor, wrote the first lines of a history that has since become synonymous with success in racing. It could have been otherwise.

Every driver craved a chance to sit behind the wheel of the 'Alfetta', seen as it first appeared at Reims in 1951 with substantial additional fuel tanks alongside the cockpit. The left-hand gear lever served a rear-mounted transaxle.

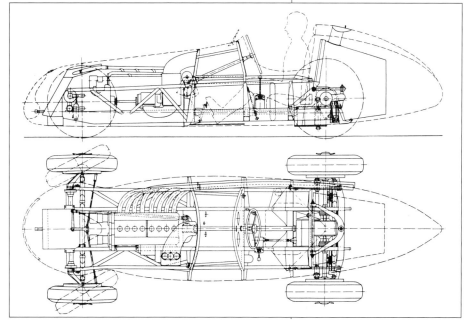

As the Type 159A the 'Alfetta' was equipped with de Dion rear suspension, its tube running behind the rear transaxle. Its basic twin-tube frame was stiffened by a welded-on superstructure of smaller steel tubes. Lightness was one secret of its success.

In one of the first Grand Prix Ferraris Raymond Sommer (number 28) makes a lively start in the Italian Grand Prix at Turin in September 1948. However, in this, its debut performance, the Ferrari was not ready to take on the Alfa Romeos alongside and Sommer placed third.

FERRARI'S REMARKABLE DEBUT

What factors at that time set Ferrari apart from the others who were seeking to make their names and fortunes as racing car builders? Only ten months passed between the first Grand Prix entry by a monoposto Ferrari and the first Grand Prix victory in 1949 for this brand-new marque. And at the end of 1951 it was accepted that Alfa Romeo would either have to come up with something quite new for 1952 (if the formula had been kept in use) or concede many victories to the outstanding unsupercharged V-12 Ferrari.

Ferrari admitted that it had been a bold decision for him to choose a twelve-cylinder engine to power his first postwar cars. Twelves, of course, had been prominent in pre-war racing,[3] but not when the engines were as small as 1,500 cc – the displacement at which Ferrari planned to begin. Expert opinion was that these tiny twelves would be temperamental and unreliable, and would lead Ferrari to regret his rash decision. Ferrari and his designer Gioachino Colombo gave the new engine reliability through simplicity, using only one chain-driven overhead cam operating two V-inclined valves through rocker arms for each bank of cylinders. Thus they built a firm twelve-cylinder foundation for many future Ferraris.

A single supercharger was used on each of the three Ferraris that came to the starting grid for the Italian Grand Prix on a road course at Turin on 5 September 1948 for a very impressive debut. Both in numbers and in readiness, the cars

---

3   Signal examples are the 2-litre Delages of the twenties, the 12C Alfa of 1936–37 and the 4½-litre Delahaye of 1938 that exploited its better fuel economy to beat the new 3-litre Mercedes-Benz V-12s at Pau that year. Auto Union also switched from V-16s to V-12s for 1938–39.

Pressure-fed by a single Roots-type supercharger, the 1.5-litre V-12 engine of the first Grand Prix Ferrari was sparked by twin vertical magnetos at the rear. The steering column crossed diagonally above the engine.

With its two-stage Roots-type supercharging system and twin overhead camshafts for each bank of six cylinders Ferrari's 1949–50 V-12 Grand Prix challenger was an impressive piece of machinery. However, problems in the design of its new cylinder heads meant that it never had a chance to perform to its full potential.

ALBERTO ASCARI

In his virtuosity, speed and success, Alberto Ascari was the shooting star among racing drivers of the forties. He became world champion twice in the Formula 2 interregnum of the fifties (1952 and 1953) and died in the midst of that decade. But in the forties Ascari made his mark as the most talented driver of the new postwar generation.

'Ascari was a driver who gave great importance to practice times and starting in pole position,' remarked Juan Fangio, who had the same objective. 'In this way he could be in front from the start and go out to win without anyone getting in his way.' Ascari was the very antithesis of the caricature Italian racing driver. Corrado Filippini wrote that for him, 'racing was not an effort, and even nervous tension seemed to require little effort, because of the store of calmness – we could almost say serenity – that he could draw on at all times'.

Born in 1918, Alberto Ascari was only seven when his father Antonio was killed while leading the French Grand Prix in his Alfa Romeo at Monthléry in 1925. Young though he was, Alberto had vivid memories of his father after rides in the co-driver's seat of his racing cars. More attracted to machinery than to the drudgery of schoolwork, he was soon astride borrowed motorcycles testing his skills on home-town streets and squares. Always on the chubby side, Alberto attracted a nickname that meant exactly that: 'Ciccio'.

Serious cycle racing began for Alberto in 1936, when at the age of eighteen he entered and began to win two-wheeled competitions. He earned a factory seat with Bianchi, for whom he rode in the last pre-war years. His first race in a car was in April 1940 in the makeshift Mille Miglia, a circuit race over a triangle of roads to Cremona and Mantua south of Brescia. The young Ascari was offered a drive in the Mille Miglia by Enzo Ferrari, for whom his father Antonio had been a role model.

Accompanied by his cousin, Giovanni Minozzi, Ascari led his class in Ferrari's Type 815 sports car, but the new car was too immature to make it to the finish. The young Ascari competed in two more car races in that year, in which Italy was the last of Europe's nations to mount motor sports events. He had his first taste of a single-seater, placing ninth in a 6CM Maserati in Libya's Tripoli Grand Prix. North Africa was familiar territory for Ascari, who managed a company transporting fuels there. This essential occupation kept him out of the clutches of Mussolini's wartime military.

One of Alberto's first races after the war was in 1947 in a one-make event with 1,100 cc single-seater Cisitalias in Egypt. He startled the field of veterans by coming second in his heat and second in the final behind the experienced Franco Cortese. Ascari was promptly invited to join the Scuderia Ambrosiana, which was racing Formula 1 Maseratis with Luigi 'Gigi' Villoresi as its lead driver. Villoresi and the nine years younger Ascari became great friends. Indeed, with scant exceptions, from then on they always raced for the same team.

Maseratis continued to be their weapons of choice at first. Ascari scored successes with the cycle-winged sports model and also with single-seaters. In 1948 he won at San Remo with the new low-chassis 4CLT/48 model, earning it the 'San Remo' nickname. Ascari was second to his mentor Villoresi in that season's British Grand Prix at Silverstone, the first to be held after the war.

For 1949 the two drivers changed to horses of the prancing variety. Enzo Ferrari was perfecting his 1½-litre

Alberto Ascari's decisive delicacy of control was well suited to the early Ferrari 1.5-litre supercharged Grand Prix car with its short wheelbase and swing-axle rear suspension. When and if these cars could succeed Alberto would be behind the wheel.

supercharged V-12 Grand Prix cars, introducing a new four-cam version during the season. Ascari took advantage of these – and of the fact that Alfa Romeo sat out the 1949 season. He won the Swiss and Italian Grands Prix, the Silverstone International Trophy and several Formula 2 races.

In 1950, the first world champion-ship year, Ferrari was developing his new big unsupercharged V-12 and his drivers were denied regular Formula 1 finishes. In Formula 2, however, Ascari and the Ferrari 166 were all but unbeatable, including the first postwar German Grand Prix at the Nürburgring. One Formula 1 win came at the end of the season when Alfa gave the Spanish Grand Prix a bye. Only the BRMs offered opposition, and they were still unready.

The culminating season for the 1½/4½ formula of 1951 found both the Ferrari 375 and Alberto Ascari ready. Although it was Froilán González who first broke the Alfa Romeo hegemony at Silverstone, Ascari showed this was no fluke by masterful victories at the Nürburgring and Monza. Only tyre trouble in the season's last race denied Ascari

Benign in appearance when out of the cockpit, Ascari was purposeful and determined in it – especially when leading. His was the only one of several 4½-litre Ferraris to succeed in qualifying at Indianapolis in 1952.

a crack at the championship; he was second in the season's points behind Fangio.

In his characteristic robin's-egg-blue helmet and jersey, Ascari dominated the next two seasons for Ferrari. With Villoresi (of course) he signed for Lancia in 1954, but the new D50 Grand Prix car was delayed. He filled his time with a superb victory in the Mille Miglia for Lancia and a drive in a borrowed Maserati 250F at Reims, vainly chasing the new streamlined Mercedes-Benz. He and Villoresi brought their smoking and clattering 250Fs back to the pits and memorably queried: 'Any more Maseratis?'

When the D50 finally appeared for the last race of 1954 at Barcelona, Ascari flaunted its tremendous pace by leading before retiring. He won at Naples and Turin with it in 1955, and then brought it to the first European Grand Prix of the season at Monaco. There he tempted his superstitious nature. 'The evening before the race,' said Juan Fangio, 'we all went to the cinema, and afterwards went for a walk round the circuit. When we got to the chicane someone said, "Whoever touches here goes into the water," and Alberto had to go and touch the wood with his hand. Next day he went into the water. When I went to see him in hospital he said, "Fortunately I can swim." Ascari was like that.'

Suffering only superficial injuries when his D50 plunged into the Monte Carlo harbour, Ascari was up and about only four days later. Visiting at Monza, he asked to take a few laps in a Ferrari sports car, borrowing another driver's kit. On his third lap the car inexplicably spun off and Alberto Ascari was mortally injured. Ciccio was dead, not yet thirty-seven years of age.

from Maranello showed from the start that they intended to be taken seriously. But their appearance was considered odd; they were small and stubby. Their wheelbase was only 85.0 inches compared to 98.6 for the Alfa Romeos and their handling on both corners and straights was visibly unsteady.

Ferrari admitted that he believed at that time that sheer engine power accounted for 80 per cent of success in racing. 'Perhaps,' he reflected, 'in designing this car as in the years that followed I underestimated the importance of the chassis.' It blended a parallel-wishbone front suspension and a swing-axle rear end in a particularly diabolical way. Englishman Raymond Mays drove one of these cars at Silverstone and lived to tell about it:

> At this stage of Ferrari's history the marque's engine performance was notoriously much in advance of the several factors contributing to controllability and I must say that I have never had a more frightening ride than the [Grand Prix Ferrari] gave me on May 14, 1949. Any attempt to take corners with the power on resulted in the tail chasing the front wheels . . .

Ferrari Grand Prix cars won four important races in 1949, helped by the absence of the Alfa Romeo team and by Ferrari's acquisition of the services of Luigi Villoresi and his protégé, the up-and-coming Alberto Ascari. At the end of the season Colombo's newest masterpiece made its bow with a victory at Monza in the Italian Grand Prix: a 94.1-inch-wheelbase chassis carrying a new engine with four gear-driven camshafts and two-stage supercharging. It seemed to be the ultimate rejoinder to the Alfas, but when the new car met them for the first time at San Remo in 1950 a single Alfa soundly defeated these exotic Ferraris. Their new cylinder heads refused to cool adequately.

By this time Enzo Ferrari had another and bigger iron in the fire. Active also in Formula 2 racing for unblown 2-litre engines, he was aware that a modern unsupercharged engine could develop a remarkable amount of power. A young engineer who had come to him in 1947,[4] Aurelio Lampredi, argued persuasively

Froilán González at Silverstone in 1951 in his 1950-type V-12 unsupercharged Ferrari. His spirited driving helped this Ferrari deliver the first unequivocal defeat to the supercharged 'Alfettas'.

---

4   Lampredi worked for Ferrari for a few months in 1946 but was only permanently engaged in 1947 after an interim period with Isotta-Fraschini.

By the final race of 1951 at Barcelona the Alfa Romeo Type 159A was as effective and purposeful a racing car as it looked. Not until the 1980s would its speed secret – supercharging – be revived as a means of building highly competitive 1½-litre Formula 1 engines.

that the best way to beat the Alfas was with an unblown 4½-litre car. The same advice was given to Ferrari by Raymond Sommer of Paris, who had driven both the unsupercharged 4½-litre Talbots and the early Grand Prix Ferraris, and before the war the 158 Alfas as well.

Before Ferrari could unleash Lampredi on a big new engine project he had to find a way to finance its construction. He turned to his tyre supplier and sponsor Pirelli, requesting and receiving a grant of some $20,000 (£8,000) for this purpose, an amount that seemed so small to Piero Pirelli that he double-checked to make sure that that was all Ferrari really needed.

The new engine first appeared in the swing-axle chassis in 3.3-litre form – because the amount of torque it generated at that size was all that the unmodified drive line could take – at the Belgian Grand Prix in 1950. The engine was progressively enlarged, first in bore and then stroke, until it was at its full 4,493 cc for the last championship race of the year at Monza. There it was breathtakingly close in speed to the Alfas. It placed second behind one of them after a hammer-and-tongs battle of attrition and car-swapping that left everyone – with the possible exception of Alfa – agog to see what would happen in 1951.

For 1951 Lampredi produced a dual-ignition version of his V-12 with improved brakes, but it was not one of these new engines that finally defeated the Alfas. It was a new driver instead, Froilán González from Argentina, at the wheel of a 1950 Ferrari, and the occasion was the British Grand Prix on 14 July. 'The iron grip of the Alfas had to be broken sometime,' wrote historian William Court, 'and it was on the anvil of Silverstone that Gonzalez performed this historic feat in real blacksmith's style.'

This victory had a profound emotional impact for Enzo Ferrari. On one level it was vindication of a major professional goal. He had left Alfa Romeo in November 1939, 'so that I might show the people in Alfa what I was made of'. This he had certainly done. But he had also defeated the cars from the factory for which he had raced with love and dedication for many years. On this level, thought Ferrari sadly, 'I have killed my mother.'

TWO-STAGE SUPERCHARGING

In the forties the principle of supercharging took an important step forward. Following a trend established at the end of the thirties, engines were supercharged in several stages rather than just one. This produced some of the most spectacular and exotic Grand Prix engines ever made.

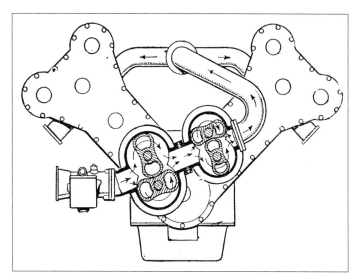

A schematic layout shows the principle of the two-stage supercharging system. A larger blower feeds a smaller one, which then delivers the charge to the engine. In this case Roots-type blowers are used, although the principle can be used with other types of compressor.

A shaft from the gear train at the front of the engine drove the two-stage blower array of the Alfa Romeo Type 158 straight-eight. A Weber downdraft carburettor sat atop the large first-stage blower on the right.

The motivation for multi-stage supercharging was that better overall performance could be achieved by a two-stage system, one in which a large blower pumps air into a smaller one, which then delivers it to the engine. Even if the final boost achieved is no greater than that realised with a single-stage system, each blower in a two-stage layout is operating at a much more favourable point on its efficiency curve. As a result the total power required to drive them is reduced and more power is delivered to the clutch to drive the car.

Multi-stage supercharging had been used by German engineers in the First World War for aircraft, employing centrifugal compressors. In 1927 a 1½-litre Miller racing car was converted to a two-stage centrifugal compressor system. This 'Detroit Special' delivered some 300 hp, a stunning 200 hp per litre – more than its front-wheel drive could apply to the road. In the thirties, with rearmament in the air, multi-stage supercharging was back on the agenda in Germany for the aircraft that would fly in the Second World War.

To explore the potential of a two-stage Roots system for its 3-litre V-12 Grand Prix engine, in mid-1938 Daimler-Benz commissioned its consultants, the Porsche organisation, to design and build one for trials. In November 1938 the first tests were made of this new kind of supercharger. Although the Mercedes single-stage system showed a higher boost reading through the range of 3,000–5,000 rpm, the two-stage-blown version out-powered it by as much as 12 per cent through the same range.

The secret, found the Daimler-Benz engineers, was that the two-stage system required less horsepower to drive it. At the highest rate of revolutions the single-stage system was delivering 35 per cent more boost, but demanding 81 per cent more horsepower to do it.[1]

Based on these findings, a new two-stage blower system was designed for the 3-litre V-12. With the new blowers, drive horsepower required was down and net output was up at every engine speed. The peak power figures of 470 to 480 bhp that had been recorded before at 8,000 rpm were now achieved at 7,500. Power was increased by

---

1   For full details of this interesting test, the reader is referred to Chapter 14 of the author's *Mercedes-Benz – Quicksilver Century*.

25 and 30 bhp handfuls all the way up the curve, while specific fuel consumption remained almost unchanged. The first such unit was ready for installation in Hermann Lang's car for the Eifelrennen at the Nürburgring on 21 May 1939. It carried Lang, then nearing the peak of his considerable skills, to another victory.

The two-stage technique was not sufficiently proven to be used on the new 1½-litre V-8 racing car that Mercedes built to race against the Italians at Tripoli on 7 May 1939; the W165 raced and won there with a single Roots supercharger. Subsequently, the V-8 engine was fitted with a two-stage system that raised its peak power from 256 bhp at 8,000 rpm to 278 bhp at 8,250 rpm.

Other Grand Prix car builders were not idle in response to the Daimler-Benz initiative. By mid-1939 Auto Union had two-stage blowers ready for its V-12 D-Type racers. In Milan new Alfa Romeo racing engines

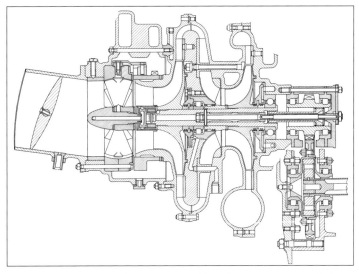

Drawing air in from the left, two centrifugal impellers on a common shaft pumped high-pressure air into the output annulus, at the bottom, of the two-stage compressor designed and built by Rolls-Royce for BRM in 1950. Adjustable stator blades in the blower inlet were intended to control the unit's air delivery but these were never made operational.

designed under Wifredo Ricart were two-stage-blown. For his 3-litre Type 162 V-16 Ricart specified two first-stage Roots blowers feeding into two second-stage Roots blowers, one for the front eight cylinders and the other for the back eight. A more conventional two-stage system was fitted to the flat-twelve engine of the 1½-litre Type 512.[2]

Carrying on into 1940, the Alfa engineers also had time to design and build a two-stage blower setup for the straight-eight Type 158 Voiturette, which of course became a Grand Prix car after the war. Alfa entered some cars with two-stage boosting in the 1947 season, and by 1948, when this had become standard, the engine was producing 275 bhp at 7,500 rpm. During a rest year in 1949, this was raised to 350 bhp at 8,500 rpm for 1950. By the end of the 1951 season this remarkable engine was producing 425 bhp at 9,300 rpm, although with a voracious appetite for fuel.

Like Alfa Romeo, Maserati found it easy enough to improve the performance of its sixteen-valve four-cylinder 4CL engine by adopting two-stage blowing. This was first experimented with in 1947 in a 4CLT driven by Raymond Sommer, and was fitted to the new 4CLT/48 for the 1948 season. Even higher boosting of this rugged base engine was carried out by Prof. Speluzzi for the Maserati-based Milans. Ferrari also used two-stage Roots supercharging for its Grand Prix cars of 1948 and 1949.

In Britain one of the most audacious features of the ambitious V-16 BRM was its use of a two-stage centrifugal supercharger developed and built for the car by Rolls-Royce. Although efficient, the centrifugal compressor was known to be very rev-sensitive, and thus an unlikely candidate for a road-racing car, which must develop torque over at least a reasonable range of engine speed. The BRM succeeded in developing more than 400 bhp, but never in a fully raceworthy form during the life of the formula for which it had been designed.

On a more modest scale, Britain's Alta built a two-stage-boosted Grand Prix car which raced from 1950. Neither its builder nor its owner/driver had the resources to develop it fully. The same could be said of the short-lived CTA-Arsenal project in France, with two-stage Roots supercharging for its V-8 engine. Only the big battalions – the Germans before the war and Alfa Romeo afterwards – had the ability and the resources to perfect the cantankerous but potent Grand Prix engines that two-stage boosting made possible.[3]

---

2   Ricart's capacity for fantastic engineering was shown by a preliminary layout for the 512. It had two second-stage Roots blowers fed by a first stage consisting of a horizontal centrifugal blower. This might have been a productive combination.

3   Many private enthusiasts have built their own two-stage supercharging setups for racing specials. The introduction of the cogged-rubber timing belt has made this relatively easy. One example among many was the two-stage Roots supercharging that Ilmor co-founder Paul Morgan gave to his 1,100 cc Lagonda Rapier special in the sixties.

That the conquering of Alfa was no fluke was adequately demonstrated twice more in 1951 by Alberto Ascari at the Nürburgring and at Monza. Yet the season ended with an Alfa Romeo comeback, a victory at Barcelona by Fangio driving a Type 159M with a more powerful engine and stronger frame that secured the driver's championship.

MASERATI'S MINOR ROLE

There were moments of glory in these years, then, for both Ferrari and Alfa Romeo, as there were for another marque from Italy – Maserati – but always in

The new Maserati 4CLT/48 introduced in 1948 mounted its front coil springs inboard, operated by arms extending inward from the upper wishbones. From the inner ends of these same wishbones, links operated rotary type hydraulic shock absorbers.

a minor key. Not for Maserati the major wins in the championship events, but through sheer force of numbers, ease of maintenance and more than marginal speed the tough four-cylinder Maseratis gained sixteen victories in Formula 1 races held from 1947 to 1951. However, it was a sign of sorts that only two of these victories came in the final two years.

Maserati of Modena carries worthily an array of laurel wreaths from this era. One of its cars won the first race held under this new Formula 1. Maseratis carried such drivers as Alberto Ascari and Juan Fangio to their first European Grand Prix victories. They were derided at the end of their careers as 'those oil-soaked Maseratis', but Grand Prix racing in the forties wouldn't have been much without them. Among the 24 cars on the starting grid for the 1949 Italian Grand Prix, 11 were Maseratis.

These successes traced their origin to the winter of 1938, when the Maserati brothers put together everything they'd learned from their earlier Voiturette models to design and build a new car, the 4CL. It was a four with four valves per cylinder, by then an unusual provision in a car engine – with the notable exception of Mercedes-Benz. Others had followed the lead of Fiat in the 1990s and adopted two-valve hemispherical combustion chambers. The brothers unveiled their lithe little car in January 1939, with its torsion-bar independent front suspension, channel-steel frame and live rear axle hanging from trailing quarter-elliptic springs. The first car was delivered to a buyer in March, and in May the 4CL model made its first race appearance, at Tripoli. To say the debut was inauspicious would be putting it mildly. All three 4CLs retired after their first lap.

Things got better after that. By the end of 1939 the Maserati was ranked about equal in speed to the Type 158 Alfa. The 4CL was the quickest car available to private teams after the war, attracting such drivers as Tazio Nuvolari in his last Grand Prix appearances, Sommer, Villoresi, Reg Parnell – Britain's best driver in the forties – Prince Bira and Nino Farina. The demand was such that the Maseratis produced an improved version of the car in 1947. It looked much the same externally but had a stiffer and lighter tubular frame that also served as an oil reservoir. Dubbed the 4CLT (T for *tubolare*, or 'tubular'), it was first raced as a semi-works car by Ascari at Reims in July 1947.

Soon after the end of the war the Maseratis started working on another improvement for the 4CL engine: two-stage supercharging. Raymond Sommer gave this version a baptismal outing in the Jersey Road Race in 1947, setting the fastest lap before retiring. Adaptable to the existing engine, the twin blowers were used on and off in 1947, and became 'standard' in 1948.

Another change in 1947 was the departure of the Maseratis from the firm they had founded. Having served the ten years that had been agreed at the time of the Orsi take-over, they simply left when the decade was up. Although ambivalent at the time about the value of racing to their enterprises, Adolfo Orsi and his son Omer decided to invest in improvements to their cars. They hired the peripatetic Alberto Massimino to design another new chassis for the sixteen-valve four-cylinder engine, now giving some 260 hp. He sharply lowered its profile with a new tubular frame and inboard coil springs for a cleaner front suspension.[5] Retained was the live rear axle, which with its high unsprung weight and vulnerability to torque reaction was a retrograde feature of the Maserati.

Thus was created the 1,400 lb 4CLT/48, also known as the 'San Remo' for the Grand Prix which it won on its first appearance on 27 June 1948. The San Remo rapidly became the staple machine of the many private teams that made up the bulk of the Grand Prix racing fields. In fact, the success or otherwise enjoyed by the 4CLT/48 depended heavily on the standard of preparation the cars were given by these (often impoverished) teams.

One team that went more than the extra mile with the San Remo was the Scuderia Milan of the Ruggieri brothers. Inspired by a $9,000 bonus promised by the organisers of the Italian Grand Prix to any team that showed up at Monza in 1949 with two new cars, they set about the substantial improvement of their 4CLT/48s. They fitted wider brakes to two cars and installed high-boost engines of a type developed by Prof. Mario Speluzzi from the basic Maserati four for speedboat racing. Called 'Milans', the cars driven by Farina and Taruffi went remarkably well at Monza, although the temperamental Farina abruptly parked his for no obvious mechanical reason.

Seen racing at Silverstone in 1949, with Siam's Prince Bira heading a sister car, the 4CLT/48 'San Remo' Maserati provided the backbone of the Grand Prix fields of the late forties.

---

5   This elegant design by Massimino foreshadowed the upper wishbones designed to work as rocker arms to inboard coil springs and dampers that Lotus introduced in the sixties.

The new six-cylinder engine of the type T26C Talbot-Lago of 1948 had two high-placed camshafts, each operating a row of inclined valves through short pushrods and rocker arms. The exhaust-valve rockers are uncovered in this view of the left-hand side of the engine.

The Ruggieris kept on improving their Milans, engaging Egidio Arzani to design completely new chassis for them. Both cars were given a new torsion-bar front suspension, while one had a de Dion rear end and the other parallel trailing arms at the rear. New light-alloy cylinder blocks were also made for the engines, with two plugs per cylinder.

The Milans often broke, however, and their best finish in a major race was fifth, with a Milan engine in a Maserati chassis at the Swiss Grand Prix in 1950, Felice Bonetto driving. A similar combination was used for the last Grand Prix entry of a Milan in the Grand Prix of Europe at Reims in July, 1951. The car lasted only two laps for its then-unknown driver, Onofre Marimon – the brilliant protégé of fellow Argentines Fangio and González, who would startle the racing world with his skill in the coming years.

THE FRENCH MAKE UP THE NUMBERS

Some big blue cars also appeared on starting grids in the forties, and surprisingly often in the winner's circle as well. The Talbot-Lagos were likened to the tortoises chasing the supercharged hares, for the unblown 4½-litre French car could go through many races non-stop while the Alfas and Maseratis were pitting twice for fuel and tyres. Yet we know who won the race in the fable,[6] and we find that the Talbot-Lagos were able to embarrass the blown cars on occasion.

With the lone pre-war car that was the prototype for the postwar Talbot-Lago racers, Louis Chiron defeated the Maseratis in the first postwar French Grand Prix at Lyons in 1947. Not long thereafter Antonio Lago, the transplanted Italian who was running Automobiles Talbot in a Paris suburb, announced that he would build a small series of newly designed cars especially for Grand Prix racing. The first new T26C appeared at Monaco in May 1948, a rugged-looking machine with a steel channel-section frame, live rear axle on semi-elliptic springs, a Wilson preselector gearbox and a six-cylinder engine with aluminium block and head and V-inclined overhead valves operated by pushrods from camshafts on both sides of the block. Its initial output was 240 hp at 4,700 rpm.

---

6   I admit that I haven't checked the fable. I'm assuming that the tortoise won.

Not until the Alfas took a year off in 1949 did the Talbot-Lagos have a chance to shine. They scored two major victories, one in the Belgian Grand Prix, driven by Louis Rosier, and the other in the French Grand Prix with Louis Chiron at the wheel. One of the cars came second just a lap behind the winning two-stage four-cam Ferrari in the 1949 Italian Grand Prix. Its driver was the energetic Philippe Etancelin, of whom it was said that he 'does seem to be taking corners all the way down the straights'. With his cap turned back to front, Etancelin had demonstrated the merits of the unsupercharged engine so clearly that day that Enzo Ferrari later confirmed his decision to design and build an unblown engine of his own.

Tony Lago contrived useful improvements to the eight or more cars he supplied to private teams, including a twelve-plug cylinder head (two spark plugs to each cylinder) and new induction system that brought the horsepower to 260 at 5,000 rpm. Rosier was the Talbot-Lago star in 1950 with an Albi victory and third-place finishes in the Swiss and Belgian Grands Prix. In 1951, however, he was able to book only two minor Grand Prix victories. One car was raced in England that year by Duncan Hamilton, who wrote:

> . . . of all the cars I have driven this one holds my special affection:
>
> When you sat in the car, the first thing of which you were conscious was the size of the rear wheels: you sat so low that they were level with your ears. When on the controls your feet actually pointed up-hill, and the prop-shaft, which was offset, ran about level with your hip. Everything about the car was big and impressive: the engine, the bonnet, the wheels and tyres, the brake drums; but what really 'sent' the enthusiast was the glorious bellow of the exhaust.
>
> In spite of its almost truck-like appearance the 1,875-pound Talbot-Lago was actually a light and easy car to handle, ideally suited to non-stop long-distance competition.

Cornering at Reims in 1951, the Talbot-Lago was an impressive machine with its in-line 4½-litre six-cylinder engine. Its relatively low fuel consumption allowed it to be surprisingly competitive with the Type 158 Alfas on a number of occasions.

SUCCESSES FOR 'THE SORCERER'

Another Italian-born engineer working in Paris built cars that played a less prominent role in the Grand Prix racing of the forties. The racing cars of Amédée (born Amedeo) Gordini, based initially on components from Simca production cars, were noted for their lightness and agility. 'The Simca was a very neat car,' recalled Juan Fangio, 'very short wheelbase, very well adapted to tight circuits, and very light. Gordini was perhaps the first European constructor to give much importance to power to weight ratio. That's how he was able to win races with cars of scarcely 1,430 cc.'

Only 74 hp sufficed for drivers like Sommer and Wimille to drive Simca-Gordinis to second places in the Albi and Nice Grand Prix races of 1947. Gordini added power to the four-cylinder engine of his little live-axle cars by bringing displacement up to 1½ litres and fitting new heads with pushrod-operated V-inclined valves. Not until late 1949, however, did he buy a British Wade supercharger and start adapting it to his engine.

Two supercharged Gordinis raced for the first time without special success at Pau in April 1950. In fact, the blowers were removed from the cars after they gave trouble in practice. For 1951 a new overhead-cam four-cylinder engine was produced by Gordini, and it was this unit, supercharged, that gave Gordini his only important triumph under the 1½/4½ formula. It came at Albi in a non-championship event in August, with Maurice Trintignant at the controls of the 150 hp Gordini.

Amédée, 'The Sorcerer', had hoped by this time to be fielding a much more ambitious Grand Prix car with a 4½-litre unblown engine. He planned it jointly in 1949 with the Maserati brothers, whom he had come to know when both he and Alfieri Maserati were working at Isotta Fraschini in Italy before the First World War.[7]

The Maseratis had now set up their own firm in Bologna, OSCA,[8] where they started building the unblown V-12 engine that they had designed together with Gordini and his former Bugatti engineer, Antonio Pichetto. They intended to make four of these clean-lined engines, one for installation in a 4CLT/48 chassis, another to power an E-Type ERA and two for Gordini. Its valve gear and combustion chamber design had much in common with that of the 1951 Gordini four, which Pichetto had also designed. Completed at the end of 1950, one engine did see use in 1951 in B. Bira's rebuilt San Remo Maserati, but it failed to achieve any placings in classic races with its 300 hp.

At Monza in 1951, the final race but one of the last official Formula 1 season, a completely new OSCA Grand Prix car appeared with a rear-mounted transaxle and de Dion rear suspension – an advanced and elaborate car. It is to the credit of the Maseratis that it did finish, although dead last. No OSCA-powered Gordinis ever materialised. Ernesto Maserati regretted the sudden end of the career of the Tipo G V-12: 'It had balance like an electric motor. And power was there too. Still, it needed refinement. We had spent a fortune on it. We couldn't afford to go on and it just stood.'[9]

---

7 Later, Isotta would machine many of the major components for Maserati racing cars.
8 Officine Specializzate Costruzione Automobili ('workshop specialised in automobile manufacture') would enjoy its greatest successes in the building of fine small-displacement sports-racing cars.
9 Two such cars were built. Both were subsequently converted into sports cars.

Backed by builder and enthusiast Kenneth McAlpine, Britain's Connaught was a lively competitor in Grand Prix racing in the Formula 2 era of 1952-53. Rodney Clarke and Mike Oliver used Lea Francis-based four-cylinder engines in their A-Series Formula 2 cars introduced in 1951, above and the two cars at left below. At right below is a $2^{1}/_{2}$-litre Connaught B-Series Formula 1 car with high-tail 'toothpaste-tube' body introduced in 1957. It used an Alta four-cylinder engine giving 250 bhp at 7,000 rpm.

The simplicity of the cockpit of the Mercedes-Benz W196 reflected the philosophy of Rudolf Uhlenhaut that the driver of one of his cars should be distracted as little as possible. Protecting the car from its drivers was his motivation for adopting desmodromic valve gear – so the valves couldn't hit the pistons – and a five-speed gearbox with Porsche synchromesh, a rarity on racing cars. Large vents released warm air from the inboard rear brakes.

Previous page: Introduced in the middle of the 1954 season, the Mercedes-Benz W196 took Juan Manuel Fangio to the World Championship – helped by his two Maserati wins – and again in 1955. It startled the racing world with its fuel-injected desmodromic-valved $2\frac{1}{2}$-litre straight-eight engine, rear swing axles and space-framed chassis, not to mention the aerodynamic body used on some circuits. This W196 is a 1955 model with outboard front brakes and a 3.0-litre 300SLR engine, as raced in Argentina at the beginning of the year.

Posing with Fiat's 1907 Grand Prix winner, Lancia's 1954 D50 shows off its side sponsons holding fuel and smoothing the flow of air between its wheels. A conception of the great Vittorio Jano, creator of the Type B Alfa Romeo, the D50 was exceptionally compact. The cars and their V8 engine, right, were given to Ferrari in 1955 and further developed by him to Fangio's World Championship mount of 1956 and the Type 801 F1 of 1957.

During the 1950s Great Britain began to raise her profile in Grand Prix racing. A maker of fire pumps and fork-lift trucks, Coventry Climax, built a V8 of 2,477 cc for the 2½-litre Formula 1 in 1953-54. Its FPE engine, above, produced a useful 264 bhp at 7,900 rpm but was not released to customers at that time. Its right-hand cylinder head and components formed the basis of Coventry Climax's FPF four, powering a Lotus Type 12, below. The FPF-engined 12 was Lotus's first Formula 1 car in 1958.

Benefiting from victory in the last championship race of 1953 at Monza, Maserati prepared well for the new 2¹/₂-litre Formula 1 in 1954 with its Type 250F, designed under Gioachino Colombo. In this 1954 form it kept the famed Maserati trident in its grille and was bodied with copious louvers. Well-balanced with a capable twin-cam in-line six, the 250F won the first two races of 1954 in Juan Fangio's hands and became deservedly popular with GP racing's privateers.

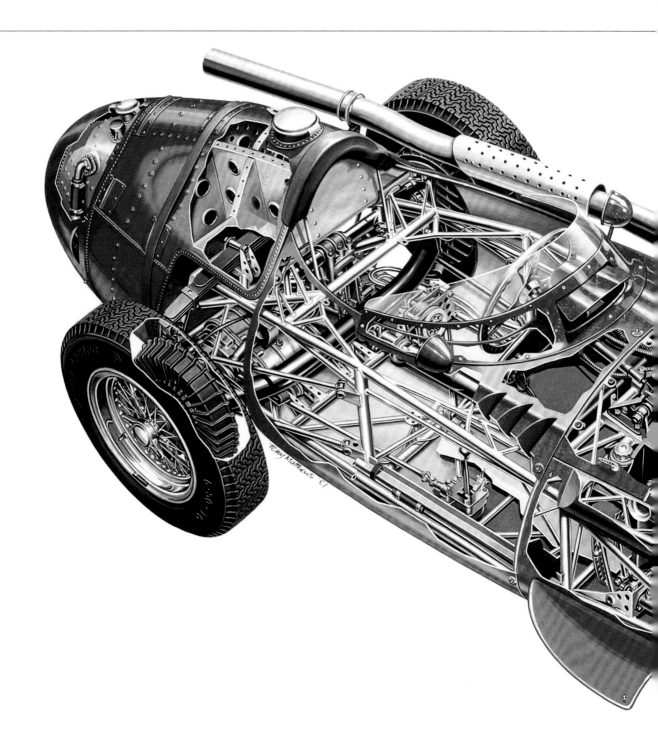

*Expressing the quintessence of the era of the classic Grand
Prix car in this superb cutaway by Tony Matthews, the
Maserati 250F in its 1957 form had a multi-tube steel space
frame within its sleek aluminium outer skin. At the end of
the era of drum-type racing brakes, Maserati's were large
and powerful, developed by the company's chief engineer
Giulio Alfieri. At the rear, a de Dion axle crossed the chassis
forward of the transaxle. Helped by judicious doses of of
nitromethane in its fuel, this Maserati model took Fangio to
his fifth World Championship.*

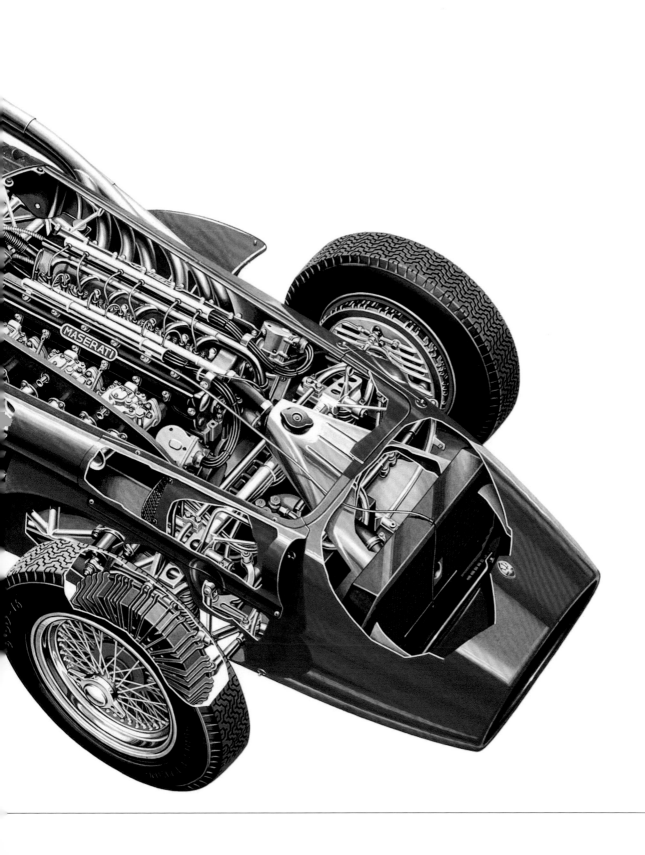

Seen above at the last race of 1957, Vanwall had broken Britain's duck in championship Grand Prix racing that season with wins at Aintree, Pescara and Monza. It used the best of British know-how with Frank Costin's body on Colin Chapman's chassis, carrying a fuel-injected four-cylinder engine based on Norton motorcycle design. Right, Tony Brooks is racing at Monaco in 1958. That season he would win for Vanwall at Spa, the Nürburgring and Monza.

Opposite: Recovering from its disastrous V16 foray, BRM, now owned by Alfred Owen's Rubery Owen, built its P25 for the 2$\frac{1}{2}$-litre GP formula. An initial semi-monocoque chassis design was replaced for 1958 by a tubular space frame, retaining a rear-mounted transaxle carrying a single central ventilated disc brake. The team's star driver, thrusting Frenchman Jean Behra, checked his pit for a signal while trying Schell's car in practice at Monaco in 1958.

New Grand Prix rules for 1958 favoured lighter cars, mandating petrol fuel and specifying shorter races. Ferrari adapted with its V6 246 Dino, scaled up from its 156 Dino Formula 2 car. At Monaco in 1958 the Dino of Wolfgang Von Trips (40) retired. This was the second race in a row won by the rear-engined Cooper-Climaxes from the Rob Walker stable. Luigi Musso's Ferrari Dino (number 34) had to settle for second place. That year Ferrari was still committed to drum brakes with unique helical finning and would only try disc brakes at the end of the season.

Opposite: By 1958 the 250F Maserati was past its best. This Scuderia Centro Sud car, number 2511, was a rebodied version of 1954 chassis 2502. Journeyman Gerino Gerini failed to qualify it at Monaco.

Moss in the light-green P25 BRM was a favourite of the crowd at Aintree in the 1959 British Grand Prix. He agreed to drive a BRM on the condition that the car be entered by his British Racing Partnership to avoid the preparation problems that he associated with the works BRMs. In this 225-mile race his strategy was successful for Moss was beaten only by Jack Brabham in the mid-engined Cooper-Climax, the combination which – to the surprise of many – won the 1959 Drivers' and Manufacturers' Championships.

The start approaches for the 1959 Italian GP at Monza. Flanking the Ferrari Dino of Tony Brooks (30) in the front row were the Cooper-Climaxes of Jack Brabham, at the left, and Stirling Moss (14). Ferraris in the second row were those of Phil Hill (32) and Dan Gurney (36). Moss defeated them all in a race that showed that the end of the road was nearing for the great front-engined Grand Prix cars.

Taking advantage of the fact that it had a suitable 2½-litre racing engine, Aston Martin entered the Grand Prix lists in 1959 with its DBR4/250. In the British GP at Aintree Roy Salvadori (2) matched the pole time of Jack Brabham's Cooper in qualifying, but could place only sixth in the race.

Not yet ready to put the horse behind the cart, Enzo Ferrari revised his 246 Dino for 1959 by giving it independent rear suspension and shifting fuel tankage to its flanks. Tony Brooks won at Reims and the Avus with the revised Ferrari, but Cooper-Climax-mounted Brabham won the World Championship.

Like Aston Martin, latecomer Scarab was caught on the hop by the new rear-engined GP cars from Cooper and Lotus. Although powered by a desmodromic-valved and fuel-injected four, America's Grand Prix hope was unable to qualify on its European debut at Monaco in 1960, above, with builder Lance Reventlow at the wheel. The two team cars are seen below in practice for the 1960 Belgian Grand Prix at Spa.

BRITAIN'S BUDDING CONTRIBUTION

Britain's smaller racing car builders enjoyed about the same level of Grand Prix success in the forties as Gordini and OSCA. 'Geoffrey Taylor is building Altas unostentatiously in his small factory' at Byfleet in Surrey, wrote Rodney Walkerley, 'slowed by every imaginable and many unimaginable difficulties inseparable from the times in which we have our being.' Taylor, who had built several competent Voiturettes before the war, announced in November 1945 that he would construct and sell an impressive new Grand Prix car with a supercharged four-cylinder engine and four-wheel independent suspension with rubber springs.

Two-and-a-half years passed before the first Grand Prix Alta was ready for the most enthusiastic exponent of the marque, George Abecassis. It was plagued by minor development problems, especially with its synchromesh gearbox,[10] and never placed better than its seventh in the British Grand Prix in 1949. The two other cars Taylor built, including one with two-stage supercharging, were run by less able drivers and had less success. 'The car did not deserve its fate,' wrote mechanic Alf Francis, who had ministered to the Abecassis Alta. 'As soon as it had been assembled, it went straight to a circuit without a trial of any sort. Fate was against the Grand Prix Alta from the very start and circumstances stunted its development.'

No such excuses could be offered on behalf of the E-Type ERA. Two such cars were on wheels when racing resumed, the last of the ERA Voiturettes built before the war by the little company backed by wealthy enthusiast Humphrey Cook. Many earlier ERAs were available too, high-rigged cart-sprung[11] cars with supercharged six-cylinder engines that were fast out of all proportion to their antiquated looks.

---

10 With a handful of exceptions (Alta, Mercedes-Benz W196, Vanwall, Formula 1 Porsches) Grand Prix cars have not used synchromesh to assist drivers in changing gear. Drivers preferred the lighter, cleaner shifting action of face-engaging dogs between constant-mesh gears. Without synchromesh, gearboxes can be shorter, lighter and more reliable. Driver skill in gear changing can be taken for granted – usually.

11 The ERA chassis had been designed by Reid Railton, the brilliant engineer who designed several cars for fur broker John Cobb, including the one with which Cobb set a Land Speed Record of 394.2 mph in 1947.

Another elegant English racing creation was the E-type ERA, seen being tested in 1946 in its original 1938 configuration. Suggesting that the English could learn from the Germans, the E-type was built low to the ground and had the latest suspension and drive systems. However, it consistently performed at less than the sum of its parts.

The ERAs raced frequently in England after the war because as, Raymond Mays put it, 'beggars couldn't be choosers and it was virtually a case of ERAs or nothing'. Nine of them, for example, started the British Grand Prix late in 1948, and Bob Gerard placed his third. Gerard and Cuth Harrison were the chief advocates of the original ERA cars in postwar racing; they placed sixth and seventh respectively in the British Grand Prix as late as 1950.

The E-Types, however, were the ERAs that seemed to hold the promise of real Grand Prix success. They'd been designed in 1938 by Peter Berthon and Arthur Barrett to include all the latest tweaks: de Dion rear end, rear-mounted transaxle, Porsche-type front suspension, side-mounted Zoller vane-type supercharger and ultra-low body, patterned after the 1938 Mercedes-Benz. They seemed to have everything, and indeed the E-Type did perform with some promise before the war. After it, however, the cars defied everything that new ERA proprietor Leslie Johnson tried to make them work. Call it a hoodoo or call them plain ornery, either way the E-Types never did behave.

NATIONS TO THE RESCUE

Contrasting sharply with these private ventures were the efforts in several countries to rally national support behind Grand Prix cars with the aim of enhancing national prestige. The effect in most cases was the exact opposite. An obvious exception was nationally owned Alfa Romeo, which received grants from the Italian Government to support its Grand Prix racing, said to be more than $150,000 in 1951 (nearly £60,000). This wouldn't have come close to covering all its costs.

The French were the first to do something about building a 'national' racing car. The ubiquitous Raymond Sommer helped plant the idea in the minds of engineers at the Centre d'Etudes Techniques de l'Automobile et du Cycle (CTA for short). They managed to get funding from French car makers, technical institutions and from the state, which made available an ordnance facility for some of the construction; hence the car's 'CTA-Arsenal' name. The car's two-stage-blown four-cam V-8 engine design showed the touch of the great Delage designer, Albert Lory, and the CTA-Arsenal's lines were pleasingly clean, but its chassis conception was agricultural, with sliding-block suspension that would have been more at home on a railway car.

It might all have worked eventually had the French not gotten the national-car bacillus out of their bloodstream remarkably quickly. The car was thought of in mid-1946, and designed by early 1947. The engine was being tested in April 1947, and that same September a car was entered in the French Grand Prix. Poor Sommer was at the wheel when the CTA-Arsenal broke a drive-line part at the standing start.

National support for the project dried up when the Communist minister supporting it, Marcel Paul, left the government. Two of the three cars built practised for the 1948 French Grand Prix but didn't race. Later the cars were turned over to Tony Lago (who had shown that France didn't need the nationalist approach), who hoped to convert them to Formula 2 cars, but ran out of time and money.

BRITISH RACING MOTOR

In Britain national support was enlisted for another Grand Prix car, the BRM (British Racing Motor). To put it mildly, the British operated on a different time scale than the French. The whole story of the CTA-Arsenal from its inception to the last abortive Grand Prix entry was played out between the beginning of design work on the BRM and the time about half the parts for the first car had been delivered.

In part this was the result of the way the car was supported by British industry. Silver-tongued Raymond Mays, trading on his ERA successes, had persuaded car and accessory companies to help by making parts for it. In some cases – and the slowest determine the pace of a project – it took them a year and a half to deliver. The other reason it took so long to make the BRM was that Peter Berthon's design was fabulously complex. It borrowed rear suspension and rear-mounted transaxle designs from Daimler-Benz, and required a sixteen-cylinder 135° V-engine with a two-stage centrifugal supercharger built by Rolls-Royce.

The centrifugally supercharged 1½-litre BRM of 1950 had a bonnet packed with sixteen cylinders surrounded by expensive machinery. Its complexity defied ready resolution of its many development difficulties.

Small wonder that the low, sleek V-16 BRM inspired 'World-Beater' headline writers on Fleet Street when it was unveiled at Folkingham Aerodrome in Lincolnshire in December 1949. However, its handsome lines flattered only to deceive.

The BRM was a car in the tectonic-Teutonic tradition of the thirties, during which the German teams had dazzled the rest of the world with their engineering skills. 'Now,' thought the BRM builders, 'we have captured their secrets, and we will use them.' Unfortunately, they had not also seized the reasoning behind the designs. Nor had they appreciated how much money, skill and effort it had taken to keep them going.

Alfred Neubauer of Daimler-Benz minced no words to Raymond Mays during a visit while the BRM was still being built: 'I'd like to congratulate your people on the design. It is one of the finest designs I have ever seen or visualised. But you'll never get that motor to win races with your present small facilities.'

Underfinanced and understaffed, delayed by indolence and indecision, the BRM didn't reach a starting line until August 1950 for a non-championship race at Silverstone. There it broke both inner universal joints on its rear axles at the start, with Raymond Sommer in the cockpit. After the CTA-Arsenal incident he got the blame, of course undeservedly. The BRM later proved it would break for

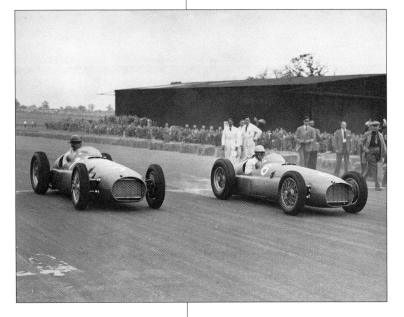

Reg Parnell, right, and Peter Walker leave the back of the grid at Silverstone in 1951 to compete in the British Grand Prix. Both soldiered on bravely to the finish in spite of suffering severe burns from the overheated cockpit components of their V-16 BRMs.

almost anybody. Its best performance in only two more race appearances during the 1½/4½-litre formula was fifth and seventh places in the 1951 British Grand Prix – barely ahead of the ancient ERAs.

Another car builder bemused by the image of German engineering superiority was former racing driver Piero Dusio, founder of Cisitalia in Turin. Flush with funds after the war, Dusio decided to follow up on his building of small 1,100 cc competition cars with a full Grand Prix car entry. Against the advice of close associates who felt he should recruit Italian talent, Dusio went to the isolated

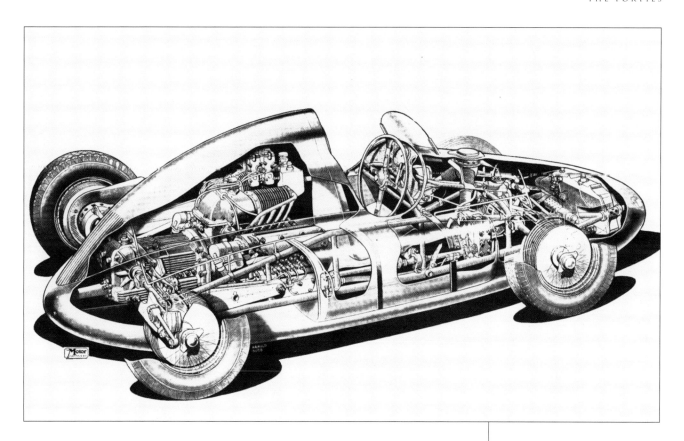

Porsche team in Austria's Gmünd for a Formula 1 Grand Prix car design. Desperately in need of money, not least to buy freedom from imprisonment in France for Prof. Porsche, the designers under Ferry Porsche and Karl Rabe made Dusio an offer he couldn't refuse.

The design sent to Turin from Gmünd in mid-1947 was, frankly, a masterpiece. It bristled with such ingenious ideas as part-time four-wheel drive, a tubular space frame, a flat-twelve mid-placed engine with two vane-type blowers, synchronised progressive five-speed shifting and an advanced independent rear suspension.[12] More to the point, these concepts were blended in a car of balance and beauty. But Dusio could not afford both to build and to race it, as he had discovered by 1949 when he journeyed to Argentina to seek financial help from the Peron regime.

One car, complete at the end of 1948, was displayed on the Cisitalia stand at the Turin Salon in February 1949. Hans Stuck said he briefly tested it in Italy in the late summer of 1949; others say it never ran in Europe. It certainly had not been raced before it was packed aboard a ship in December 1950 bound for Buenos Aires. There it immediately gave rise to rumours that Fangio and Gonzalez would be racing for an Autoar (née Cisitalia) team in Europe in 1951![13]

Designed as its Type 360 by the Porsche engineering office exiled in Austria, the Cisitalia Formula 1 car of 1949 was a technical masterwork – far beyond the development ability of Cisitalia. It foreshadowed the multi-tube space frame and parallel-link rear suspension.

---

12 The synchronising rings specified for this gearbox were conceived by Porsche engineer Leopold Schmid. He later developed them into the patented ring synchroniser that was lucratively licensed by Porsche to companies throughout the world.

13 The Type 360 was made to run while in Argentina, and made some track appearances, driven by Clemar Bucci, but never raced in anger. Perhaps the most notable might-have-been in Grand Prix history, the one complete car is in the Porsche collection and parts of another are in Tom Wheatcroft's collection at Donington.

The Mercedes-Benz W165 was the pre-war world's most advanced 1½-litre supercharged racing car. Fate decreed, however, that it was never to race in anger in the forties or fifties. Its sole race and sole victory was at Tripoli in 1939.

DAIMLER WEIGHS A COMEBACK

Nobody knew better than Daimler-Benz what it would take to win Formula 1 races in the forties. Realistic assessment accounted to no small degree for the firm's reluctance to return to racing after Germany was readmitted to the FIA in 1949. A comeback had to be a tempting idea, especially after the Daimler-Benz Swiss importer bought title to the two 1½-litre W165 Voiturettes that had been 'captured German property' since their arrival in Switzerland early in 1945. After all, these were improved versions of the cars that had beaten the Type 158 Alfa Romeo in a straight fight (Tripoli 1939). They'd been further developed, with two-stage supercharging and revised dampers and fuel tanks, early in 1940.

A Daimler-Benz contingent was conspicuous (could it be otherwise with the bulky Neubauer?) in the pits at Reims for the French Grand Prix on 1 July 1951. They kept to themselves the knowledge that Daimler-Benz had decided two weeks earlier to build a brand-new team of W165 cars: five cars plus five spare engines. They'd have gone racing in 1952, almost surely with Fangio as team leader, because the 1½/4½-litre formula had officially been extended through 1953.

But at the end of July, after watching a record-smashing German Grand Prix in which Ferrari defeated Alfa Romeo, they changed their minds. The little W165, they had to admit, wouldn't be able to beat those red cars. In fact, their drivers had been unable to reach their pre-war lap times at the Nürburgring with the same car; Fangio had been reluctant to annoy Alfa Romeo by accepting Neubauer's entreaties to set a bogey Nürburgring lap time. Fritz Nallinger's engineers started working on a new V-12 which was also cancelled when it became evident, during 1952, that the existing formula would no longer be used for world championship racing.

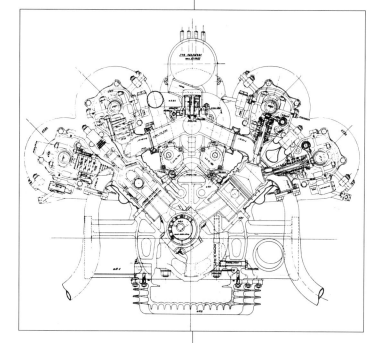

EXPIRATION OF A FORMULA

The 1952 and 1953 Formula 1 seasons could have been quite something. Alfa might have removed from mothballs its plan for a smaller and much lighter edition of the Type 159, and Ferrari would have completed the four-cam version of the 4½-litre V-12 on which work had begun. BRM was starting to show some promise; Mercedes-Benz was coming back, and even Talbot was making a lighter and more powerful car.

For race organisers, however, the immediate outlook was bleak: dominant Ferraris racing against the most notorious non-starters/scratchers/DNFs of the era, the BRMs. This the organisers eschewed in favour of the then-current Formula 2, which was elevated to world championship status for two years.

Thus it transpired that the Grand Prix formula of 1948–51, which had grown in part from a preceding Voiturette category, was succeeded by one as well. Later formulas kept provisions for supercharged engines, but not for a quarter-decade would one be remotely in contention. The first era of the high-pressure Grand Prix car died at dusk on 28 October 1951 in Barcelona with the last victorious bellow from the twin tailpipes of Fangio's Alfa Romeo. It was a thrilling sound that made it hard to remember there had ever been a war at all.

The 90-degree V-8 engine of the W165 Mercedes-Benz could have been a sound basis for postwar development with its four valves per cylinder and roller-bearing bottom end. Daimler-Benz had to acknowledge, however, that it had fallen behind Alfa Romeo in racing engine development during the forties.

THE FINISH.—Wimille (Type 158/47) Alfa Romeo, on the left, crosses the line to win by a lap, while Villoresi (Maserati) and Sommer (Ferrari) scrap for second place.

THE ITALIAN GRAND PRIX

Jean-Pierre Wimille (Type 158/47 Alfa Romeo) Wins
Finest Post-war Race

THE Italian Grand Prix run on the 2.79-miles circuit in the Valentino Park, Turin, last Sunday, September 5, fulfilled all expectations of being the finest race of the post-war years. Run in pouring rain, the race provided yet another victory for Jean-Pierre Wimille driving the latest high-supercharged Alfa Romeo, known as the type 158/47, by a clear lap after leading the race with ease from start to finish. On the other hand, this was the first race in which the all-conquering Alfa Romeo team has been faced with real opposition and the other two Alfas of the familiar type 158 retired from the race as a result of the hot pace set by the latest low chassis Maserati and the new Grand Prix 1½-litre Ferrari which is illustrated elsewhere in this issue. Throughout the 75 laps of the 223.75-mile race, Villoresi on one of the type 4 CTL/48 Maseratis and Sommer on a new 12-cylinder Ferrari fought a memorable duel.

Had there been another four laps Villoresi's tired engine must have yielded to Sommer's Ferrari, which was as powerful at the end as at the start. Reg. Parnell and Leslie Brooke both drove the new type Maseratis; Parnell finished 5th although without a clutch after the second lap and Brooke, after

losing his oil pressure, overshot a corner, stalled and pushed in to finish. Bira and Farina on the other two Ferraris both retired.

From "Grande Vitesse." From Turin by telephone Sunday night.

AS I telephone this account of the 29th Italian Grand Prix I am still a little breathless, for we have witnessed a fight for second place between Villoresi and Sommer which lasted throughout the entire race and ended only when they crossed the line a few lengths apart with the winner Wimille sandwiched in between. The entry of over 30 cars was whittled down

in practice to the fastest 20. On the first day, when the road was dry, Wimille lapped in 2 mins. 16.6 secs., which equals 78.61 m.p.h., Trossi next, with 2 mins. 18.4 secs., and Villoresi 3rd in 2 mins. 20 secs. On the second practice day there was heavy rain and the speeds dropped off. Finally the practice times gave the following starting order.

Row 1.
Wimille, Trossi, Villoresi, Sommer.
Row 2.
Sanesi, Farina, Ascari, Chiron.
Row 3.
Parnell, Comotti, de Graffenried, Cortese.
Row 4.
Taruffi, Rosier, Bira, Etancelin.
Row 5.
Manzon, Brooke, Cabantous, Chaboud.

Both Parnell and Brooke drove the new low-chassis type 4 CTL/48 Maserati. John Gordon, who was entered on Brooke's B. Type E.R.A., had trouble with his lorry on the road from Geneva and arrived after astonishing adventures—which included driving the racing car itself down the Grand St. Bernard Pass—20 mins. too late to qualify.

ITALIAN GRAND PRIX RESULTS

Distance, 75 laps; 223.75 miles. One lap measures 2.97 miles.
1. Wimille (Alfa Romeo Type 158/47), 75 laps, 3 hrs. 10 mins. 42.4 secs.; 70.38 m.p.h.
2. Villoresi (Maserati 4CTL/48), 74 laps, 3 hrs. 13 mins. 24.2 secs.
3. Sommer (1½-litre Ferrari V12), 73 laps, 3 hrs. 10 mins. 43 secs.
4. Ascari (Maserati 4CTL/48), 72 laps, 3 hrs. 12 mins. 28.4 secs.
5. Parnell (Maserati 4CTL/48), 72 laps, 3 hrs. 13 mins. 6 secs.
6. Rosier (Talbot Lago), 70 laps, 3 hrs. 12 mins. 1.8 secs.
7. Comotti (Talbot Lago), 70 laps, 3 hrs. 13 mins. 35 secs.
8. Etancelin (Talbot Lago), 69 laps.
9. De Graffenried (Maserati 4CL), 67 laps.
10. Chaboud (4½-litre Delahaye), 67 laps.
11. Brooke (Maserati 4CTL/48), 67 laps.
Fastest lap: Wimille (4th lap), 2 mins. 22.4 secs.; 75 41 m.p.h.

BS

PUSH-FINISH.—H. L. Brooke (Maserati) pushes his car across the finishing line.

THE CARS

Alfa Romeo.—(Sanesi, Trossi.) Normal type 158. 280 b.h.p.
Alfa Romeo.—(Wimille.) Type 158/47. 300 plus b.h.p.
Maserati.—(Parnell, Brooke, Villoresi, Ascari.) Latest type 4CTL/48. 240 b.h.p. approximately.
Maserati.—(de Graffenried, Taruffi.) Normal type 4CL single supercharger, 215 b.h.p.
Ferrari.—(Sommer, Farina, Bira.) New Grand Prix 1½-litre, single-seater, single supercharger, V12 single camshaft to each bank, short tubular chassis, 7-ft. 6-in. wheelbase, independent suspension all round, transverse leaf at front, torsion bar at rear, weight approximately 10 cwt. 230 plus b.h.p., front tyres 5.50 x 15, rear tyres 7.00 x 15.
Simca Gordini.—(Cabantous, Manzon.) Four-cylinder 1,440 c.c. approximately 80 b.h.p.
Talbot-Lago.—(Etancelin, Comotti, Rosier.) 1948 model, 4½-litre two-camshaft, 240 b.h.p.
Talbot.—(Chiron.) 1946-47 model, 4½-litre, single camshaft. 220 b.h.p.
Delahaye.—(Chaboud.) 4½-litre, single-seater, 200 b.h.p. approximately.

The weather had changed from the famous Italian summer to a very English day of steady rain and grey skies which hung low over the hills flanking the river Po, on the near-side banks of which the circuit lies in Valentino Park, ten minutes from the centre of Turin. All the afternoon the rain alternated between a steady drizzle and torrential showers, so that the road was awash and one could hear the sudden rise of engine revs. as the wheels spun on the glassy circuit.

At the drop of the flag, Sommer shot into the lead with Wimille a length behind and Sanesi and Ascari wheel to wheel. Cortese (Maserati) was late away with a plug oiled on the line and began a series of pit stops until he eventually retired.

Wimille, driving the latest "super" Alfa, sang past in the lead on lap 1, in clouds of spray and, as the field tore past, the spray was blown across into the grandstand and the cars were almost hidden from sight. How the drivers managed to see where they were going, especially when overtaking, is highly remarkable.

There was no doubt about the superior speed of Wimille's Alfa, but it was equally obvious that the normal type Alfa had met its match at last in the Ferrari and Maserati. On the first lap the order was Wimille, Sommer (4 seconds behind), Sanesi (3 seconds behind), Ascari, Farina, Trossi, Villoresi and Parnell all howling past in a smother of flying water, Brooke lying 13th behind assorted Talbots and Maseratis.

Thereafter Wimille began to pile up a commanding lead of several seconds a lap and, on his fourth time round, he put in the fastest lap of the day at 75.41 m.p.h (2 mins. 22.4 secs.) and led by nearly half a minute already. There is little doubt that he is the fastest driver in Europe to-day.

The new Ferraris were remarkably fast, running their first race with only one supercharger instead of the three which are to be used later. It was noticeable that they cornered faster than any other car on the course although their front wheels appeared to cant over astonishingly under the strain.

Position at 5 Laps (14.85 Miles)

1. Wimille, 12 mins. 4.6 secs. 73.92 m.p.h.
2. Sommer, 12 mins. 33.4 secs.
3. Villoresi, 12 mins. 38.8 secs.
4. Ascari, 12 mins. 39 secs.
5. Sanesi, 12 mins. 41 secs.
6. Farina; 7, Trossi; 8, Parnell.

By lap 5, Villoresi had got into his stride, passed several cars and lay third behind Sommer, who was driving like a demon in the true Sommer style. Now began a battle royal between these two inveterate rivals which lasted the whole race.

Sanesi and Trossi could not command the situation and lay fifth and seventh respectively.

At this stage Parnell, driving bare-headed, very fast and in high delight with his new car, found his clutch give up and drove the rest of the race without it; he lost the top of his gear lever as well.

Etancelin (Talbot) fell back with a pit stop to change a plug. There was a good deal of plug trouble, probably owing to the water flying about on the course.

Parnell-Bira Duel

By seven laps, Parnell and Bira were locked in combat, separated by 18 seconds and, as Parnell was slowed by the lack of a clutch, Bira's Ferrari began to creep up. At ten laps the order was:

Position at 10 Laps (29.7 Miles)

1. Wimille, 24 mins. 20.6 secs. 73.34 m.p.h.
2. Villoresi, 25 mins. 2.2 secs.
3. Sommer, 25 mins. 3.4 secs.
4. Ascari, 25 mins. 11.8 secs.
5. Trossi, 25 mins. 26.6 secs.
7. Etancelin; 8, Sanesi; 9, Farina.

A lap later Ascari, driving with great calmness and very fast—obviously a coming man—stopped 50 seconds for plugs and fell back to 12th place, such was the speed of the race, while Wimille sailed around 50 seconds in the lead, Villoresi about 2 lengths ahead of Sommer, and already Wimille was easing up and no longer crowding on the power. He dropped to 2 minutes 25 and 2 minutes 26.

On the 15th lap Sanesi's Alfa came in for plugs and was delayed over 2 minutes and, at the same time, Cortese gave up on the course and walked in.

At 19 laps, Wimille having lapped the rest of the entire field, driving as always as though touring but taking his corners in a steady slide, was about to lap Parnell running 6th and then the crowd roared, for Trossi came tearing into his pit, fighting his way through a solid mass of people in front, over half of whom appeared to be soldiers policing the area, and lost 1 minute changing plugs; then Bira passed Parnell, so that at 20 laps the order was:—

Position at 20 Laps (59.4 Miles)

1. Wimille, 49 mins. 6 secs. 72.72 m.p.h.
2. Sommer, 50 mins. 6.6 secs.
3. Villoresi, 50 mins. 8 secs.
4. Farina, 51 mins. 6.6 secs.
5. Bira; 6, Parnell; 7, Trossi; 8, Rosier.

Next lap Sanesi was in again. The pace set up by the Maseratis and Ferraris was at last beginning to tell for the first time in post-war history.

Sommer and Villoresi dashed on through the rain, passing and repassing lap after lap and never more than a length or two apart. They swirled into the corners nose to tail and, thrashing their engines out on the far side, held their revs. in second gear right up to valve bounce, and the spray from the wheels shot up 15 or 20 ft. Running in fourth place Farina's Ferrari bore traces of having hit something.

On lap 29 Bira dashed in for fuel while Parnell repassed. Bira was off again in pursuit in 45 secs., refilling from a pressure hose.

- - - - - - - Contd.

Position at 30 Laps (89.10 miles)
1. Wimille, 1 hr. 13 mins. 57 secs. 72.44 m.p.h.
2. Villoresi, 1 hr. 15 mins. 14 secs.
3. Sommer, 1 hr. 15 mins. 14.2 secs.
4. Farina, 1 hr. 16 mins. 28.8. secs.
5. Parnell; 6, Trossi; 7. Bira; 8, Ascari.

Two laps later Farina refuelled, clapped on a new vizor and was away in 32 secs., still fourth, and Parnell was still holding Bira at bay, almost a minute away.

At 35 laps, Sommer refuelled, to immense applause, changed his goggles, adjusted the front brake and was off again in 1 min. 3 secs. His car was filled from churns, for the pressure hose inconsiderately packed up. At this point it was noticeable that Sanesi, lying 11th, was unable to pick up any ground and could not close on Comotti's Talbot which lay just ahead.

Villoresi refuelled at lap 37 with a pressure hose and was back in the race 1 min. later and, as he accelerated away. Sommer rushed past in a smother of spray. A mile farther on, coming out of a fast curve, Villoresi repassed back into second place. Trossi refuelled on that lap and dropped to 11th place. Wimille, thanks to all this, was now a steady lap and a half in the lead.

Brooke refuelled on lap 38 (55 secs.). Parnell on lap 40 (39 secs.) and at this stage the order was:—

Position at 40 Laps (118.8 Miles)
1. Wimille, 1 hr. 38 mins. 55.4 secs. 72.21 m.p.h.
2. Villoresi, 1 hr. 41 mins. 31 secs.
3. Sommer, 1 hr. 41 mins. 44.4 secs.
4. Farina, 1 hr. 43 mins. 14 secs.
5. Parnell, 1 hr. 45 mins. 9 secs.
6. Bira; 7. Trossi; 8. Ascari.

On the 41st lap Wimille came in for his refuel and was away in 32 secs., still with just over a lap lead. At this moment Chiron came in, the lid of the Talbot was taken off and after a scrutiny the car was withdrawn. At the same time Taruffi and his old Maserati also retired.

A lap later came sensation, for Sanesi was in with front wheels at a drunken angle—he had rammed the straw bales on a slow corner—and the car was wheeled away. The first Alfa was out. Two laps later they flagged Trossi in and Sanesi took over the car. Two laps later the car was in again and six laps later came in for good with what sounded like supercharger trouble and the second Alfa was out of the race. Thus, at 50 laps the order was:—

Position at 50 Laps (148.5 Miles)
1. Wimille, 2 hrs. 4 mins. 19.4 secs. 71.81 m.p.h.
2. Villoresi, 2 hrs. 7 mins. 10.6 secs.
3. Sommer, 2 hrs. 8 mins. 37.6 secs.
4. Farina, 2 hrs. 11 mins.

Now the pattern of the race was set. The rain poured monotonously down; the awnings of the stand sagged; the flags drooped miserably; the road was covered with deep pools through which the racing cars charged as if through water splashes, almost hidden as they went.

Wimille, a good lap in the lead, was easing up still more, but behind him Villoresi tore along, with Sommer in pursuit and with Farina doing all he could to close on Sommer, but on the 51st lap Farina went a shade too fast on a slow corner, slid with locked brakes and slammed the straw bales

A SKETCH OF THE VALENTINO CIRCUIT, TURIN.

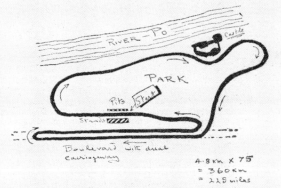

4.8 km × 75
= 360 km
= 225 miles

hard with the radiator of his Ferrari so that he limped into the pit and retired. Score so far: two Alfas, one Ferrari out. Brooke's Maserati too was in trouble with spasmodic oil pressure and now Villoresi's engine began to sound as if the valve seats were no longer what they should be. Sommer's Ferrari, on the other hand, sounded as hearty as ever although his brakes did not seem to respond to his increasing demands. He made a second fuel stop on lap 56 and was away in 34 secs., still third, with Ascari fourth, coming up faster now behind him. Bira, steady as ever and making no mistakes, lay fifth, and Parnell always sixth, despite his vanished clutch. Now at 60 laps the order was:—

Position at 60 Laps (178.2 Miles)
1. Wimille, 2 hrs. 29 mins. 40 secs. 71.57 m.p.h.
2. Villoresi, 2 hrs. 33 mins. 6.6 secs.
3. Sommer, 2 hrs. 35 mins. 32.6 secs.
4. Ascari; 5. Parnell.

At 61 laps Villoresi made his second fuel stop and changed his plugs, dropping one minute 25 seconds, re-starting a lap behind Wimille, but still the Maserati sounded very tired. At 67 laps Wimille did his second refuel, merely topping up to make sure of the race and was off in only 15 seconds with almost a lap (three miles) lead.

Uncatchable Wimille

There was no catching Wimille, but the Sommer-Villoresi duel marched to a crisis. On lap 68 Sommer was 24 seconds behind him; on lap 69 it was 22 seconds, then 17 seconds, then 11 seconds and, on lap 72, only 6 seconds. Villoresi roared along soaked to the skin with his engine sounding as if it would not go much farther, but it was driven flat out just the same for this was no time for sparing engines.

On lap 66, Bira suddenly found his Ferrari make its usual noise without proceeding up the road and on the far side of the course he parked the car with its transmission in a muddle and walked back through the rain. At the same time Brooke, worried about a lack of oil pressure, overdid a hairpin and hit the straw bales so hard that he stalled the engine and could not restart. Thereupon, with the gallant idea of finishing at all costs, he began to push the car as fast as he could in the direction of the pits, half a mile away, for the race was nearly over.

Position at 70 Laps (208 Miles)
1. Wimille, 2 hrs. 56 mins. 57 secs. 70.51 m.p.h.
2. Villoresi, 3 hrs. 2 mins. 18.8 secs.
3. Sommer, 3 hrs. 2 mins. 35.4 secs.
4. Ascari, 3 hrs. 6 mins. 25.4 secs.
5. Parnell, 3 hrs. 7 mins. 0.8 sec.

Thus, Wimille was almost exactly a lap in the lead—a shade under three miles—in three hours' motor racing and at lap 73 Sommer was two seconds behind Villoresi.

The entire crowd of 25,000 people was on its feet yelling—and a crowd shouting in Italian must be heard to be believed. Round they came again on Wimille's last lap and, as the cars grew clearer in the clouds of spray, we saw Villoresi first, then Wimille streaking for the finishing line and, just behind, Sommer madly trying to catch Villoresi. Sportingly Wimille shot out of the way as they crossed the line in that order, Sommer about five lengths behind his quarry—foiled again.

Wimille was flagged on the spot as winner, Villoresi went on and was credited with the next lap, while Sommer, coming in behind the flag, was reckoned to have finished, which explains the oddity of the official results.

One by one the ten survivors of the twenty starters came in dripping, and lastly, with the crowd shrieking encouragement, and clapping him to the echo, came the exhausted Brooke, still pushing his Maserati and, as he tottered breathless across the line, he received the chequered flag all to himself—11th man home.

So ended a tremendous race. For the first time the Alfas could not arrange their finishing order. Two of them, out of three, retired, but the high supercharge "super" Alfa in the hands of Wimille ran away with the race. The new Ferrari covered itself with glory on its first appearance and the new Maserati proved itself again to be a vast step forward in this factory's design. It looks as though we are on the verge of a new phase in Grand Prix racing.

Parnell, finishing fifth in such a gallery, indicates that, given good cars, British drivers can hold their heads up in any company. Incidentally, the moment Parnell stopped after the race, the drain plugs fell out of the sump.

TURIN RETIREMENTS

Manzon (Simca), 9 laps, 27 miles; engine.
Cortese (Maserati 4 CTL/48), 12 laps, 35 miles, engine.
Giraud-Cabantous (Simca), 40 laps, 119 miles; engine.
Chiron (Talbot), 41 laps, 122 miles; gasket.
Taruffi (Maserati 4CL), 41 laps, 122 miles; engine.
Sanesi (Alfa Romeo), 42 laps, 125 miles; bent front axle.
Farina (Ferrari), 50 laps, 148 miles; split radiator after crash.
Trossi (Alfa Romeo), 53 laps, 158 miles; supercharger while the car was being driven by Sanesi.
Bira (Ferrari), 66 laps, 198 miles; transmission.

CHAPTER SIX

THE FIFTIES

I had an awkward moment when travelling flat out down the Masta Straight towards Stavelot. There were two pigeons standing in the road and they rose much too slowly to get out of the way of a racing car travelling at about 150 mph. I missed one, but the other went straight into the air intake and hit the radiator. The news of my incident with the pigeon was reported in the press and next time I got back to England I found a letter waiting for me, saying what a swine I was to go around killing birds. You have to keep a sense of proportion!

Mike Hawthorn at Spa-Francorchamps, 1955

A summary of the state of Grand Prix racing during the fifties will not detain us long. Juan Manuel Fangio was the outstanding driver, with four World Drivers' Championships from 1954 through 1957 to prove it. If we were counting 1951, which we covered in Chapter Five, we would include Juan's five championships in all. Next equal in brilliance were Alberto Ascari, champion in 1952 and 1953, and Stirling Moss, who placed his personal brand on the fifties with many great victories. Mike Hawthorn was champion in 1958 and Jack Brabham in 1959 and 1960.

Nor are many names necessary in reviewing the outstanding marques of Grand Prix cars of the fifties. Ferrari predominates. Impressively, he provided prancing-horse mounts for the world champions of 1952, 1953, 1956 and 1958. Cooper was the star in 1959 and 1960, as was Mercedes-Benz in 1954 and 1955 – though in the former year Fangio collected some of his points with Maserati, for whom he won the championship in 1957. Individual successes came the way of BRM, Lotus and Vanwall.

WATERSHED YEARS OF TRANSFORMATION

This bald summary gives no sense of the incredible turbulence and change that transformed Grand Prix racing in the fifties. These were watershed years for the highest level of motoring sport, years when the dramatic new design techniques that we saw originated in the thirties and carried over by necessity through the forties were exploited to the full and finally thrust aside in favour of a generation of cars with engines behind the driver – a state that has continued to prevail. In the fifties we said farewell, not without nostalgia, to the handsome, long-nosed, front-engined Grand Prix cars, evoking a classic profile, that we celebrate in this book.

A few examples will suggest the magnitude of the transformation that took place during the fifties. At the beginning there were only a few rear-engined cars; at the end there were only a few front-engined cars. De Dion rear suspension, all but universal since 1938, had given way to full independence at the rear. Disc brakes and disc wheels had taken over from drum brakes and spoked wheels.

From 1954 to 1960 the Type 250F Maserati was a fixture of the Formula 1 scene. At Monza in 1957 Guerrino Bertocchi warms up Juan Fangio's car while Maserati's Omer Orsi watches, right. More Chianti bottles will be opened after the race.

Fuel injection had shown its superiority over carburettors, albeit tentatively. And the multi-tube geodetic chassis frame, the so-called 'space frame', had finally conquered the twin frame rails that traced their origins back to Wilhelm Maybach's 1901 Mercedes. In all respects save the monocoque frame (and even that was tried in the fifties) and the generation of aerodynamic downforce, the elements that make up the modern Formula 1 car were already being glimpsed by the end of the fifties.

Several yeasts gave rise to this extraordinary fermentation. One was the change in the Grand Prix formula that took place during these years. When the fifties opened, two formulas were in place. Formula 1, for Grand Prix racing cars, admitted engines of 1½ litres supercharged and 4½ litres unsupercharged. In parallel with it was, since 1948, Formula 2, which allowed 2-litre unsupercharged engines and 500 cc engines with superchargers.[1] Both were scheduled to expire at the end of 1953. In the measured pace that was typical of the time, the deliberations over their successor(s) took place during 1951.

In February of 1951 France and Italy suggested that both formulas be given up in favour of one new formula for 2½-litre unsuper-charged engines and 750 cc supercharged engines. As in the previous Formula 2, the supercharged engines were kept very small to discourage their use. Much influenced by Ferrari, the framers of the formula had the aim of creating a less expensive form of racing. In October 1951 the FIA confirmed that the proposed new formula would take effect in 1954. It remained the guideline for Grand Prix racing until 1960, with the added requirement in 1958 that only petrol of aviation quality be allowed as fuel. Hitherto, fuels had been unrestricted.

In ways the framers could not have foreseen in 1951, the formula was adopted by *fait accompli* for Grand Prix racing, in slightly different form, the following year. The plan had been to carry on in 1952 and 1953 with the existing Formula 1, but after the retirement from racing of Alfa Romeo and the celebrated and frequent non-appearances of the V-16 BRM, race organisers despaired in the spring of 1952 of having decent fields of cars for their events. They chose instead – with the approval of the FIA – to run races counting for the world championship according to Formula 2. Allowing engines only half a litre smaller than the 1954 formula, this was in effect a preview of the 2½-litre era.

NEW NAMES ON THE GRIDS

Another source of the explosion of creativity in the fifties was the rise of new car builders. Older names were still present, to be sure. Ferrari, Maserati, BRM, Alta

---

1   To the author's knowledge, the latter option was never taken up, although it was certainly meant to appeal to the makers of 500 cc cars that were competing in the lowest category, Formula 3. A 4:1 equivalency ratio against the supercharged engine was a heavy burden.

and Gordini carried on, and such pre-war names as Bugatti, ERA and Mercedes-Benz returned. From the world of Formula 2 racing, new marques saw no reason not to leap into racing's top echelon: HWM, Cooper, Connaught, Frazer-Nash, Veritas and OSCA. The Grand Prix gene pool was further enriched by the entry of Lancia, Vanwall, Lotus, Aston Martin and Scarab. While some of the new builders made appearances that can best be described as fleeting, others substantially and lastingly advanced the Grand Prix art.

Completely new to Grand Prix racing in this decade was the building of cars by companies that did not also make the engines that powered their cars. Whether they were large or small, Fiat or Bugatti, prior Grand Prix entrants, had designed and built the entire automobile. This ceased to be uniformly the case as a result of the quirk of history that admitted the Formula 2 brigade to Grand Prix racing in 1952. They brought with them a different way of building racing cars. Three proprietary engines – if the term may be so used – were prominent in the Grand Prix racing of 1952 and 1953.

Two of them were close cousins, the BMW 328 in-line six and the British engine that had been derived from it as a form of reparations by Germany after the war, the Bristol. In spite of their long stroke and complex pushrod valve gear,[2]

Strategically placed thin tubes helped Cooper's designers plan the shape of the body of their new T20 Formula 2 car of 1952. Although its six-cylinder Bristol power was modest, the Cooper's light weight and agility helped it scare more imposing cars.

---

2   Its V-inclined overhead valves were operated by pushrods from one camshaft in the block. It opened the inlet valves by rocker arms, and the exhaust valves by bell-cranks and another set of pushrods across the head. The design had always been regarded as a temporary expedient by its originators, BMW.

CHARLES AND JOHN COOPER

How would Grand Prix cars have evolved if the Coopers hadn't been around? We can safely assume that the front-engined era might have lasted much longer, certainly through the fifties and the expiration of the 2½-litre Formula 1. All the big players – Ferrari, Vanwall, Maserati, BRM, Aston Martin – were comfortable, thank you, with the classic Grand Prix car configuration. Why would they want to change to engines in the rear like those quirky Auto Unions? Weren't they a real handful for anyone except Bernd Rosemeyer?

It would be fair to say of Charles Cooper and his son John that the need to make this transition hadn't been all that obvious to them either. The senior Cooper was steeped in motor sports, having been both mechanic and manager for the racing efforts of Kaye Don between the wars. Don was a dedicated Brooklands competitor and challenger for speed records on land and water. After Don retired in 1934, Cooper built up a substantial garage business in Surbiton, Surrey.

After the war British enthusiasts, keen to get racing again, came up with the idea of building small single-seaters around ½-litre motorcycle engines in what became known as the '500' movement. In 1946, for his son John and family friend Eric Brandon, Charles Cooper whipped up suitable cars using the transverse-leaf suspension of Fiat Topolinos at both front and rear. Like most '500' builders – though not all – Cooper put the engine behind the driver.

A justifiably proud John Cooper poses with one of his first series-production racing cars. Its wire-mesh grille belied the fact that its motorcycle engine was behind the driver.

With his central-seated 'Bobtail' sports-racing car of 1955 Cooper engineered the vehicle that was fated to create a successful transition from the minor leagues of single-seater racing to Formula 1. Roy Salvadori in a 'Bobtail' leads the sliding Lister of Archie Scott-Brown.

Unlike most of the devices being bolted together by enthusiasts, the first Coopers looked like proper racing cars. They even had mock grilles on their noses that gave them a 'serious' mien. They were also quick, as both Brandon and John Cooper demonstrated with racing successes, and this led to demand from enthusiasts. Suddenly the Coopers were in the car business.

For the 1948 season Cooper produced a dozen Mark 2 cars, now with their brake drums integral with the light-alloy wheels in the Bugatti tradition. Stirling Moss was one of their customers. Cooper remained a leader in the '500' category, which in 1950 was officially designated as international Formula 3.

Fitted with twin-cylinder 1-litre engines, these rear-engined Coopers were able to make a decent showing in Formula 2 races, even though they gave away a full litre of capacity. But when they decided to build a pukka Formula 2 car for the 1952 season, Charles and John put its engine in the front, as they had with the various MG-powered sports cars they had produced. Powering this T20 Cooper was the ubiquitous Bristol six, tuned to produce up to 150 bhp.

Front-engined though they were, these Cooper-Bristols were practical and useful racing cars, launching the international careers of Mike Hawthorn and Jack Brabham, and providing successful mounts for Ken Wharton, Bob Gerard and Alan Brown. Cooper also built some big front-engined Jaguar-powered sports cars. But the serendipitous breakthrough came with creation of the 'Bobtail' centre-seated sports car in 1955.

From this sports car, by chance more than choice, the mid-engined Cooper single-seaters were derived for both Formula 2 and Formula Junior in 1957. From them in turn keen owners and teams derived the Formula 1 Coopers. Behind this evolution were the practical driving and development skills of Jack Brabham, supported by the rising talent of New Zealander Bruce McLaren. The result: the 1959 and 1960 world championships and a dazzling and convincing demonstration of the efficiency of a mid-engined racing car.

Jack Brabham stayed with Cooper for the first year of the 1½-litre formula in 1961 and then left to build his own Brabham cars. His departure was taken hard by the Coopers, especially by Charles, and they did not extend the same intimate involvement with the cars to Bruce McLaren.

Cooper Grand Prix cars failed to find form in the rest of the 1½-litre years up to 1965. Some compensation came in the form of the Mini Cooper, the hugely popular tuned Mini which became the leading rally car of its day and was all but unbeatable in small-capacity saloon-car races.

After Charles Cooper's death in 1964 the company was sold to the Chipstead Group for 1965. Chipstead being the UK Maserati importer, V-12 engines from Modena were supplied for the new Grand Prix Cooper for the 3-litre formula. Although these cars had some success, the momentum of the effort was slowed by serious injuries to John Cooper in a road-car accident when testing a Mini powered by two engines, one in front and the other in the back. After 1969 – a decade after company and team had transformed Formula 1 racing – Cooper was no longer a maker of racing cars.

Drivers such as Stirling Moss and Peter Collins raced across the continent in the Alta-powered HWMs of John Heath in the years when the Grand Prix championship was run to Formula 2 rules. The car's purposeful practicality helped to keep the small HWM team solvent.

these hemispherical-head engines were effective performers in light cars. A distinctive and positive feature was their use of inlet ports that flowed down to the valves from the top of the cylinder head. In Germany the BMW was used by AFM, by Veritas before it built its own overhead-cam six, and by privateers, even in one rear-engined car.

In Britain the similar Bristol powered a Frazer-Nash single-seater, the G-type ERA – which failed to sparkle even in the hands of Stirling Moss – and, most notably, the front-engined T20 Cooper-Bristol which Mike Hawthorn drove with virtuosity in his Grand Prix debut year of 1952. From their successful Formula 3 cars and sports cars, Charles and John Cooper (father and son respectively) used the Bristol engine to graduate to the Grand Prix circuits. They would dominate it by the end of the fifties.

For Formula 2 Britain's Geoffrey Taylor continued to build his lovingly made Alta single-seaters, but they did not excel. Much more successful were other cars using his twin-cam four-cylinder Alta engines, which Taylor was only too happy to sell. Some Cooper chassis were Alta-powered, to the buyer's order. John Heath's HWM made its mark with Alta power, but failed to achieve a successful transition to the more competitive post-1953 era.

By contrast the Connaught racing cars built by Rodney Clarke and Mike Oliver for Kenneth MacAlpine only came into their own when they replaced their original modified Lea-Francis engines with 2½-litre Altas for the new formula, leading to Tony Brooks's victory in the 1955 Syracuse Grand Prix – the first Grand Prix win for Britain since Segrave's for Sunbeam in 1924.

ARRIVAL OF COVENTRY-CLIMAX

Alta planned a V-8 for the 2½-litre formula but never raised the funds to build it. Another British V-8, the Brooke-Weston with a three-valve cylinder head, reached the prototype stage but was not developed further. Only one British company had both high-performance engine ideas and the ability to execute them. This was Coventry-Climax, a British Midlands maker of fork-lift trucks and fire pumps.[3] Producing its own ultra-light engines for its fire pumps, it gave them designations beginning with 'FP'.

Without trying too hard, Climax achieved gratifying success in sports car racing with its single-overhead-cam fours. Enjoying the services of racing engine engineers Wally Hassan and Harry Mundy, it decided to build a pukka four-cam Formula 1 V-8. Both Kieft and Connaught were eager to use it in their new Grand Prix cars. Officially designated the FPE, the V-8 was nicknamed 'Godiva' after the legendary lady who rode naked through the streets of Coventry, home town of Coventry-Climax.

---

3 Coventry-Climax had been a pre-war maker of proprietary engines for road cars, Morgan among them. It would take up this role again as the maker of the engines powering the Lotus Elite coupé.

The 2.5-litre version of Geoffrey Taylor's Alta four-cylinder engine was put to best use by the British Connaught team. Although this small team could never attract the best drivers, the intelligent design of its B-Type brought it some surprising successes.

The Godiva V-8 was built and tested with promising results, but when it was new it was never installed in a car.[4] Coventry-Climax decided to abandon its development because the power figures it obtained (264 hp at 7,900 rpm) did not compare well, in its view, with those of other Grand Prix engines in 1954. Only later did Climax discover that the publicly quoted figures of its rivals were exaggerated and that its V-8 would in fact have been highly competitive.

The effort was not wasted, for one cylinder head of the V-8 became the basis of the 1½-litre FPF four-cylinder Climax engine, which was built for the new Formula 2, at that displacement size, in 1957. Among the users of the FPF in Formula 2 were British chassis makers Lister, Cooper and Lotus.

The latter two companies, at the urging of their drivers, began entering their cars in Formula 1 as well. For this Climax produced a 2-litre FPF. So powered, Coopers astonished the Grand Prix world by winning the first two races of 1958. Next, a 2.2-litre FPF was made. Then, for the 1959 season, an extensive redesign took it to a full 2.5 litres. With this engine Jack Brabham and the Cooper-Climax won the last two drivers' world championships of the fifties.

Thus was born the concept of the off-the-shelf engine for Grand Prix racing. Cooper had grown up with such engines, from the JAP, Norton and Triumph

---

4 In 1966 one such engine failed to complete the first lap of the British Grand Prix in a rear-engined car called the Shannon. Their subsequent fate is unknown.

motorcycle units of its Formula 3 days to the Bristol, and finally to the Climax, and Lotus followed suit with its entry into Formula 2 in 1957 and Formula 1 in 1958. With the adaptable Cooper chassis available, the inevitable happened and other engines were installed in it. Starting in 1959, Maserati made a suitable 2½-litre four available, and Ferrari fours were also fitted in the backs of Coopers.

At the end of the fifties only Ferrari and BRM were still active as companies able and willing to build a complete Grand Prix car from scratch. Vanwall had joined them during the decade, but then had faded from the scene. Around them on the starting grids were products of the joint efforts of engine builders and chassis builders, with some help from gearbox specialists. The age of the 'British kit car', or the '*garagistes*', as they were pejoratively known on the Continent, had begun.

Installed in the back of a 1958 Cooper, the four-cylinder Coventry-Climax FPF engine proved surprisingly competitive. This car's engine at the Nürburgring was equipped with two special twin-throat SU carburettors.

At Reims in 1959 Jack Brabham was chasing another Cooper in his works Cooper-Climax on his way to third place. Brabham was among the first drivers to think of tailoring his car's tyres and suspension to the particular requirements of each circuit.

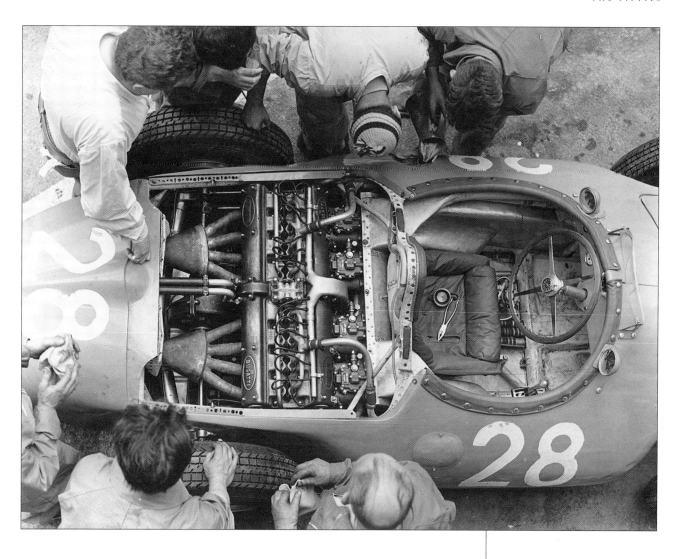

REAR-MOUNTED ENGINES ATTEMPTED

The little Cooper works in Surbiton, Surrey, led the way in the transformation during the fifties of Grand Prix cars from front engines to rear engines. Logical though the rear-engined car may look from the modern perspective, its advantages were not so obvious in the fifties. Still bright in the memory were the pre-war Auto Unions, said by many to be very difficult to drive, with their weight at the rear and their far-forward cockpits. Overlooked were both their compelling simplicity and the high level of success that they had achieved in the face of the much greater resources of Daimler-Benz.[5]

Little happened immediately after the Second World War to reverse the poor reputation given to rear engines by Auto Union. Tests carried out during the war by Alfa Romeo on its rear-engined Type 512 only confirmed its view that the

The Type 251 Bugatti of 1956 was notable in having its straight-eight engine placed transversely behind the cockpit. Steering wheel and exhaust manifolds were fabricated very much in the Bugatti tradition and a leather cockpit surround was an elegant touch.

---

5   From the perspective of outside observers, both German companies seemed to have limitless resources. However, the Auto Union conglomerate could not afford to fund its racing as lavishly as could Daimler-Benz, which was already benefiting from its large government orders for engines for military aircraft.

layout was dangerous; we recall that it killed its test driver. The beautiful rear-engined Formula 1 car built by Cisitalia to Porsche's Type 360 design had the potential to demonstrate the merits of an engine behind the driver. However, it was fully evaluated neither in Europe nor in Argentina, to which it was exported.

News came from France about an exciting rear-engined racer designed by ex-Porsche engineers and financed by a film producer, but the Sacha-Gordine failed to reach a starting grid. Following the Auto Union model some German privateers built rear-engined Formula 2 cars with BMW engines; one was the Monopol of Helmut Polensky. None was able to challenge the front-engined efforts of AFM and Veritas.

At Reims in 1956 Maurice Trintignant drove the Type 251 Bugatti (number 28), seen in company with Robert Manzon (number 30) in the latest eight-cylinder product of the Gordini works. Neither car was able to contribute greatly to the glory of France.

In 1954 the exciting news came that Bugatti, still precariously in business in Molsheim, was readying a car for the 2½-litre formula as part of a bid for its rebirth as an automotive company. Just as significant was the news that the car would be designed by Gioachino Colombo, who was responsible for the Type 158 Alfa, the first V-12 Ferraris and the best of the early fifties Maseratis. Most remarkably Bugatti, maker of some of the most classical racing cars, was now to build a rear-engined racer.

The new Bugatti placed its in-line eight-cylinder engine transversely behind its driver. The eight had central gearing, between two blocks of four cylinders, to both the camshafts and the gearbox. Two such Type 251 Bugattis were built, but only one race entry by a single car was attempted in the French Grand Prix of 1956. It started near the back of the grid and lasted less than one-third of the race. The Bugatti venture did nothing to dispel the common perception that engines belonged in the front of Grand Prix cars.[6]

The elite Formula 1 ranks took little notice of the flea-sized ½-litre Formula 3 cars, among which the most successful were rear-engined, and principally British Coopers. Based on its Formula 3 experience, in 1955 Cooper built its T39 sports car to suit the new single-overhead-cam FWA Coventry-Climax engine. The 1.1-litre Climax was behind the driver, who was seated centrally, and it was bolted to a converted Citroën transaxle. The T39's truncated rear end earned it the nickname 'Bobtail'.

COOPER BLOODLINES

Two lines of development into Grand Prix racing may be traced from this Cooper. One was early and, indeed, premature. At the instigation of Australian Jack Brabham, who had raced successfully down under with the T20 Cooper-Bristol, a 2-litre Bristol six was installed in the back of a lengthened T39 Cooper in 1955. This created the envelope-bodied T40 Grand Prix Cooper, which Brabham built largely with his own hands, using Cooper's chassis jig.

---

6 In fact, its engine location was one of the better features of the heavy, complex, solid-axled and underfinanced Type 251 Bugatti.

Underpowered by some 100 hp compared to the rest of the field, the T40 was no threat to the established runners in the 1955 British Grand Prix held at Aintree. Even worse, Brabham had clutch trouble before the race and had to start from the back of the grid. He retired with an overheated engine.

Lesser men might have been discouraged by this debut, but Jack Brabham persevered. He cured the T40's teething troubles and entered it for a minor race at Snetterton that same year. He surprised all present by holding third place (behind two Vanwalls) ahead of Stirling Moss in his own Maserati 250F. Three laps before the end Brabham took to the grass and let Moss slip by; the Cooper-Bristol placed fourth 'with a small haystack firmly attached to its undershield', wrote *The Motor*. This was a defining moment for Jack Brabham. 'If it hadn't been for that race,' he wrote, 'I might have gone back to Australia for good.'

Meanwhile, at Cooper Cars the other line of development from the T39 sports car led towards the building of an open-wheeled single-seater racing car for the new Formula 2, using many components from the T39 'Bobtail'. Such Coopers first ran in 1956 and were ready, when Formula 2 commenced again in 1957, to do more than their share of winning.

So quick did these Cooper-Climax racers prove to be, in fact, that Cooper could not resist taking a car with a 2-litre FPF engine to Monaco for the Grand Prix in May 1957. After practice problems and a change of cars, Jack Brabham just squeaked it into the sixteen-car field. Astonishingly, he rose to third place near the end of the race, helped by a heavy rate of retirements, before falling to sixth (and last) at the finish after his fuel pump failed.

This debut of the rear-engined Cooper-Climax in Grand Prix racing was successful enough to encourage more such Formula 1 entries. In 1957 the first world championship points for a Cooper-Climax driver were earned by Roy Salvadori in the British Grand Prix at Aintree in July, an achievement that was overshadowed by the outright victory by Vanwall, the first-ever win by a

At the Ring the Polish mechanic who changed his name to 'Alf Francis' when he moved to England sits in the cockpit of one of the Coopers he tended in 1958 for the Rob Walker stable. What began as an annoyance for the established teams would turn into dominance for the Cooper-Climax in 1959.

British car in a championship race. Together, the two successes were signs of things to come.

As mentioned earlier, the combination of the Cooper chassis and the 2-litre version of the FPF engine produced victories in the first two championship races of 1958 in Argentina (Moss) and Monte Carlo (Trintignant). Both had been driving the same car entered by the private Rob Walker team – the first successes in the modern era for a privately owned Grand Prix car. Cooper works driver Roy Salvadori placed second in the German Grand Prix and collected enough points to rank fourth in the world drivers' championship in 1958.

The Cooper's agility and simplicity gained greatly in effectiveness in 1959 when more power was extracted from the new 2½-litre FPF Climax engine at a time when the opposition was losing power from its engines as a result of the restriction after 1958 to aviation-quality petrol fuel. Also from 1958 new rules curtailed championship Grand Prix races to 300 km or two hours, compared to the previous 500 km or three hours. Both changes favoured the production of smaller, lighter cars – like the Coopers – which would be easier on their tyres. On very fast circuits Ferrari won two races and BRM won one – its only victory of this era.

The five remaining championship Grands Prix were won by Cooper-Climaxes, two of them by Jack Brabham, who became champion. His second championship in 1960 with Cooper-Climax, the cars now with a lower profile, was even more convincing with five wins in a row. Second in the points table was Bruce McLaren, the other Cooper team driver, thus underlining the superiority that the cars from Surbiton had achieved.

OTHERS – BUT NOT ALL – ADAPT

The transformation to the rear-engined layout at the end of the fifties was so complete that in the last Grand Prix of the 2½-litre formula in 1960, at Riverside, California, only 2 of the 23 starters had their engine in the front. Ferrari, who did not send a team to Riverside, never did relinquish the front-engine layout for his Formula 1 cars during the fifties. After his decades of racing the superb Alfa Romeos and his own long-nosed Ferraris, Enzo Ferrari was reluctant to conclude that the Coopers represented anything other than a transient phenomenon. He was supported in this view by others in his organisation, including engineer Giotto Bizzarrini.

More open-minded on the subject at Ferrari was its chief engineer since November 1957, Carlo Chiti. For the 1960 season he produced a new front-engined Grand Prix Ferrari which was intended to adopt the more concentrated central mass distribution of the mid-engined car, to gain a lower polar moment of inertia that would make it more nimble in corners. The engine was shifted rearward within the wheelbase, and the main fuel tanks were at the sides instead of at the rear.[7] This car won only one race in 1960, however, and that an Italian Grand Prix at Monza which the British teams boycotted because the bumpy banked track was used as part of the circuit.

In parallel with this car, Carlo Chiti developed a mid-engined Ferrari. 'We argued a lot and we discussed it a lot,' Chiti recalled. 'Facts proved its

---

7   These were very much Bizzarrini's ideas. He used the same concepts in the sports cars he produced in his own name after leaving Ferrari following the 1961 season.

effectiveness and the drivers themselves wanted to have mid-engined
cars. There was nothing much
we could really do when ugly
ducklings like the 210-hp Coopers
(our cars developed 280 hp) left
us well behind.'

The first such Ferrari was
driven by American Richie Ginther
at Monaco in 1960. Although he
qualified with the same lap time as
team-mate and friend Phil Hill in
a front-engined Ferrari, Ginther
fell back through the field, this
being his first experience of a
Grand Prix. This car was not
entered again. Instead it was
converted into a 1½-litre Formula
2 car that raced three times in
1960 to gather experience for the
new Formula 1 that took effect
in 1961.

In Britain one company that
might have led the way was
Connaught. When this small
racing car builder was liquidated
at the end of 1957, among its
properties were the components
of its never-completed rear-

engined Type D Formula 1 car. Always progressive in its engineering – as it
had to be to exploit the modest power of its Alta engines – Connaught had
planned an advanced rear-engined car with a semi-automatic five-speed
gearbox. Connaught had been thinking along exactly the right lines.

In 1959 BRM decided it was time to react. Its chief engineer, Tony Rudd, built
the rear-engined P48 model, using many parts from the front-engined four-
cylinder P25 BRMs, and brought its prototype to Monza for the 1959 Italian
Grand Prix practice session.[8] As refined for 1960 the P48 was fast enough to
win, but was let down by unreliable engines and by BRM's stubborn retention of
a single central disc brake at the rear which exerted stopping power through the
transmission and half-shafts.[9] In theory it was a good idea, but theories do not
win races.

The more successful adaptation was that of Lotus, which gave up its
troublesome front-engined designs in favour of the Climax-powered rear-engined
18 in 1960, the car that Colin Chapman considered to be his first true Formula 1
design. It was certainly the first successful Formula 1 Lotus, placing well and
winning two championship races in 1960 in the hands of Stirling Moss. The

*When he could field such handsome
and rapid cars as the 1959 Dino
246, Enzo Ferrari was disinclined
to consider that he would do better
by putting the engine in the rear. By
1960, however, he and some of his
engineers would begin to think
otherwise.*

---

8   It was, and remained, something of a tradition for BRM to bring prototypes of its latest
     racing cars to Monza, often to practise, but not necessarily to race. This was viewed by
     Ferrari as a generous gesture, granting as it did to his engineers a preview of the British
     opposition for the coming season.
9   The season was a crushing disappointment for Dan Gurney, who had joined BRM from
     Ferrari. His previous year at Ferrari had led him to think that Grand Prix cars were
     generally reliable. His one and only BRM season was to prove the contrary.

Very pretty in the Aston Martin tradition, the light green DBR4/250 Grand Prix Aston first raced in 1959. It was no more than a footnote to the final years of the 2½-litre Formula 1. Driver Carroll Shelby and team manager Reg Parnell stroll alongside it.

Lotus 18 was also noteworthy as the first front-line Grand Prix car to use fibreglass bodywork, which became universal in the sixties.

The transition to rear-placed engines took place so suddenly that teams that had planned traditional cars were still introducing them toward the end of the fifties. In one case, that of Aston Martin, the delay was intentional. Aston began work on a Grand Prix twin of its DBR1 sports car in 1957, much like a Maserati with its in-line twin-cam six and rear-mounted transaxle with its shafts transversely placed.

The resulting DBR4/250, which was first tested at the end of 1957, could have raced in 1958 but was put aside to allow concentration on Aston's sports car programme. By the time it first competed in 1959, however, it was outpaced by the competition. As John Wyer of Aston Martin said: 'by 1960 rear-engined cars were firmly in the ascendant and it was a dead duck'. A new DBR5 design, though lighter, proved a step backwards rather than forwards, and a rear-engined chassis was initiated but never completed.

This rapid transition also put an end to the dream of wealthy American Lance Reventlow to field a successful Formula 1 car. In 1957 his Reventlow Automobiles Inc. near Los Angeles started work on a front-engined Scarab car designed by aerospace engineer Marshall Whitfield. Reventlow hoped to be competing by 1959, but making the Scarab's unique four-cylinder engine took longer than expected. When the Formula 1 Scarab appeared in 1960 it was neither fast nor reliable. Chuck Daigh drove a much-revised Scarab to its sole Grand Prix finish, tenth at Riverside at the end of the season – and of the formula.

IMPORTANT SUSPENSION ADVANCES

Closely linked to the rear-engine revolution was the progress made in parallel in suspension design, especially at the rear. During the fifties, telescopic tubular shock absorbers came into use, replacing the arm-operated Houdaille rotary dampers that had hitherto been common, especially on Italian cars. Pioneers of the use of direct-acting tubular dampers were Cooper, Mercedes-Benz and Lancia. Another refinement was the fitment of anti-roll bars at the rear as well as the front of the chassis to provide more precise tuning of the handling and balance of the car.

A sharp contrast began to develop between the old 'perfect car' posture of Ferrari and the resourceful adaptability of the British teams, led by Jack Brabham at Cooper. Suffering from severe understeer at Monte Carlo in 1955, Paul Frère begged the Ferrari engineers to unhook his car's front anti-roll bar. They refused as this was considered to be 'part of the car'. Brabham and Cooper, in contrast, began perfecting the art and science of 'tuning' the springs, dampers, anti-roll bars and tyres to the conditions at each circuit to extract the maximum grip in cornering.[10]

At the beginning of the fifties a few Grand Prix cars still used live rear axles, in spite of their known disadvantages for racing: high unsprung weight and torque reaction which tended to lift the right rear wheel on acceleration. Amédée Gordini of Paris used live axles in his very light Gordinis, which were able to challenge the Ferraris occasionally in 1952 and 1953. In fact, he did not give them up until an all-new and ambitious eight-cylinder Gordini was introduced at the end of 1955.

The modest looks of the six-cylinder Formula 2 Gordini were belied by the high performance that the man known as 'the sorcerer' conjured from its lightness and simplicity. Such drivers as Jean Behra and Robert Manzon starred in these blue cars.

The other live-axle advocate was Maserati, which in 1953 was increasingly able to match Ferrari's pace with its A6GCM, sprung by quarter-elliptic leaves and radius rods at the rear. Juan Fangio won the Italian Grand Prix at Monza for Maserati in September 1953, scoring the last-ever Grand Prix victory for a live-axle car.

As it had since 1950, Ferrari used de Dion rear suspension, which had been reintroduced to Grand Prix racing by Mercedes-Benz in 1936. In a sense a half-way house between the live axle and full independence, de Dion suspension uses a dead axle – usually a large-diameter tube – to connect the hubs, and mounts the differential on the frame of the car so it doesn't have to bounce up and down with the wheels.

---

10 It is relevant to mention that in the fifties the science of car handling in general and racing car handling in particular was still in its infancy. In November 1956, at a historic meeting in London, the seminal findings of Cornell Aeronautical Laboratory engineers concerning automobile handling and stability were presented; from them the modern understanding of car cornering has been developed. Not until the sixties would this scientific comprehension begin to have an influence on racing car design.

Others using de Dion suspension as the fifties opened were Connaught, HWM, OSCA and ERA. Among the new cars built for the 2½-litre formula in 1954, de Dion was adopted by Maserati for the 250F, by Lancia for the D50, by BRM for its P25 and by Vandervell Products for the new Vanwall. The late-arriving Aston Martin DBR4/250 also had a de Dion rear suspension. The Bugatti Type 251 went a step further, having de Dion suspension at the rear and a similar tubular dead axle at the front at the specific request of Roland Bugatti, who felt that this would be appropriate for a car bearing the Bugatti name.[11]

Notably, the people who had pioneered de Dion suspension in Grand Prix racing, Daimler-Benz, did not choose it when they introduced the W196 in 1954. Knowing that the axle tube's connection of the wheels led to undesirable bounce and tramp under some conditions, Daimler-Benz chose instead a low-pivot swing-axle layout, fully independent, sprung by torsion bars. With this independent rear suspension the Mercedes-Benz W196 joined Cooper, which had never used anything but all-independent suspension on its single-seater cars.

De Dion axles remained dominant through the mid-fifties. Mercedes-Benz's use of an all-independent rear suspension led to some experiments with similar layouts by Ferrari, but no adoption of the system at that time. In 1958, however, the fine Cooper performances started designers thinking about the merits of full independence at the rear.

Lotus used it for its Formula 2 car of 1957, which went Grand Prix racing in 1958. Gordini made the leap from live axle to full independence in the 1956 season. Ferrari brought an independent-rear car to the last race of 1959 and adopted independent rear suspension for its 1960 team cars. Cooper, admitted

In the chassis of the 250F Maserati the de Dion rear-axle tube passed forward of the differential. The Modena rumour mill had it that this layout was cribbed from the design of an experimental 1952 Ferrari, the first side-tanked 'Squalo' model.

---

11 Roland was the youngest son of Ettore Bugatti. He did his utmost to bring the Grand Prix project to fruition after Colombo had left Bugatti.

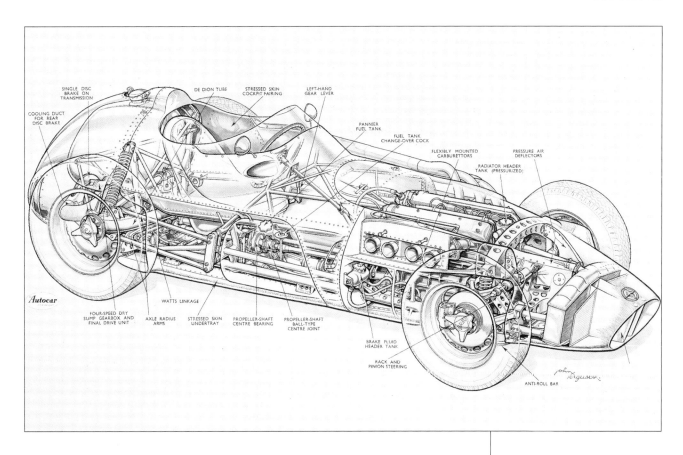

SINGLE DISC BRAKE ON TRANSMISSION

COOLING DUCT FOR REAR DISC BRAKE

DE DION TUBE

STRESSED SKIN COCKPIT FAIRING

LEFT-HAND GEAR LEVER

PANNIER FUEL TANK

FUEL TANK CHANGE-OVER COCK

FLEXIBLY MOUNTED CARBURETTORS

PRESSURE AIR DEFLECTORS

RADIATOR HEADER TANK (PRESSURIZED)

Autocar

FOUR-SPEED DRY SUMP GEARBOX AND FINAL DRIVE UNIT

AXLE RADIUS ARMS

WATTS LINKAGE

STRESSED SKIN UNDERTRAY

PROPELLER-SHAFT CENTRE BEARING

PROPELLER-SHAFT BALL-TYPE CENTRE JOINT

BRAKE FLUID HEADER TANK

RACK AND PINION STEERING

ANTI-ROLL BAR

Ferrari engineer Chiti, 'proved that if a good double-wishbone configuration was applied to both the front and rear suspension, you could obtain excellent results. This is what triggered off the revolution in this field.'

All the new rear-engined cars used independent rear suspension except one: Brian Naylor's JBW-Maserati, which retained de Dion suspension. It remained the exception, for the conversion to full independence at the rear was otherwise total by the end of the fifties. Thus was completed the transition that began with the Grand Prix Benz of 1923.

NEW CHALLENGES TO FRAMES

As racing car designers discovered during this decade, fully independent suspension makes special demands on the stiffness of a car's frame. With a live axle or de Dion tube holding the rear wheels parallel, high frame stiffness was not essential to obtain good handling. Frames needed to become much more rigid in torsion with the adoption of independent suspension. Loads on the frame were also increased by the achievement of higher cornering speeds thanks to the work of both Pirelli and Dunlop on tyre compounds giving greater cornering grip.

At the beginning of the fifties, Grand Prix car frames were like those of the late thirties: two large tubes with ladder-like connections between them. Only Cooper had a more three-dimensional frame concept. In the new cars built for 1954, frame design took a dramatic step forward. Lancia and Mercedes-Benz used small-diameter steel tubes placed wide apart to make full use of the depth of

A de Dion axle tube running forward of the rear transaxle was a feature of the design of the P25 BRM of 1956. It was sprung by concentric coil/damper assemblies. This four-cylinder BRM had a semi-monocoque frame construction.

the car body, giving the frame a truss-like structure which, when properly designed, is very stiff for its weight.

For his Lancia D50 space frame, designer Vittorio Jano went a step further: he used the cylinder heads of the V-8 engine as part of the upper structure of the frame. This was the first modern hint at a reversion to the pre-war practice of making the engine an active part of the car's frame. This feature was given up when the Lancias were taken over by Ferrari in 1956; we can attribute this as much to increased ease of servicing as to mistrust of the merit of this design solution.

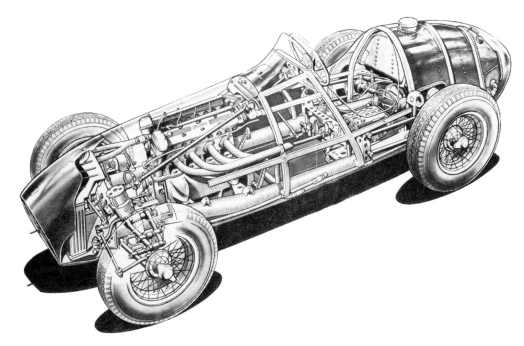

The main frame stiffness of the successful Type 500 Ferrari of 1952–53 was provided by its two large oval-section steel frame rails. A light superstructure supported the body and provided some additional overall rigidity.

Excellence in tubular frame design was exhibited by the W196 Mercedes-Benz of 1954–55. It used carefully placed small-diameter steel tubes in a shrewdly planned truss-type structure that was rigid in both bending and torsion.

At Lotus, Colin Chapman sought to deploy small-diameter tubes intelligently in the space-type frame of his Type 16 Grand Prix car of 1958–59. The need to be able to install and remove its engine did little for the integrity of its design.

One of the most elegant space frame designs of the fifties came from the drawing board of Colin Chapman for Tony Vandervell's Vanwall car. The first Vanwall of 1954 had a frame built by Cooper based on Ferrari principles.[12] This was replaced by Chapman's design in the 1956 Vanwall, laying a foundation for the 1957 and 1958 success of the Vanwall team.

Chapman himself used an intricate space frame design in his front-engined Lotus 16 of 1958–59, but had greater success with the much simpler layout of his rear-engined 1960 Lotus 18. Colin Chapman became the leading advocate of this more efficient type of frame, and in the sixties would be the first to render it obsolete by the introduction of the monocoque frame.

EMPHASIS ON AERODYNAMICS

Entirely peculiar to the fifties, and made impossible by later Grand Prix regulations, was intense experimentation with – and successful use of – fully enclosed bodies to reduce aerodynamic drag. Most designers were well aware that

---

12 In its suspension design and rear-mounted transaxle the first Vanwall was also directly derivative of current Ferrari practice.

Extensive analysis by Daimler-Benz demonstrated that a fully aerodynamic body could offer advantages for Grand Prix racing in some circuit conditions. This radical conception – seen at the Nürburgring – shattered the complacency of the Formula 1 world of 1954.

Only Britain's Connaught sought to follow the Mercedes-Benz lead with the design of a fully enclosed body for its B-type Grand Prix car, first raced in 1955. However, a conventional body proved more practical for the financially constrained Connaught team and its customers.

the exposed wheels of the conventional Grand Prix car greatly increased its drag. They knew that higher speeds would be achievable with enclosure of the wheels, in spite of the greater frontal area this would impose. Having verified this by wind tunnel tests before the war, in the fifties Mercedes-Benz decided to build its 1954 W196 with two types of body: open wheels for slower tracks where lightness counts, and fully enclosed for fast circuits where lower drag gives faster lap times.

Stupefaction greeted the first showing in March 1954 of the W196, with its fully enclosed body. Ultra-low and packed with machinery, it was clearly a car in another class from the 'Italian traditional' designs. Its July racing debut was equally impressive with a victory on the fast Reims track – ideal for the fully enclosed body. Daimler-Benz used the enclosed bodies in the next race, at Silverstone, because the open-wheeled bodies weren't ready yet. It made them its principal choice in only two other championship races: the Italian Grands Prix at Monza in 1954 and 1955, both of which were won by Fangio in the W196.[13]

---

13 At the race on the fast Barcelona circuit that ended the 1954 season, Mercedes-Benz practised with both body types, and elected to compete with the open body. At Monza in 1955 the difference was not great; Piero Taruffi finished close behind winner Fangio in an open-wheeled Mercedes.

The first competitor to follow the Mercedes-Benz lead was the small but progressive Connaught company in Britain. Introduced at the end of 1954, its new B-type Grand Prix car had a handsome, one-piece, fully enclosed body with a high fin behind the driver. In its 1955 race appearances the aerodynamic body seemed to offer no special advantage and was replaced by conventional bodywork. The sports-car-based Cooper-Bristol raced by Brabham in 1955 was another enclosed-wheel Grand Prix entrant of the era.

The Lancia D50 showed that Vittorio Jano had also considered the question of aerodynamic drag. Its fuel tanks were strut-mounted between the wheels to serve as fairings which usefully reduced drag. In mid-1955 these cars were given to Ferrari, which modified them for 1956 by blending the fairings into the sides of the body. For most of the 1957 entries of the Lancia-Ferraris, as they became known, the fairings were removed altogether.

The very fast Reims circuit, where lap speeds exceeded 120 mph, continued to attract aerodynamic experiments. Based on the results of tests with models in the Milan University wind tunnel, Maserati built a special 250F for the 1956 race with its wheels enclosed, apart from openings at the top. It practised at Reims and was tested at Monza, but it was not used in a race.

Vanwall brought a car to a non-championship race at Reims in 1957 with fully enclosed front wheels and rear 'fenders'. Made to a Frank Costin design, it showed little advantage and was not raced. The same held true of a later Cooper enclosed-body experiment for Reims. The effects of aerodynamic lift, not fully appreciated at the time, caused the unsatisfactory behaviour of some of these cars, and led to the abandonment of these closed-wheel ventures by the end of the fifties.

Vittorio Jano used the fuel tanks as drag-reducing aerodynamic fairings between the front and rear wheels of his 1954 Lancia D50. Mike Hawthorn is finding one of the V-8 Lancias quick but a handful at Oulton Park in 1955, where he placed second to the Maserati driven by Moss.

WHEEL AND BRAKE ADVANCES

If the front-mounted engine was a hallmark of the classical Grand Prix car, so too were bright-spoked wire wheels, usually by the Italian firm of Borrani. Their splined centre-lock hubs with knock-off retainer nuts allowed the wheels and tyres to be changed quickly in a pit stop at a time when tyres were not always able to last the length of a Grand Prix.[14] This was an important factor during 1957, when a Grand Prix had to run for 500 km or three hours, but it ceased to be essential in 1958 and afterwards, when the minimum race duration was reduced to 300 km or two hours.

The new British arrivals on the Grand Prix scene, having previously engaged principally in short-distance sprint racing, used bolt-on light-alloy disc wheels. Connaught did so, as did Cooper, which on its Cooper-Bristol used a wheel with an integral brake drum, scaled up from its Formula 3 cars – a modern tribute to Bugatti's innovation of the twenties. For its Cooper-Climax cars it separated the wheel from the brake; this would have been necessary later in any case to accommodate disc brakes.

The new BRM P25 of 1955 had Dunlop disc wheels with knock-off hubs. The Lotus single-seater of 1957 introduced that company's 'wobbly-web' design of light-alloy wheel. Similar wheels were adopted by Vanwall during 1958. By 1960 only Ferrari remained true to the wire-spoked wheel.

At Aintree in 1959 Harry Schell is hustling a P25 BRM to fourth place with its light-alloy Dunlop disc wheels equipped with three-eared knock-off caps. In the shorter races of 1958 and later, such quick-change hubs provided only needless extra weight.

Changes in wheels paralleled those in brakes, which were dramatic during the fifties. Drum brakes, still used during much of the decade, appeared in their most developed form on the Maserati 250F and the Mercedes-Benz W196, which in its 1954 edition had all four drum brakes mounted inboard on the chassis; those at the front were driven by universal-jointed shafts.[15] The capabilities of even the best drum brakes were limited, however. As Stirling Moss said of the 1955 Mercedes-Benz and its contemporaries: 'No one at that time was really using brakes to their limit; this in fact would have been impossible with the linings and drums then used.'

The disc brakes that arrived in racing in the early fifties were derived from aircraft techniques developed in America and Britain. In 1952 they were fitted and raced on cars from the previous Formula 1 that were still competing in Formula Libre events. Based on Goodyear patents, Tony Vandervell made his own disc brakes for his modified 4½-litre V-12 Ferrari, the Thinwall Special. BRM fitted Girling discs to its 1½-litre supercharged V-16.

The first car to use disc brakes in Grand Prix events was the Cooper-Alta Special built in 1953 by Cooper, Ray Martin and Alf Francis for Stirling Moss.

---

14 From 1953 these knock-off nuts generally had three instead of two ears, following Ferrari's introduction of three-eared nuts after seeing them in use at Indianapolis that year.

15 Juan Fangio was especially unhappy about the 1954 design, which had the inboard front brakes in the path of the heat thrown off by the radiator. He lobbied hard for the introduction of outboard front brakes, which Mercedes introduced on most versions of the W196 for 1955 and on the 1956 prototype of the 300SLR sports-racing car.

Moss, who had raced the disc-braked Jaguar sports cars in 1952, insisted that discs be fitted to the Special, with which he competed at Reims in 1953 without success. The Special had chassis faults that led to its abandonment, but in braking it had shown the way.

When the first Vanwall raced at Monza at the end of 1954 it was braked by the Vandervell-Goodyear discs. During that season BRM entered a 250F Maserati to which it had fitted Dunlop disc brakes and wheels; it was racing the Maserati until its own cars were ready. When the P25 BRM was shown in 1955 it was seen to have Lockheed disc brakes, with an unique feature at the rear: a single disc mounted on the transmission to brake both rear wheels through the differential. In spite of its faults, which included a tendency to collect dirt and oil, this was kept through the mid-engined P48 models to 1960. A pioneering feature of this BRM brake was internal vane cooling for the single rear disc.

In 1956 Maserati experimented inconclusively with disc brakes on the 250F it had bodied with fairings between the wheels. Dunlop discs were used, of a type which required a powerful servo to assist the driver in applying them. This turned out to be incompatible with the five-speed gearbox that was needed for best performance, so Maserati was unable to extract the desired benefit from discs, and reverted to its own highly developed drum brakes for its last Grand Prix cars of 1957 and 1958.

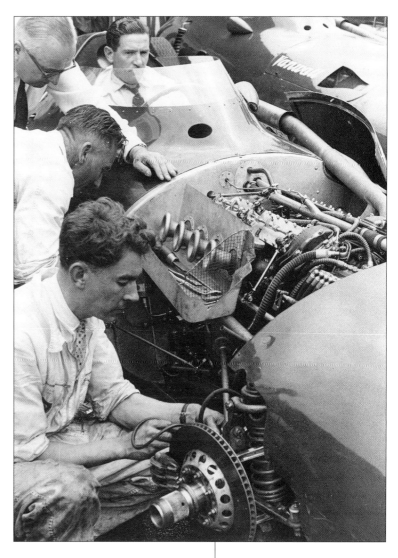

Vandervell's development of its own disc brakes, using Goodyear aircraft patents and designs, was a rare accomplishment in the Grand Prix world. Most competitors adopted disc systems engineered by Dunlop, Girling or Lockheed.

Adding to the disc-braked British Grand Prix contingent were the Coopers in 1957 and the Lotuses in 1958. In the Italian Grand Prix at the end of 1958 Ferrari tried discs on one car for the first time, installing a set that was patterned after the brakes that had been fitted to Peter Collins's road Ferrari. In 1959 and subsequently, all Grand Prix Ferraris were disc-braked. The conversion to these more consistent, fade-resistant brakes was complete.

DOMINANCE OF TRANSAXLES

In the thirties a new pattern for the arrangement of the elements of a Grand Prix car was created by both German and Italian entrants. They placed the transmission at the rear in unit with the axle gears in order to distribute more weight toward the rear of the chassis and improve traction. This transaxle layout was continued through the forties and used in most of the front-engined cars of the fifties. In fact, among the principal makes taking part after 1954 only Connaught and Gordini did not adopt the transaxle. Some, like Maserati, Lancia, Aston Martin and Ferrari in 1958 (influenced by Lancia), placed the gearbox

In the 250F Maserati the transaxle was placed transversely and offset to the right side of the car, providing a very compact arrangement at the rear and placing its weight low in the chassis. Final drive to the differential was by helical gears.

shafts transversely, while Vanwall, Lotus, Mercedes-Benz and BRM located them longitudinally. Rear-engined cars, of course, were all equipped with transaxles.

A deviation in Grand Prix design practice unique to the fifties was a sudden interest in synchromesh transmissions.[16] Synchromesh uses small clutches inside the transmission to synchronise the speeds of the gears being engaged. Introduced on normal road cars in the thirties to make gear engagement easier, this seemed a needless complication to racing car designers. In any case, they had skilled drivers at their disposal who were able to make smooth shifts without this crutch. In the fifties it was given a try in Formula 1.

No special attention was given to its use in the 2-litre Altas or the Type 251 Bugatti, but there was greater significance in the choice of Porsche-type synchromesh for the W196 Mercedes-Benz. The latter used the system to reduce the chance that a car could be damaged by its driver. Tony Vandervell, who greatly respected the work of the Stuttgart firm, had synchromesh installed in the transaxles of his Vanwalls. This did not have great appeal to his drivers, who hated the balky, heavy shift of the Vanwall. Apart from its use by Porsche in its single-seaters of 1961–62, synchromesh made an unlamented departure from the Grand Prix scene.

NATURALLY ASPIRATED ENGINE ADVANCES

The racing car formula rules of the fifties were framed to discourage supercharged cars, and in this they were successful. Only naturally aspirated cars took part in the championship races of this era. For a non-championship Formula 1 event at

---

16 Strictly speaking this is a trade name, originally spelled Synchro-Mesh. The one-word version describes the generic principle.

Pau in 1955, René Bonnet produced two little front-drive air-cooled twin-cylinder 750 cc DB single-seaters with Roots superchargers, but they were not remotely able to hold the pace and these DBs were not raced in this form again.

Although engineers concentrated totally on the unsupercharged engine during the fifties, only fitful progress was made in the perfection of the type. One reason for this was that four-cylinder engines were remarkably popular during these years. Not since before the First World War had so many four-cylinder engines been used, utterly reversing the trend that had seen eights and twelves become most numerous, even in sizes as small as 1½ litres, from the twenties until the forties.

Ferrari, with his 2-litre four designed by Aurelio Lampredi, was responsible for this trend. Designers could hardly overlook Ascari's success with the four-cylinder Type 500, which won sixteen championship races in 1952 and 1953. Ferrari enlarged his fours for the 2½-litre formula, but by 1955, with his cars quite outclassed, he welcomed the gift of the eight-cylinder D50 Lancias.

Connaught sought to make do with the Alta 2½-litre four, but it was not powerful enough, and the Connaught team was dissolved in 1957. The Vanwall engine was a four – in concept four short-stroke Norton 500 cc motorcycle engines placed in a row and mounted on a Rolls Royce military engine crankcase. In 2½-litre form it was developed to give the most power of any four-cylinder engine of the fifties, 285 hp at 7,400 rpm on alcohol fuel (308 hp with a nitromethane additive) and 270 hp at 7,500 rpm in 1958 pump petrol tune. By racing standards, however, these rates of crankshaft revolution were moderate, constrained as they were by the heavy reciprocating parts of these big fours. We recall that a 2-litre Mercedes eight was reaching the same rotational speed in 1924.

BRM also elected to develop a four-cylinder engine for the 1954 formula. It chose a short-stroke design with very large valves which, throughout the five-year racing life of the engine, resisted all attempts to make them reliable. Cooper and Lotus made good use of the Coventry-Climax four toward the end of the fifties, and Maserati and Ferrari fours were installed in Cooper chassis. The last to introduce a new four-cylinder engine for Grand Prix racing, until the eighties, was America's Scarab in 1960.

Equipped with fuel injection and dual ignition, the four-cylinder Alta engine powered all the Connaught racing cars of the 2½-litre formula. Alta engines were also used in the front of Cooper chassis, although with less success.

During the 2½-litre years, sixes enjoyed success, at first in in-line form in the 250F Maserati and later in V form in the Dino 246 Ferrari. The most successful eights were those of Lancias (V) and Mercedes-Benz (in-line); both factories withdrew from Grand Prix racing in 1955, thus ending their own development of the engines that should by rights have dominated the later years of the formula. (Ferrari persevered for two more years with the Lancia V-8.)

HAIRPIN VALVE SPRINGS

The fifties were notable for a craze that swept the world of Grand Prix engines: hairpin valve springs. The 'hairpin' spring in fact looks nothing like a hairpin. It much more closely resembles the springs used on clothespins. Used in pairs on opposite sides of the valve stem, each such spring consists of a single piece of spring wire which is bent at its centre and then wound into coils from which the bend at the centre and the two ends protrude. The curved central element of the spring engages the retaining collets at the top of the valve, while the two protruding ends of the wire are retained against the cylinder head surface.

Although generally called 'hairpin' springs, these valve springs in a Ferrari engine more correctly resemble 'clothespin' springs. They were fitted to all Ferrari engines from the outset until the end of the fifties.

Hairpin springs were popular for motorcycle engines, especially in the thirties, for a number of reasons. Most motorcycles had exposed valve springs; the hairpins allowed cooling air to flow more freely around the stem of the valve than coil springs did, especially when the latter were doubled. Their added bulk at both the sides of the valve was easy to accommodate on motorcycle singles and twins.

These qualities enhanced the basic merit of the hairpin spring, which is that the main mass of the spring is not part of the reciprocating mass of the valve/spring assembly. With a coil spring, the part nearest the cylinder head doesn't move at all, but the rest of the spring oscillates up and down, and is effectively part of the mass of the system that it is also trying to control.

In addition, hairpin springs can be short vertically, which in turn allows the valve stem to be shorter and thus the valve to be lighter. Their design, which stresses the spring steel in the bending mode rather than the torsion of the coil spring, applies a more constant closing force than the coil does.

With the technology of the time, engine designers found that these features in combination allowed hairpin-spring engines to gain satisfactory valve performance with less spring pressure. Alternatively, they could use hairpins to reach higher engine speeds safely with the same spring pressure.

Hairpin springs had rarely been used in automobile engines.[1] They were found in several Alfa Romeo engines of the thirties, including the exhaust valves of a two-stroke Alfa diesel engine. They were also used on the Type 512 flat-twelve and Type 162 135° V-16 engines built and tested by Alfa Romeo for racing (but never raced) during 1939–40.

An engineer who was familiar with these Alfa Romeo developments – which were highly secret at the time – was Gioachino Colombo. Thinking back to their work together on the Type 158 Alfa Romeo, in 1946 Enzo Ferrari asked Colombo to design his postwar car, the first true Ferrari. He introduced a feature that was highly exotic for an engine that was intended to serve both for racing and as the basis of a production series. He chose hairpin valve springs. These continued to be used for all Ferrari engines of all categories, racing and production, for a decade.

What was Colombo's motivation? In the postwar Ferrari project he was assisted by Giovanni Nasi, who had headed Alfa's diesel engine department and certainly knew of the two-stroke project. Colombo also mentioned in his memoirs that when designing the new engine, he 'kept in mind certain experiences in the world of motorcycling which interested me'. Hairpin valve springs were among those experiences.

---

1   A company with ample experience of motorcycle engines, BMW, used hairpin springs for the valve gear of the twin-cam 2-litre six-cylinder Type 318 engine it built experimentally in 1939 as a potential successor to the Type 328 sports-car six, which it had always regarded as a provisional stop-gap design. Only two prototypes were completed of the 318, which embodied one of the faults of the hairpin-spring layout: the springs impinged on space that was needed to smooth the flow of air into the inlet valves.

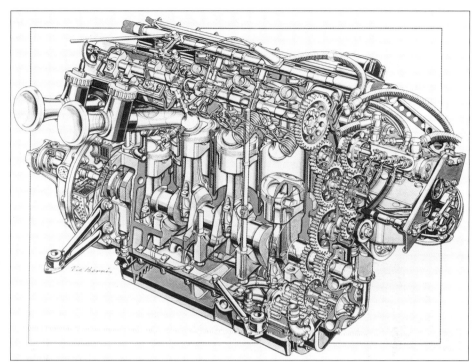

Exposed hairpin-type valve springs were fitted to the four-cylinder Vanwall engine in the tradition of the Norton motorcycle engine that inspired its configuration. Achieving adequate durability with these parts in the big four gave the Vandervell engineers many sleepless nights.

Another early hairpin adopter was Peter Berthon, designer of the 1½-litre BRM V-16. Former ERA engineer Berthon was clearly influenced strongly in the layout of the BRM by the Alfa Romeo Type 162 mentioned above.[2] His V-16 had the same V-angle, the same finger cam followers and the same hairpin springs as the Alfa.

Among the engineers on the BRM project was Harry Mundy. Moving to Coventry-Climax, Mundy specified hairpin springs for the ambitious 2½-litre FPE V-8 that Climax produced in 1953 for the new Grand Prix Formula. He managed to position them longitudinally rather than laterally so that they impinged less on the ports than was the case with the BRM. Nevertheless, getting good reliability from the springs was always a problem, and when Climax derived the FPF four from the V-8 it reverted to coil valve springs.

Maserati was a late adopter of hairpin springs, not using them for the 250F, but installing them in the new 2½-litre V-12 that it began racing in 1957. Inspired both by Ferrari practice and the Norton motorcycle engine that was the basis of its design, Vanwall used hairpin springs. Its design was a startling throwback to the first twin-cam Peugeots of the 1910s, with its springs out in the open air between the cam cases and the cylinder heads. For Vanwall, wrote Edward Eves:

> The valve gear was one of the biggest headaches, and all concerned must have rued the decision to use hairpin valve springs. All the British spring makers tried their hand at making springs that would stand the pounding [of the Vanwall's heavy valves], and so did Scherdel in Germany. Exotic materials, finely ground and finished, were used, but all of them failed eventually. The eventual solution was to run every spring on a rig for several hours before fitting it.

Problems like these contributed to a general disenchantment with hairpins by the end of the fifties. Beginning in 1959, Ferrari made a transition to coil springs. Advances in manufacturing methods and materials had improved the performance of coil springs, as had a better understanding of the dynamics of valve trains and cam-lobe design. From that time Formula 1 valve gear and springs changed little until the introduction by Renault in 1986 of pneumatically closed valves.

---

2   A likely source of cross-pollination in this case was the English engineering-consulting firm of Ricardo. Ricardo had consulted with Alfa chief engineer Wifredo Ricart and his team on the design of these new racing engines at the end of the thirties. At the end of a war in which Italy and Britain had been enemies, any such technology would have been seen by the victors as fairly exploitable.

Britain's BRM went from one extreme to the other by giving up its 1½-litre V-16 to build a four-cylinder 2½-litre engine for the 1954 Formula 1. It carried to an extreme the concept of a large bore and short stroke to allow large valves and matching Weber carburettors. The materials technology of the time was unable to cope with this concept.

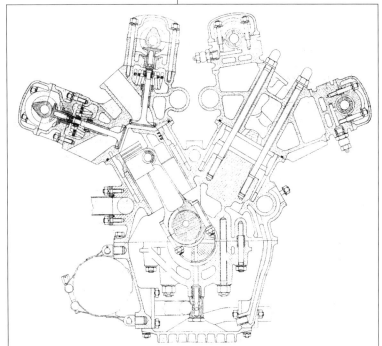

Hairpin-type valve springs were still in fashion in 1957 when Maserati introduced its 2½-litre V-12 with its banks at a 60-degree angle. With its 'downdraft' inlet ports it was the most powerful engine of the formula but the power was not necessarily available just when the Maserati drivers required it.

Twelves, which were so prominent in previous Grand Prix eras, were all but invisible in the fifties. Alfa-Romeo built but never raced its Type 160 2½-litre flat-twelve, designed for a front-engined four-wheel-drive chassis. In 1957 Giulio Alfieri introduced his Maserati V-12, which fitted into the 250F chassis. It made only a few appearances in 1957, Maserati's last season for works Grand Prix entries. Its 300 hp at some 10,000 rpm showed effectively at Monza at the end of 1957, where Jean Behra briefly pushed his low-chassis V-12 into the lead before retiring with overheating.

FOUR-VALVE HEAD ECLIPSED

Unsupercharged engine development was retarded by the almost complete, and to some extent arbitrary, eclipse of the four-valve cylinder head in Grand Prix racing during the fifties. Designers uniformly considered the hemispherical head with two valves to be ideal, and looked on the four-valve layout as an antique suitable only for the huge cylinders of the Indianapolis Meyer-Drake Offy.

The only Grand Prix cars with four-valve heads competing during the fifties were the 4CLT/48 Maseratis converted by Enrico Platé from their original supercharged 1½-litre trim to unblown 2 litres to take part in Formula 2 and, subsequently, the world championship in 1952. The best performance by one of these cars was sixth in the 1952 Swiss Grand Prix.

The fifties also represented a period of obsession with hairpin-type valve springs, popular on motorcycle engines, but until this period relatively rare in cars. They were thought to be advantageous in permitting shorter valve stems and reducing the spring mass that had to be moved together with the valve, but they were space-consuming and very sensitive to faults in manufacture.

At Ferrari, Lampredi had been highly partial to hairpin springs, and used them on his four-cylinder engines. They were also used by BRM, Vanwall and by Maserati on the V-12. After trials with hairpins, however, both Lancia and Coventry-Climax went back to coil springs, and so did Ferrari with his Dino V-6. By the end of the fifties the fad had run its course.

The other dramatic valve gear development of the fifties was the use by Mercedes-Benz of cams instead of springs to close as well as open the valves of its racing engines. Desmodromic valve gear, used just before and after the First World War, as related in Chapter Two, had long been forgotten when it was reinvented for the 1954 M196 engine. In the Mercedes-Benz racer it was used to prevent damage to the engine from inadvertent over-revving, and also to improve torque as well as horsepower by providing very rapid valve acceleration.

The Mercedes-Benz initiative sparked desmodromic experiments in other engineering offices. None, however, was able to devote to the project the resources and skills the Stuttgart company could dispose. Maserati built and tested a desmodromic six, but never raced it. OSCA experimented with the technique, as did BRM. The only other marque that raced with desmodromic valve gear in the fifties was one of the smallest, the American Scarab. Its four-cylinder engine used valve gear patterned very much after the Mercedes-Benz example, although without its sophistication of adjustment. It was the last to use the principle in Grand Prix racing.

INTRODUCING FUEL INJECTION

One technique that might have been expected to move rapidly ahead in an unblown era made only uncertain progress: fuel injection. Working closely with Ferrari and Maserati, Weber of Bologna perfected at the beginning of the fifties a carburettor with two straight throats served by a common float bowl. This provided near-unrestricted air flow to each cylinder and allowed the all-important adjustment to the length of the separate ram pipes to each inlet valve that gave optimum cylinder filling, with volumetric efficiencies in excess of 100 per cent, and permitted tailoring of power and torque curves. Consequently, the simple and efficient Weber carburettor was used on every world champion driver's mount during the fifties except Mercedes-Benz. And even Mercedes had used Webers on its engines in the early development stages.

RAM TUNING AND WEBER CARBURETTORS

From the early twenties until the forties it was taken for granted that first-rank racing cars in all categories would be supercharged. The first Formula 1 to seek equivalency between blown and unblown engines was introduced in 1938, with unsupercharged engines allowed 4½ litres and supercharged units 3 litres. After the war, Formula 1 kept the larger size for atmospheric engines and reduced the allowable limit for supercharged engines to 1½ litres. For the first time this ratio gave unblown engines an opportunity to compete for top honours.

Enzo Ferrari's was the first company to build new Formula 1 racing cars designed expressly to take advantage of the opportunities granted to unsupercharged engines.[1] Correctly, he perceived that the trend in Formula 1 racing

was towards the less costly and less troublesome unblown engine. Indeed, by building and racing his own 2½-litre four-cylinder single-seater as early as 1951 he did much to encourage the selection of that unsupercharged engine size for the new Formula 1 in 1954.

Between the wars a few pioneers, such as Harry Miller in America and Freddie Dixon in Britain,[2] had begun to realise that the successful extraction of power from an unsupercharged engine requires careful individual tuning of its inlet and exhaust tracts. Advantage must be taken of the natural resonances that occur in these tracts to create an over-pressure at the right moment in the combustion chamber to ensure that as much as possible of the fresh fuel/air mixture is packed in. This can only be achieved when each cylinder has its own separate ducting and fuelling system.

We take this for granted now, but it was relatively new science in the early fifties when the first modern atmospheric-induction racing engines were being designed. Italian competitors were able to pioneer in this important area as a result of their close relationship with Edoardo Weber's carburettor firm in Bologna. Maserati had used Webers since the early thirties, and Ferrari had worked

Unlocking the full potential of the unsupercharged Formula 1 engine required the genius of Edoardo Weber in the design of a horizontal carburettor that combined a pair of straight-through throats with a single central float bowl. These are seen fitted to an early Ferrari 2½-litre four-cylinder engine.

with Weber before the war on developing special carburettors for the supercharged Alfa Romeo competition cars. Weber was thus the successor to Claudel in the 1910s and Memini in the 1920s as the master of Grand Prix carburetion.

Ferrari's new four-cylinder car for Formula 2, the 2-litre Type 500, would need an individual ram-tuned inlet for each cylinder if it were to reach its full potential. Maserati was facing a similar challenge to get the best performance from its new twin-cam Formula 2 six-cylinder engine. To meet these needs Weber built a new horizontal carburettor that combined two straight-through throats with a single central float chamber.

---

1   Talbot-Lago racing cars had long competed under the unblown 4½-litre provision of the formula, but this had been simply by default; these were the types of engines that Tony Lago had available. OSCA and Gordini co-operated on the design of such an engine after Ferrari had shown the way forward.

2   Miller was by profession a carburettor expert as well as an engine genius. This helped him reach this conclusion. Dixon came from the world of racing motorcycles, where he was accustomed to seeing each cylinder equipped with its own inlet pipe and carburettor

A 2-litre Maserati six of 1953 is fitted with three Weber twin-throat carburettors. The long ram tubes are configured to assist the engine's volumetric efficiency through the middle of its speed range.

Some of the first such twin-throat Webers were used by unsupercharged six-cylinder sports-racing Alfas, although not with ram-tuned inlet piping. The first formula-car appearance of the large twin-throat Weber 50DCO carburettor was on 2 September 1951 in the non-championship Grand Prix at Bari, Italy. Two of them were used to feed Ferrari's new four-cylinder racing engine, which made its debut as a 2½-litre unit.

With their large 50 mm throats, these Webers were only suited to an engine of that size. The smaller-diameter units that were needed to feed the new 2-litre formula cars were not ready at the beginning of 1952. So Weber provided four individual 45DOE carburettors, each one feeding its individual cylinder. These were used through much of the successful racing career of Ferrari's 2-litre four-cylinder cars.

A special feature of the Weber design was an auxiliary central venturi that pre-emulsified the fuel/air mixture before it reached the main venturi. The main jet assemblies were completely surrounded by the float chambers, assuring a good supply of fuel under braking, cornering and acceleration. Under full-throttle conditions the accelerator-pump circuits took on an added high-speed-jet function.

Lancia used twin-throat Solexes at first for its D50, and later installed Webers as well. But Weber carburettors did not long remain an exclusively Italian speed secret. The Alta-powered HWM team heard about them during their jaunts to Italy and soon began fitting them. So did BRM to its new four-cylinder engine for the 2½-litre formula. France's Gordini could not abstain. Even Daimler-Benz fitted Weber carburettors to its new 1954 W196 Grand Prix car during testing and as a precaution in case its Bosch fuel injection didn't mature in time.

In the fifties Webers were standard wear for Maserati, Ferrari, BRM, Gordini and Climax-powered Formula 1 cars. Fuel injection was championed not only by Mercedes-Benz but also by British competitors Connaught and Vanwall, the latter using Bosch systems with the benefit of advice from Mercedes after its retirement from racing. By the early sixties fuel injection advanced toward the norm with the introduction of the Lucas system.

Webers, in the meantime, never lost their appeal. They continue to be the carburettors of choice for high-performance non-injected engines. And the principle of tuning the inlet-passage length to extract the best performance from an engine is widely accepted in power units for both road cars and racing cars.

A bird's-eye view of the 1958 Vanwall showed its four-cylinder layout and the pipework radiating from the Bosch fuel-injection pump at the front of the block. The Vanwall enjoyed considerable success in spite of its creator's decision to endow it with only four cylinders.

Downdraft inlet porting was a feature of the eight in-line cylinders of the Mercedes-Benz M196 engine of 1954–55. Welded-steel construction allowed the cylinder walls and the exhaust-valve guide to be finned for better heat dissipation to the cooling water.

It was not for want of trying. In the 2-litre era Connaught was one of the first to try injecting fuel, using the American Hilborn-Travers constant-flow system. Later it also tested, without great success, British SU injection on the Alta four. Stirling Moss arranged for SU injection to be installed on his privately owned 250F Maserati, but no great benefit was gained. The SU system was tried on the new P25 BRM four as well, but its erratic throttle response made it a non-starter.

At Maserati, Guilio Alfieri conducted tests on a system of his own based on a diesel-type injection pump that added some 20 hp at the peak (to 265 hp). However, he said, 'the power curve was too sharp, the power came in too hard and made the car difficult to control as the cornering power of the tyres of the time was really very small'. The system was raced several times in 1956 – Moss won with it at Goodwood – but the effort to develop it was too great in the midst of a racing season, and it was set aside.

Only two marques in the fifties used fuel injection effectively. One was Mercedes-Benz, which did so as a follow-through from the pre-war experiments it had conducted in co-operation with Bosch. Daimler-Benz also used injection during the war in its V-12 aero engines. In its M196 engine, fuel was injected through an aperture in the cylinder wall and squirted towards the exhaust valve. By 1955 this system was performing well in the roller-bearinged M196 eight, which delivered 290 hp at 8,500 rpm from a fuel mix of 25 per cent methanol with gasoline and benzol.

As early as 1952 Tony Vandervell started working with Bosch to obtain fuel injection for his Vanwall four. But his systems squirted fuel into the inlet ports, not directly into the cylinders. After Mercedes-Benz retired from racing at the end of 1955 it made some of its know-how available to Vandervell. When many teething troubles were overcome – including breakage of injection pumps and throttle linkages on the vibratory Vanwall four – Bosch injection was made to work very well in the Vanwall, contributing significantly to its success.

At the end of the fifties the Scarab used Hilborn injection, and Aston Martin made a disappointing trial with Lucas fuel injection, which, however, would have a part to play in the coming decades.

ROLE MODEL

In 1960 a car was built that summed up the state of the Grand Prix art as it stood at the end of the fifties. It used a Lotus 18 chassis, rear-engined, with a space frame, all-independent suspension and disc brakes and wheels. It was powered by a fuel-injected Vanwall engine. This car, built as an experiment by Vandervell, embodied all the many advances that had taken place in a dramatic decade. That it never raced in a championship Grand Prix is not important. Its features would prove their worth many times over in the years to come.

At a rainy Silverstone in 1960 John Surtees drove the rear-engined Vanwall that incorporated many of the technical characteristics that would feature in the Grand Prix cars of the coming decade. Trailing it was one of the last of the classic Grand Prix cars, a Reventlow Scarab.

WELL DONE, TRINTIGNANT

A Second Grand Prix Win This Season
for Rob Walker's Cooper - Climax

ONCE AGAIN Monaco's sunny, colourful, theatrical Grand Prix has opened the European season—a season which, traditionally, is anticipated by the Argentine G.P. in January; equally true to tradition, the race was spectacular to a degree found on no other circuit in the world. As the cars raced through the streets, the shops, hotels and houses of the uninhibited little Principality, and round by its sparkling, blue harbour, it was as difficult as ever to believe one's eyes—and ears.

By no chance of fate, but because it was faster on this circuit than the opposing Ferraris, and more reliable than ten of the 16 starters in the race, Rob Walker's 1,960 c.c. Cooper-Climax, driven by Maurice Trintignant, won the day; having already won the Argentine G.P. this season, Rob Walker is in the unique position of being the only private owner ever to have won two successive

grandes épreuves—a remarkable record. It was Trintignant's second success in this event since the war, the first being for Ferrari in 1955, and—immensely heartening to British enthusiasts—it was the fourth successive grande épreuve to be won by a British car. As ever, the race took a tremendous toll of cars, only six finishing out of 16—among them one of the two B.R.M.s—but all three Vanwalls, undoubtedly, on practice showings Britain's main hopes, retired through mechanical trouble early in the race.

Maurice Trintignant, twice winner of the Monaco G.P. since the war

RESULTS
(100 laps of 1.9-mile circuit; 199 miles)
1. Cooper-Climax. (M. Trintignant), 2hr 52min 27.9sec, 67.98 m.p.h.
2. Ferrari (L. Musso), 2hr 52min 48.1sec.
3. Ferrari (P. Collins), 2hr 53min 6.7sec.
4. Cooper-Climax (J. Brabham), 97 laps.
5. B.R.M. (H. Schell), 91 laps.
6. Lotus-Climax (C. Allison), 87 laps.
   Fastest lap (record): Ferrari (J. M. Hawthorn), 1min 40.6sec, 69.93 m.p.h. (fastest practice lap, Brooks, Vanwall, 1min 39.8sec, 70.22 m.p.h.).

The Practice Periods

VANWALLS, running in their first G.P. of the season—and, indeed, their first race—brought four cars: Moss' (No. 28), Brooks' (No. 30), Lewis-Evans' (No. 32), and a fourth car without an engine. Subsequently, an engine was flown out for this car, but the aircraft crashed on the way. Serious enough was

Wheels spinning, raucous exhausts echoing out across the harbour, the sixteen starters get away from the grid, in the shadow of the fir trees that line the pits. In the distance is the Gasometer hairpin

With the yachts and blue harbour in the background, Jean Behra's B.R.M. comes round at the end of the first lap—in the lead, a lead that was to last for 26 of the 100 laps

the loss of the engine, but more serious still was that of the fuel injection pump, for it is through the development of this critical component, since the change-over from free fuel to 100-130 pn Avgas, that Vanwalls have been so slow in starting.

During the Thursday afternoon practice session Brooks, in No. 30, tied with Behra's B.R.M. for fastest lap in 1min 40.8sec; thus the two drivers shared the £100 prize for fastest lap of the first period. Moss, unhappy about his car's handling under braking, and suffering from tummy troubles, could do no better than 1min 46.7sec; he did, however, lap in 1min 42.4sec in Brooks' No. 30. It was, unfortunately, the drivers' times in their own cars that qualified for the sixteen starting grid positions, and Moss' put him 14th on the list. Lewis-Evans' best time was 1min 43.5sec.

Both Moss' and Brooks' cars were fitted with new, light-alloy disc wheels to reduce unsprung weight. These were knock-off at the rear and bolt-on in front —a somewhat unexpected arrangement as, with the many kerbs round the circuit, it is the front wheels that are most likely to become damaged, and these would take about ten minutes to change. The cars were also fitted with new, extractor-type exhaust systems.

On Friday, when the practice started at 5.45 a.m., Brooks did a lap in 1min 39.8sec in his own No. 30; this remained unbeaten, and secured for him pole position on the grid. Moss managed to get No. 28 round in 1min 45.4sec, and Lewis-Evans improved his time to 1min 41.8sec.

During Friday, however, the engine of Moss' No. 28 was removed and fitted to Brooks' car, No. 30; at the same time, Moss' racing number (28) was transferred to the erstwhile No. 30. Brooks' engine, from this car, was transferred to the engine-less spare car, together with Brooks' number, 30. The reason for this game of musical chairs was that Brooks' engine occasionally spluttered on pick-up after corners, and Moss, as No. 1 driver, was given first choice.

On Saturday afternoon, Moss, still unwell, lapped in his new car in 1min 42.3sec. Neither Brooks nor Lewis-Evans improved on on their times of the second period, so that in the list of qualified drivers, Brooks came first (1min 39.8sec), Lewis-Evans seventh (1min 41.8sec), and Moss eighth (1min 42.3sec).

B.R.M.s brought three cars—Behra had a brand-new one about which he could not speak highly enough, and in which his time of 1min 40.8sec earned second position on the list of qualified drivers; Schell had a 1958 car in which he lapped in 1min 43.8sec during the first period, ensuring for himself a place on the grid; the third, practice, car was one of the 1957 Casablanca-type models. After Behra's success during the first period, B.R.M.s did not appear during Friday; on Saturday neither he nor Schell improved on their Thursday's times, which qualified them for second and eleventh positions on the list.

Cooper Strength

No fewer than four Coopers turned up for practice—two works cars (Brabham, No. 16, and Salvadori, No. 18), and two from Rob Walker's stable (Trintignant, No. 20, and Flockhart, No. 22). Brabham's car was fitted with the new 2.2-litre Climax engine, and all the rest with 1,960 c.c. versions. During the first period Trintignant lapped in 1min 42.2sec, putting him third on the list, and Brabham in 1min 42.5sec.

During the second period both Brabham and Salvadori lapped in 1min 41sec, making them equal third on the final table of qualifications, and Trintignant lapped in 1min 41.1sec, gaining him fourth place; as none of these times was improved during the Saturday session, the first five positions on the grid were taken by British cars (Brooks, Vanwall; Behra, B.R.M.; Brabham, Cooper; Salvadori, Cooper; Trintignant, Cooper). What is more, all these—and, in fact, the next three (Hawthorn, Ferrari; Lewis-Evans, Vanwall; Moss, Vanwall)—bettered the existing lap record of 1min 42.4sec set up

by Fangio's Mercedes-Benz in 1955— though this was due in part to the fact that the chicane had been widened, which was worth about 2sec a lap.

Lotus brought two works cars (Allison and Hill), both with 1,960 c.c. engines. Though a 2.2-litre engine was flown out, it was not used; Graham Hill was unfortunate enough to damage his car during Friday's practice, and the mechanics burnt much midnight oil repairing it; time was short and it was thought better to leave things as they were. Both cars qualified to start, Hill's 1min 45sec being recorded on the Thursday, and Allison's 1min 44.6sec on the Friday.

Nine Maseratis—all in the hands of private owners, since the works have withdrawn from racing—were down on the entry list. Of these, Godia's should have been fastest; it is the slightly shorter chassis version, built for Fangio last season; as it was, this car did not even qualify. Gould tried hard in the Centro-Sud car with which Gregory finished third at Silverstone (the car being virtually untouched since then), but could not get near a qualifying lap time. He did a few laps in Gerini's car, gradually bettering his times—1min 55sec, 1min 53sec and 1min 51sec—before he was told to give it back.

Marie-Teresa de Filippis did an astonishing number of laps both on Thursday and Friday, getting down to 1min 48.8sec; on Saturday a piston broke, scattering the track with oil, so that was that. This car had been, in fact, the first of the 12-cylinder conversions; because of the demand this season for secondhand 250Fs, Maseratis have had to scrape the barrel to satisfy all customers, and had fitted a six-cylinder engine, retaining the 12, at the factory. Of the formidable strength of Maseratis, only two qualified to start —Scarlatti's (1min 44.7sec) and Bonnier's (1min 45sec).

Four Ferraris were entered (Collins, Hawthorn, Musso and von Trips), and all four qualified. All were new Dino 246 cars, fitted for the first session with Perspex windscreens round the protruding air intakes, and subsequently with Perspex hardtops. After the first session the gear ratios were changed, as they were too high for the tight circuit. Handling did not appear to be quite right, the cars seeming to suffer from a considerable understeer; it is noteworthy that the only Ferrari G.P. cars that appeared to handle really well were those taken over from Lancias. Mike Hawthorn's time of 1min 41.5sec gained him sixth place on the grid, Collins' 1min 42.4sec ninth, Musso's 1min 42.6sec tenth, and von Trips' 1min 44.5sec put him twelfth on the list.

In addition to this strong field of challengers for starting positions, there were two 1,500 c.c. formula 2 Oscas—looking very strange indeed with their enclosing, two-seater bodywork. These, driven by Cabianca and Piotti, lapped in 1min 52sec and 1min 52.4 respectively, and failed to qualify. The Connaughts also were too slow.

Race Day

AS the last half-hour before the race ticked by in brilliant sunshine, an enormous cluster of coloured balloons was released, and soared into the blue sky. . . . Prince Rainier and his Princess drove round the circuit in a large, open car, pulling up in front of the Royal stand . . . and the 16 starters were wheeled out to the grid: British racing green predominant—the front two rows were uninterrupted green, the third row having Hawthorn's red Ferrari to add colour. Of the 16 cars lined up, ten were British, and ten were driven by British drivers—a state of affairs that has never before occurred in a *grande épreuve*. After the engine reshuffle, all the Vanwalls were fitted with Lotus-type disc wheels.

From the turmoil at Gasometer hairpin immediately after the start, Behra's B.R.M. emerged in the lead, followed by Brooks' Vanwall . . . Brabham's Cooper . . . Moss' Vanwall . . . Trintignant's Cooper . . . Lewis-Evans' Vanwall—and the first of the red cars, Mike Hawthorn's Ferrari, lying seventh. There had been all but an "incident" at the hairpin, when Salvadori's Cooper and one (two, some

say) of the Vanwalls touched; at the end of the lap Salvadori came in with "one-wheel steering"; a track rod had become detached in the mêlée. The first standing lap—as unbelievable as ever, with the cars tearing through the narrow streets and their exhausts echoing across the sunny harbour—was covered in 1min 53.8sec.

While Salvadori stood at the pit for well over a couple of laps, Behra held his lead; Hawthorn, driving on top of his form, began to climb up through the field —sixth on the second and third laps, fifth on the fourth, fourth on the fifth, sixth and seventh, and third on the eighth, putting Moss' Vanwall, which had in the mean-

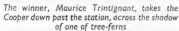
The winner, Maurice Trintignant, takes the Cooper down past the station, across the shadow of one of tree-ferns

time passed Brabham's Cooper, back into fourth place.

Lewis-Evans' Vanwall, having dropped back to 10th position, came into the pits at the end of the 12th lap to retire. The official reason was that the pressurized header-tank had expanded, binding the steering column. However, when head mechanic Derek Wootton wheeled the car away, there seemed to be about a third of a turn's free movement on the steering wheel—which may have resulted from the Gasometer hairpin incident at the start; the air intake at the front of the car was dented. By now the order was Behra, Brooks, Hawthorn, Moss, Trintignant, Brabham and Musso duelling for sixth place, Collins, Trips, Schell, Bonnier, Allison (Lotus), Scarlatti, Hill and Salvadori.

Soon Hawthorn, on his magnificent drive, began to challenge Brooks' second place and, six laps later (lap 18), he moved up behind Behra.

After only three laps of chasing Hawthorn, Tony Brooks' Vanwall was out of the race. It was suffering a loss of power —which, no doubt, made Hawthorn's move into second place easier—and, as the engine began to sound sick, rather than wreck it Brooks stopped on the climb up into the town.

In fact the trouble was no worse than a sparking plug that had fallen out, but to fit it himself meant disqualification as work may be carried out only at the pit; restarting was possible only by running backwards downhill—also rewarded by disqualification, for it is not permitted to proceed in the opposite direction to the race. So Brooks was left with no alternative but to call it a day, and the second of the Vanwalls dropped out.

On lap 21 Brabham, lying eighth, brought the 2.2-litre Cooper in to the pit with the front anti-roll bar adrift. This was refitted in 3min 1sec, and he rejoined

On the twisting descent from the Casino Square down to the water's edge, Mike Hawthorn's Ferrari, which held the lead for nine laps, prepares to lap Cliff Allison's Lotus

MONACO G.P. . . .

the race in 13th place, ahead of Salvadori; a lap later Behra, still leading, though only by 3.3sec, had lapped the three tail-enders. By now many cars had acquired "white-wall" tyres by clipping the white-washed kerbs. Soon Scarlatti's Maserati was to retire after a spectacular blow-up near the pits.

Behra's lead lasted until the end of the 27th lap when, as the leaders came through the narrow tobacco kiosk corner at the start of the pits "straight," it was a red car in front, Mike Hawthorn had moved up from seventh place in a quarter of the race.

The B.R.M. stopped at the pit for only 15sec, but it was enough to drop it back to third place. Two laps later it was in again—and, a lap later, in again, to retire this time; the central, rear disc brake had once more given trouble.

At the end of the next lap, Schell, lying 9th, was called in to hand over his car—but this, too, was running badly, and it was decided to save time by letting him carry on. A lap later and he was in again, a carburettor needle having stuck, causing flooding and wetting the plugs. The plugs were changed, and Schell rejoined the race in final position.

While all this had been going on, Moss had managed to bring the Vanwall up into the lead, passing Hawthorn's Ferrari during the 32nd lap. Hawthorn went all-out to retake his lead, tailing the Vanwall for almost seven laps—almost, for during the 38th, Moss slowed and as they came back to the pits it was the Ferrari in front again, and Moss, to everyone's horror, stopped at the pit. Quietly he climbed out of the car, and the mechanics went to work on it. One could not help but admire his coolness when the second event of a World Championship which he already led was at stake.

After a few minutes the electric starter was connected up and switched on; the Vanwall engine popped and banged; then the starter was taken out and the car wheeled away. A valve cap—"jampot"—had broken, increasing the clearance between valve stem and cam follower so that the valve was not opening. Thus, the third and last Vanwall was out of the

Tony Brooks (Vanwall), chased by Hawthorn's Ferrari, swings round the narrow Tobacco Kiosk corner on the approach to the pit area. A few laps later both these cars were out of the race

race; and, by now, every green car save Hill's Lotus and Trintignant's Cooper had been at the pits for one reason or another; Scarlatti's Maserati had retired, but the four Ferraris and Bonnier's Maserati were free from trouble so far.

Hawthorn re-took his lead some 13sec ahead of Trintignant's Cooper, now in second place. Third was Musso's Ferrari, followed by Collins' and von Trips' Ferraris and Bonnier's Maserati. At some distance came Hill (Lotus), Brabham (Cooper), Allison (Lotus), Salvadori's Cooper and Schell (B.R.M.); only 11 remained of the 16 starters, with the race not yet half run.

Suddenly, as they came round to complete the 47th lap, it was Trintignant in the lead—and no Hawthorn. After his wonderful drive, the casing of the fuel pump had cracked and come adrift, and the Ferrari was out of the race. Trintignant led by some 45sec, and out went the signal

to Musso (second), Collins (third), and Trips (fourth) to increase speed. Though both Musso and Collins were clearly doing their utmost to catch the Cooper, they made no appreciable difference to the gap —42.4sec, 41.6, 40.1, 40.3, 40.5, 43.4sec, thus it varied between the 53rd and 69th laps.

With this sole British car—and a privately owned one at that—battling against the Ferraris, it required only that Trintignant should suffer mechanical trouble for the race to become a 1, 2, 3 Ferrari victory; and the Ferraris have proved reliable so far this season. Very slowly the gap decreased; at one time it was down to 27.3sec, but never, despite their highly spirited efforts, did the Ferraris look like catching.

But for this tension, the latter half of the race lacked incident; the order settled down to Trintignant, Musso, Collins, Trips, Bonnier, Hill, Brabham, Schell and Allison—who had spun the Lotus and lost several places. Hill's Lotus dropped out with a broken half-shaft on the 69th lap, letting Brabham into sixth place; Bonnier's Maserati took to the pavement close to the Casino, burst a couple of tyres, and retired, letting Brabham up into fifth place, Schell into sixth, and Allison into seventh—seven left out of 16 by the 72nd lap.

With only nine of the 100 laps still to run, von Trips' Ferrari, which had been sounding rough for some time, coasted to the pit with a seized engine; Musso, for a lap or two, came round pointing at his fuel filler, but completed the race without coming in, and Trintignant sat out in front, holding off the challenge.

Six cars finished the race, four of them British.

To win this most taxing of all Grand Prix races is evidence of sound and thorough preparation by Alf Francis; in addition, and demonstrated in full at Buenos Aires, Rob Walker's race management is shown to be first class.

Mike Hawthorn, who, after driving a brilliant race, was put out by a cracked fuel pump, takes the Ferrari Dino 246 along the harbour's edge, past the pit area

CHAPTER SEVEN

POSTSCRIPT TO THE CLASSIC ERA

It is, of course, logical to put the engine at the rear (or between the axles: central-engined is the correct term) – it avoids the difficulty of running the drive-shaft past the driver, and the steering column past the engine; it is also a saving in weight – as the 100 lb weight reduction in the rear-engined BRM demonstrates – and reduces the frontal area. When an engine has reached its peak of development, and there is little more power to be coaxed out of it, this is the only way to increase performance. It remains, now, for John Cooper to move his engines to the front!

Peter Garnier, *The Autocar*, 18 September 1959

The appeal of the classic front-engined Grand Prix cars is durable and profound. Whenever and wherever they appear – at shows, vintage races, demonstrations, in articles and books – these great cars attract both attention and admiration. They are the classic beauties of the century – the 3-litre Ballot, the 1921 Duesenberg, the Type 35 and 59 Bugattis, the 1½-litre Delage, the Maserati 8CTF and 250F, the Alfa Romeo Type 159, the Ferrari Supersqualo, the Mercedes-Benz W154, the Lancia D50. These are only the most outstanding of the magnificent cars that populated the first fifty-plus years of Grand Prix racing.

These pages have been dedicated to the evolution of these racing cars and to the final chapter, at the end of the fifties, that saw them supplanted by the new generation of mid-engined Grand Prix racers.[1] These in turn encouraged the design and production of mid-engined sports-racing cars. Mid-engined design is now the norm for sports-racers, although American Panoz entries were showing at the end of the nineties that a well-designed front-engined car could still offer stiff competition.

Roadgoing sports cars moved to mid-placed engines as well, starting with cars like the Lamborghini Miura, Ferrari Dino and de Tomaso Pantera. In this category, however, the mid-engined car has not achieved the domination that it has among racing cars. Front-engined Jaguars, Ferraris, Aston Martins, Vipers, Corvettes and Maseratis still express the long-bonneted look of the classic Grand Prix cars and the great road cars that were associated with them in their salad days.

---

1 In American Indianapolis-car racing the transition took longer, after its initiation by Cooper and Lotus entries. By the end of the sixties the American racing car was mid-engined as well.

Shockingly advanced for the late forties, the Grand Prix racing car designed for Cisitalia by Porsche was an un-raced masterpiece. Had it competed with adequate backing it might have accelerated the arrival of the rear-engined era in Formula 1 by more than a decade.

Thus we have no reason to look back with any sense of regret at the decades during which Grand Prix cars were front-engined. Quite the contrary. But could they have made an earlier transition to mid-engined design? This is a question worthy of our attention.

LIBERATION OF ENGINES IN FRONT

All the first cars, and the first racing cars as well, had their engines under the floorboards, close to the rear axle for convenient connection by chains or belts. Benz racing cars of 1899 and 1900 followed this principle, including the flat-four-powered car of the latter year.[2] In America, Winton built a racing car with a massive single-cylinder under-floor engine; it took part in the Gordon Bennett Trophy race of 1900.

Three liberating influences led to the front-engined racer thereafter. One was Panhard's placement of its engines in the front of the chassis in 1891, and its success in racing with this arrangement from 1894. Out in front, there was no constraint on an engine's size. A second influence was the ease of cooling a front-mounted engine. Efficient cooling was a major preoccupation for the early auto engineers. And the third influence was Daimler's introduction of the pressed-steel chassis frame. This allowed longer chassis, and thus longer and larger engines.

Grand Prix car designers cheerfully exploited all these opportunities. Bonnet lengths stretched out to accommodate the in-line eights that powered successful racing cars through the twenties, thirties and forties. In-line sixes enjoyed a

Light, aerodynamic and efficient, the mid-engined Benz Grand Prix car convincingly demonstrated the merits of a racer with its engine placed behind the driver in 1923. One of its drivers was instrumental in convincing Ferdinand Porsche to adopt a mid-engined layout for the Auto Unions of the thirties.

2 Founder Karl Benz halted these excesses with a warning to his board in 1901 that motoring progress was being threatened by 'the newly prominent passion for surpassing others in speed in competitions, for vying with fast trains, thereby wantonly endangering the lives of those people driving as well as those using the roads'.

vogue as well, although only in the fifties. V-12 and V-16 engines also lived under long bonnets in the twenties, thirties and forties.[3] These trends were paralleled in the designs of the great luxury cars of these years, from Duesenbergs to Cadillacs, Hispanos and Isottas.

In the twenties, however, forward-looking engineers began having second thoughts. Aviation was the exciting new technology, and from it came an awareness of aerodynamics and its effect on the performance of vehicles moving through the air. We saw the impact of this awareness on the Grand Prix Fiats, Bugattis, Benzes, Ballots and Voisins of the early twenties. But road car designers were considering aerodynamics too, and some of them were concluding that a low-drag shape was best achieved by putting the engine in the rear.

Rear-engined road cars were planned and built in most countries. In Britain Oliver North and Sir Charles Dennistoun Burney were rear-engine advocates, as were Emile Claveau and Jean Andreau in France. In America John Tjaarda and Bill Stout argued the case for engines in the rear, as did Edmund Rumpler in Germany. Rumpler's ideas were the direct inspiration for the rear-engined Benz racing cars of 1923.

FROM BENZ TO AUTO UNION

For many engineers, however, moving the engine to the rear seemed to add rather than reduce complication. If the radiator remained in the front it had to be piped to the rear engine. Gear-shift linkage was awkward to arrange. Where should the fuel tank go? The spare wheel? Luggage space? Worst of all, a rear engine usually called for an independent rear suspension – this at a time when independent suspensions of any kind were *terra incognita* for car designers.

Engine length was a problem too during the heyday of the in-line eight. This would have contributed to an awkward automobile. Although some production cars already had shorter V-8 engines, the layout would remain virtually unknown for racing engines until the thirties, and then be embraced only by Maserati (and in 1939 by Mercedes-Benz for a Voiturette) in Europe.

The Benz Tropfen-Wagen, with its compact in-line six, coped adequately with most of the challenges facing the mid-engined racing car engineer. In spite of being well down on power to the supercharged opposition, it performed creditably in its only Grand Prix in 1923.

Converted to a sports car configuration, the Benzes were very successful in their class through the twenties. Awareness of their merits by their frequent driver, Adolf Rosenberger, Ferdinand Porsche's business partner, led directly to the mid-engined configuration of the P-Wagen for Auto Union. And Mercedes-Benz thought well enough of the idea to produce both sports cars and road cars with rear engines in the thirties.[4]

That a mid-mounted engine could contribute to a light and efficient racing car was conclusively demonstrated by the V-16 Auto Union. In its original form, however, the Auto Union suffered from its use of a simple swing-axle rear suspension. It continued with this layout from 1934 to 1937, while Mercedes-Benz gave it up in favour of a de Dion rear suspension – keeping the drive wheels vertical to the road surface – in 1936 and 1937. This gave the Mercedes cars a handling advantage.

---

3   The Auto Union was unique in placing its V-16 engine under a long bonnet at the rear of the car.

4   The road cars had their engines overhung behind the rear wheels, in the manner of the Czech Tatras and the later Volkswagen, while the 1½-litre Type 150 sports cars were mid-engined.

The mid-engined Auto Union of 1938–39 was a well-developed and effective Grand Prix racing car. Ironically, in the thirties Mercedes-Benz built and sold rear-engined production cars while Auto Union's four marques did not.

Torsion-bar springing was one of the least exotic features of the Type 512 Alfa Romeo of 1940, with its flat-twelve supercharged 1½-litre engine. With its spindly frame and far-forward driving position it did little credit to the concept of the mid-engined racing car.

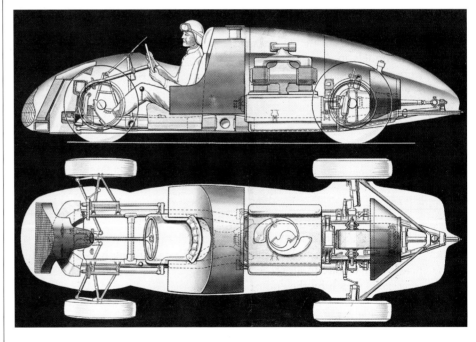

Confirmation of the disadvantage suffered by the Auto Union was given by Hans Stuck before the race at Brno in Czechoslovakia at the end of the 1937 season, as related by Laurence Pomeroy Jr:

When the Mercedes-Benz team had ended their official practice he was invited to try one of the W125 cars on which the fastest practice [lap] had been put up by Lang at 93.8 mph. After only one lap to gain experience of the car Stuck did a circuit at an average of 94.2 mph without, as he has explained, taking more risks than were normal in his previous experience with Auto Unions.

Although Mercedes had fought back well in 1937, Auto Union had enjoyed a good season in 1936. Soon thereafter, when it was time to design new cars for the 1938 Grand Prix formula, mid-mounted engines were given deeper consideration. In a March 1937 meeting the Daimler-Benz directors were shown two possible mid-engined layouts by their new engineering consultant, Ferdinand Porsche. One had the gearbox overhung behind the rear axle gears, and the other, giving more balanced weight distribution, placed the gearbox between the engine and the final-drive gears.[5]

By this time Auto Union was so closely identified with the mid-engined racing car that Daimler-Benz could hardly have adopted it even if it was convinced it was the better layout – which Daimler wasn't. It liked neither its forward driving position nor its concentration of masses toward the centre of the chassis. Ironically, however, Mercedes-Benz was a producer of rear-engined passengers cars in the thirties, while all the models in Auto Union's four brands were front-engined, and some of these (DKW, Audi Front) were front-drive as well.

A rear view of the chassis of Porsche's Type 360 design for Cisitalia revealed its side-mounted fuel tanks and the nearly parallel links guiding its rear hubs. A lever just under the steering wheel allowed the driver to select four-wheel drive when required.

MID-ENGINE MOMENTUM BUILDS

Drawing on its internal engineering resources, Auto Union produced its new Type D for 1938, a car that addressed many of the drawbacks of its predecessor. De Dion rear suspension replaced the swing axles. By fitting a shorter V-12 engine and placing much of the fuel tankage along the car's flanks, the driver's position was moved more towards the centre of the car, giving him a better feel for the chassis as a whole. In all respects the Type D was a soundly realised mid-engined racing car which by the end of 1938 was the equal of its Mercedes-Benz opposition. Only superhuman efforts by Mercedes over the winter – and during the season itself – restored their superiority in 1939.

By now the merits of the mid-engined layout for competition cars were beginning to win some converts. The Porsche office used it for the Type 114 sports car it intended to manufacture on its own account, designed in 1938-39.[6] We recall that Alfa Romeo designed and built a mid-engined racing car for the Voiturette formula in 1940, the Type 512; it had also begun building sports-racing cars to the same pattern. Planning its own new car for the same 1½-litre

---

5   Both designs still had swing-axle rear suspension – an apparent blind spot of the Porsche design office.

6   The Type 114 was to have been powered by a V-10 engine of 1½ litres – the first time that this layout, later universal in Grand Prix cars, was proposed for a high-performance car.

A regrettable non-starter in racing of the early 1950s was the French Sacha Gordine. One of Formula 1 racing's most intriguing might-have-beens, the Sacha Gordine reached an advanced stage of completion but was never driven in anger.

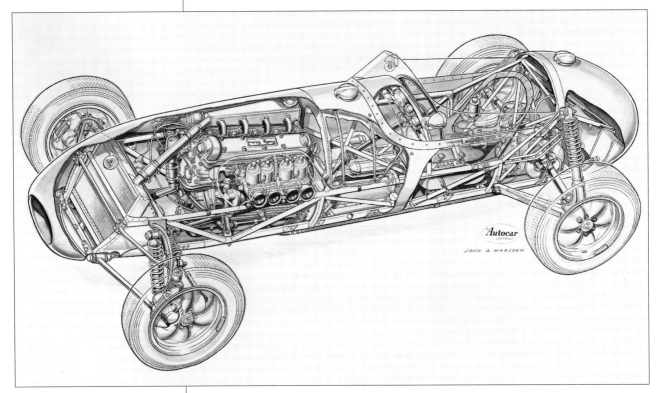

Originally produced as a 1.5-litre Formula 2 car, Colin Chapman's first single-seater Lotus was this Type 12. With a larger Coventry-Climax engine it began competing in Formula 1 races in 1958, driven by Graham Hill and Cliff Allison.

Formula, Auto Union had a mid-engined layout in mind – but prepared designs for a front-engined installation of its V-12 engine as a precaution.

Engineers preparing for the postwar resumption of racing were thinking of mid-mounted engines as well. Among the ambitious designs prepared for Maserati by Alberto Massimino in 1944–45 was one, clearly influenced by the Alfa 512, with the fuel tank, engine and gearbox between the driver and the final drive gears. Such a design was far beyond the modest means of Maserati in war-torn Italy, however.

At their Austrian postwar base the Porsche engineers were thinking on the same lines in their Type 360 design for Italy's Cisitalia, except that they followed the lead of the 1939 Auto Union and placed the fuel along the flanks of the frame – not an uncontroversial location from the standpoint of the driver's safety in a crash – allowing the driver to be seated more to the rear. The Cisitalia was an extremely accomplished design with a form of parallel-arm independent rear suspension, and had it raced it might well have advanced the mid-engined era by a decade. Although the car was built, it was beyond Cisitalia's capacity to bring to race-readiness.

If any car accurately foreshadowed the shape of mid-engined Grand Prix cars to come it was the astonishing Sacha Gordine funded by a French film producer of that name.[7] Originally intended by engineers Vigna and Perkins for the 1½-litre supercharged formula, the Sacha Gordine's V-8 was converted to 2 litres for Formula 2 racing in 1952–53, but regrettably never reached a starting line.

With its low-built lines and separate nostrils for two ducted radiators, the Sacha Gordine could easily be taken for a Ferrari Formula 1 prototype of a decade later. It used side-mounted fuel tanks, many magnesium castings and a transversely mounted five-speed gearbox. Gordine had also put in train the building of 3-litre sports cars on the same lines, and announced André Simon as his driver. His funds ran out, however, before his project could reach fruition. Another potential mid-engined role model fell short of its realisation.

CHAPMAN VERSUS COOPER

There matters rested until Charles and John Cooper came along with their simple, light and practical Climax-powered cars, as related in Chapter Six. When the new 1½-litre Formula 2 was announced for 1957 it was a veritable gift to Cooper. It rejected the front-engined design it had used for the previous Formula 2, and had its new mid-engined single-seaters built and racing in 1956.

Purposeful rather than attractive, the Lotus 18 married the genius of Colin Chapman in chassis design with the logic of the rear-engined racing car. This is a 1961 model being driven at Goodwood by Innes Ireland.

---

7   Not to be confused with Gordini, in spite of the similarity of names.

Even for latecomer Lance Reventlow the writing was on the wall. He built this new mid-engined chassis using a Cooper-Knight transaxle and his own desmodromic four-cylinder engine. The car was not ready to compete before the 2½-litre formula expired.

For the same Formula 2 Colin Chapman at Lotus produced his first-ever single-seater racing car – front-engined. 'He followed the front engine principle,' said his technical biographer, Hugh Haskell, 'simply because he was working from existing vehicles of this system.' Lotus single-seaters began racing in Formula 1 in 1958, when Chapman introduced more advanced versions of his front-engined Grand Prix car designs, and persevered with them into 1959.

During 1959 Chapman and Lotus began a transition to rear engines. Haskell recalls:

Plainly, he felt some reluctance at doing what his arch rival Cooper had been doing for so long and in admitting that the firmly established layout was not ideal. Chapman's clear understanding of the fundamentals involved, in which he was not unusual, was allied to a single-mindedness of purpose, which was less common. This meant that he overcame this reluctance more readily than some others.

Chapman himself put it simply: 'We went to rear engines because they make the cars very much easier to build, they remove some handling problems, and they eliminate the power losses we were having last year.'

By 'last year' Chapman meant 1959, when he introduced his first mid-engined car, the Formula Junior Lotus 18. This grew into the successful Formula 1 Lotus-Climax of 1960, which won two championship Grand Prix races under Stirling Moss that season.[8] From the 18 evolved the Formula 1 Lotuses of the future.

This capitulation by Lotus, and later by Ferrari, marked the end of the front-engined Grand Prix car era. Both Aston Martin and Scarab started building mid-engined cars, but neither raced before the 2½-litre formula expired at the end of 1960. From 1961, in the new 1½-litre formula all the entrants were mid-engined – with one notable exception.

LAST FRONT-ENGINED GASP

In 1950, Ulsterman Harry Ferguson, wealthy through the exploitation of his tractor designs and patents, established a research company to pursue the idea of four-wheel drive for cars. Headed by former racing driver Tony Rolt, Ferguson Research did not wait long before trying out its ideas in the form of a racing car.

The Climax-powered P99 racing car build by Ferguson was front-engined because its designers believed that this would best balance its mass among its four driven wheels. Peter Westbury, seen here, demonstrated its attractive attributes in hillclimbing.

---

8 It also badly injured Moss when a wheel came off during practice at Spa. The early 18s were notoriously fragile.

Driving the Ferguson P99, Stirling Moss is flagged to victory in a Formula 1 race at Oulton Park in September 1961. This was the final hurrah in Grand Prix competition for a racing car with the engine in front of the driver.

Former Aston Martin engineer Claude Hill led the design of the Ferguson Project 99, which was ready to take to the tracks by the end of 1960.

Rolt and Hill decided to make the P99 a front-engined car because they felt that this would make it easier to obtain the equal distribution of weight between the front and rear pairs of wheels that they believed was desirable for four-wheel drive. The driver was offset to the right, with the gearbox and drive shafts to his left. The Ferguson's body was wrapped tightly around its machinery and a Coventry-Climax four-cylinder engine.

Rolt's friend Rob Walker agreed to enter the P99 in some 1961 races. Stirling Moss had a chance to try it during a rainy British Grand Prix and was very impressed by its grip and performance. After private tests he drove it in a non-championship 166-mile Formula 1 race at Oulton Park in September. All the top Formula 1 opposition was there, save Ferrari.

Wet or dry (and both were experienced during the weekend), Moss was among the fastest. In the race he took the lead on the fourth of sixty laps and won by a ¾-minute margin. He set the fastest lap as well, a new Oulton Park Formula 1 record. 'To me,' said Stirling later, 'the advent of four-wheel drive in the Ferguson was as momentous, and as great a change from anything I had been used to, as the famous "rear-engined revolution" which for me was marked by the move from Vanwall to Cooper-Climax.'

Moss's victory at Oulton Park on 23 September 1961 was the last in a Formula 1 race for a front-engined car – an exceptional one at that. Four-wheel drive had given the front-engined Grand Prix car one last hurrah. However, the advantages of the rear engine are so overwhelming in the Formula 1 car, with its centrally placed driver, that the front-mounted engine will never make a comeback in that category – with or without four-wheel drive.[9]

The position is different for the sports car, with its seats disposed at the sides of a central propeller shaft. The front-mounted engine is still feasible. In making the transition from its Testarossa to its replacement, the 550 Maranello, Ferrari's change from mid-engine to front-engine met with general acclaim. In sports-racing categories as well, long-bonneted front-engined racers are still taken seriously.

HORSE BEFORE THE CART

By late 1959 it had been obvious to Enzo Ferrari's drivers that the 'rear-engined revolution' was well under way. 'I realised that the front-engined car was no longer going to be in the front line,' Dan Gurney recalled. 'As "the word" trickled down to me, Enzo Ferrari's reaction to the rear-engine versus front-engine debate was said to be, "The horse belongs in front of the carriage!"'

Putting the horse in front of the carriage had served Ferrari and his contemporaries very well indeed for the first half of the twentieth century. It had also created some of the most emotionally involving and technically stimulating racing cars of all time. It is an era we can, and do, enthusiastically celebrate.

Streaming away from the starting grid at Monza in 1957 were Ferraris, Maseratis and Vanwalls – elegant alcohol-fuelled exemplars of the glorious front-engined era of the Formula 1 car. Hot on their heels – metaphorically – were the rear-engined racers that would make them all obsolete within two years.

---

9   Four-wheel drive was experimented with by most of the Formula 1 teams towards the end of the sixties, but tyre improvements mean that it was never required. It was subsequently banned by the international racing authorities.

APPENDIX

SELECTED SPECIFICATIONS OF CLASSIC GRAND PRIX CARS FROM THE FIRST

Year	Marque	Model	Cyls	Bore (mm)	Stroke (mm)	Stroke/ Bore Ratio	Piston Area (sq ins)	Capacity (cc)	Super- charged	Peak Power (hp)
1903	Mercedes	60 HP	4	140	151	1.08	95.4	9,293	no	65
1904	Fiat	Gordon Bennett	4	165	165	1.00	132.6	14,112	no	76
1904	Mercedes	90 HP	4	165	140	0.85	132.5	11,972	no	98
1905	Mercedes	120 HP	4	175	146	0.83	149.3	14,065	no	120
1906	Mercedes		6	140	120	0.86	143.1	11,080	no	106
1906	Renault		4	166	150	0.90	134.2	12,985	no	105
1906	Richard-Brasier		4	165	140	0.85	132.6	11,974	no	105
1907	Lorraine-Dietrich		4	180	170	0.94	157.8	17,304	no	120
1907	Fiat	130 HP	4	180	160	0.89	157.8	16,286	no	130
1907	Mercedes		4	175	150	0.86	149.1	14,432	no	120
1908	Fiat	100 HP	4	155	160	1.03	117.0	12,076	no	115
1908	Benz		4	154.9	160	1.03	117.0	12,076	no	120
1908	Mercedes		4	154.7	180	1.16	116.5	13,533	no	135
1911	Fiat	Tipo 14 (S74)	4	150	200	1.33	109.6	14,137	no	190
1912	Peugeot	L76	4	110	200	1.82	58.9	7,603	no	130
1913	Delage		4	110	185	1.68	58.9	7,032	no	105
1913	Peugeot		4	100	180	1.80	48.7	5,655	no	115
1913	Mercedes		6	105	140	1.33	80.3	7,250	no	91
1913	Mercedes		4	140	150	1.07	95.4	9,230	no	100
1914	Mercedes	18/100	4	93	165	1.77	42.1	4,483	no	106
1914	Peugeot		4	92	169	1.84	41.2	4,494	no	112
1919	Ballot		8	74	140	1.89	53.3	4,817	no	140
1920	Ballot		8	65	112	1.72	41.1	2,973	no	108
1921	Duesenberg	183	8	63.5	117	1.84	39.3	2,964	no	125
1921	Fiat	Tipo 801	8	65	112	1.72	41.1	2,973	no	120
1922	Fiat	Tipo 804	6	65	100	1.54	30.9	1,991	no	92
1923	Benz	RH	6	65	100	1.54	31.0	1,997	no	90
1923	Fiat	Tipo 805	8	60	87.5	1.46	35.1	1,979	yes	130
1923	Mercedes	Indianapolis	4	70	129	1.84	23.9	1,989	yes	125
1923	Miller	122	8	58.8	89	1.51	33.7	1,933	no	120
1923	Sunbeam		6	67	94	1.40	32.8	1,988	no	108
1924	Alfa Romeo	P2	8	61	85	1.39	36.2	1,987	yes	140
1924	Bugatti	Type 35	8	60	88	1.47	35.1	1,991	no	100
1924	Mercedes	Targa Florio	4	70	129	1.84	23.9	1,989	yes	150
1924	Mercedes		8	61.7	82.8	1.34	37.2	1,988	yes	170

*Mean piston speed at maximum power is divided by the square root of the stroke/bore ratio, providing a correction factor that gives a more accurate indication of the engine's stress level in accord with the Lanchester Theory.

SIX DECADES OF THE TWENTIETH CENTURY

@RPM	Piston Speed* (ft/min)	Engine hp/litre	Ratios Forward	Wheelbase (inches)	Weight (lbs)	Car hp/ tonne	Max Speed (mph)	Front Tyres	Rear Tyres
1,100	1,049	7.0	4	108.2	2,200	59.1	73	910x100	920x125
1,200	1,299	5.4	4	113.6	2,215	68.6	95	920x90	920x120
1,150	1,147	8.2	4	105.9	2,190	89.5	97	810x90	820x120
1,200	1,259	8.5	4	115.0	2,200	109.1	100	870x90	880x120
1,400	1,191	9.6	4	105.9	2,215	95.7	95	880x105	880x120
1,200	1,242	8.1	3	114.2	2,180	96.3	92	870x90	880x120
1,400	1,396	8.8	3	108.3	2,220	94.6	94	870x90	880x120
1,250	1,435	6.9	4	116.1	2,205	108.8	95	870x90	880x120
1,600	1,782	8.0	4	112.0	2,260	115.0	98	875x105	880x120
1,400	1,488	8.3	4	112.2	2,290	104.8	100	880x105	880x120
1,400	1,447	9.5	4	108.3	2,655	86.6	110	875x105	880x120
1,500	1,550	9.9	4	110.0	2,650	90.6	101	880x105	935x145
1,400	1,533	10.0	4	106.0	2,460	109.8	105	880x120	895x135
1,600	1,818	13.4	4	107.1	3,310	114.8	102	880x120	895x135
2,200	2,141	17.1	4	109.0	1,980	131.3	100	875x100	895x135
2,300	2,153	14.9	5	108.0	2,270	92.5	100	870x90	880x120
2,500	2,201	20.3	4	106.0	2,290	100.4	108	875x105	880x120
1,400	1,114	12.6	4	113.2	2,450	74.3	90	5.5x34	5.5x34
1,350	1,284	10.8	4	113.2	2,550	78.4	95	5.5x34	5.5x34
3,100	2,520	23.6	4	112.0	2,385	88.9	112	815x105	820x135
2,800	2,291	24.9	4	106.3	2,335	95.9	116	875x105	880x120
3,000	2,004	29.1	4	108.0	2,350	119.1	118	5.0x33	5.0x33
3,800	2,127	36.3	4	104.5	1,735	124.5	112	820x120	835x135
4,250	2,404	42.2	3	106.0	2,020	123.8	114	4.50x32	4.50x32
4,400	2,463	40.4	4	108.3	2,030	118.2	110	820x120	820x135
5,200	2,751	46.2	4	98.4	1,455	126.5	105	760x90	760x105
5,000	2,645	45.1	3	109.4	1,620	111.1	110	765x105	765x105
5,500	2,615	65.7	4	103.1	1,500	173.3	115	797x120	797x135
4,500	2,806	62.8	4	107.5	2,150	116.3	119	4.50x29	4.50x29
5,000	2,373	62.1	3 or 4	100.0	1,350	177.8	116	4.50x29	4.50x29
5,000	2,604	54.3	3	98.0	1,490	145.0	112	765x105	765x105
5,500	2,599	70.4	4	103.5	1,654	169.3	135	5.25x19	6.00x19
5,000	2,384	50.2	4	94.5	1,455	137.5	112	710x90	710x90
4,800	2,993	75.4	4	107.5	2,030	147.8	118	765x120	765x105
7,000	3,283	85.5	3	102.3	1,715	198.3	130	5.00x29	6.00x31

Year	Marque	Model	Cyls	Bore (mm)	Stroke (mm)	Stroke/ Bore Ratio	Piston Area (sq ins)	Capacity (cc)	Super- charged	Peak Power (hp)
1924	Sunbeam		6	67	94	1.40	32.8	1,988	yes	138
1925	Delage		12	51.3	80	1.56	38.4	1,984	yes	190
1926	Bugatti	Type 39	8	52	88	1.69	26.3	1,495	yes	110
1927	Delage		8	55.8	76	1.36	30.3	1,487	yes	170
1927	Talbot	8 Cylindres 1500	8	56	75.5	1.35	30.5	1,488	yes	155
1927	Fiat	Tipo 806	12	50	63	1.26	36.5	1,484	yes	187
1928	Bugatti	Type 35B	8	60	100	1.67	35.1	2,262	yes	135
1930	Maserati	26M	8	65	94	1.45	41.1	2,495	yes	185
1931	Alfa Romeo	8C2300 Monza	8	65	88	1.35	41.1	2,336	yes	165
1931	Bugatti	Type 51	8	60	100	1.67	35.1	2,262	yes	160
1932	Alfa Romeo	Tipo B	8	65	100	1.54	41.1	2,655	yes	215
1932	Maserati	8C3000	8	69	100	1.45	46.4	2,991	yes	220
1933	Maserati	8CM	8	69	100	1.45	46.4	2,991	yes	240
1934	Auto Union	Type A	16	68	75	1.10	90.1	4,358	yes	295
1934	Bugatti	Type 59	8	73	100	1.37	51.9	3,348	yes	240
1934	Mercedes-Benz	W25	8	78	88	1.13	59.2	3,360	yes	314
1935	Alfa Romeo	Tipo 8C	8	78	100	1.28	59.3	3,823	yes	330
1935	Auto Union	Type B	16	72.5	75	1.03	102.4	4,954	yes	375
1935	Maserati	V8R1	8	84	108	1.29	68.7	4,788	yes	320
1935	Mercedes-Benz	W25	8	82	94.5	1.15	65.5	3,992	yes	370
1935	Mercedes-Benz	W25	8	82	102	1.24	65.5	4,309	yes	402
1936	Alfa Romeo	Tipo 12C	12	70	88	1.26	71.6	4,064	yes	370
1936	Auto Union	Type C	16	75	85	1.13	109.6	6,008	yes	520
1936	Mercedes-Benz	W25 Kurz	8	86	102	1.19	72.0	4,740	yes	453
1937	Mercedes-Benz	W125	8	94	102	1.09	86.1	5,663	yes	575
1938	Alfa Romeo	Tipo 312	12	66	73	1.11	63.6	2,997	yes	350
1938	Auto Union	Type D	12	65	75	1.15	61.7	2,986	yes	420
1938	Delahaye	Type 145	12	75	84.7	1.13	82.2	4,490	yes	220
1938	Maserati	8CTF	8	69	100	1.45	46.4	2,991	yes	360
1938	Mercedes-Benz	W154	12	67	70	1.04	65.6	2,962	yes	453
1939	Alfa Romeo	Tipo 316	16	58	70	1.21	65.5	2,959	yes	440
1939	Auto Union	Type D	12	65	75	1.15	61.7	2,986	2-stage	485
1939	Mercedes-Benz	W154	12	67	70	1.04	65.6	2,962	2-stage	480
1939	Mercedes-Benz	W165	8	64	58	0.91	39.9	1,493	yes	246
1940	Maserati	8CL	8	78	78	1.00	59.3	2,982	yes	430
1940	Mercedes-Benz	W165	8	64	58	0.91	39.9	1,493	2-stage	278
1946	Maserati	4CL	4	78	78	1.00	29.6	1,491	yes	220
1947	Alfa Romeo	Tipo 158/47	8	58	70	1.21	32.8	1,480	2-stage	275
1948	Ferrari	125 F1	12	55	52.5	0.95	44.2	1,497	yes	225
1948	Maserati	4CLT/48	4	78	78	1.00	29.6	1,491	2-stage	260

@RPM	Piston Speed* (ft/min)	Engine hp/litre	Ratios Forward	Wheelbase (inches)	Weight (lbs)	Car hp/ tonne	Max Speed (mph)	Front Tyres	Rear Tyres
5,500	2,864	69.4	4	102.5	1,680	164.3	125	765×105	765×105
7,000	2,943	95.8	5	102.0	1,455	261.2	134	765×120	765×120
5,500	2,441	73.6	4	94.5	1,680	131.0	110	710×90	710×90
7,500	3,205	114.3	5	98.5	1,650	206.1	128	765×105	765×120
7,000	2,987	104.2	4	103.0	1,765	175.6	130	5.35×29	5.35×29
8,500	3,130	126.0	4	94.5	1,545	242.1	135	800×130	800×130
5,300	2,694	59.7	4	94.5	1,655	163.1	125	4.75×29	4.75×29
5,600	2,872	74.1	4	108.3	1,810	204.4	136	5.00×18	5.50×18
5,400	2,680	70.6	4	104.3	2,030	162.6	130	5.50×19	5.50×19
5,500	2,795	70.7	5	94.5	1,675	191.0	134	5.00×19	5.00×19
5,600	2,963	81.0	4	104.3	1,545	278.3	140	5.50×18	5.50×18
5,500	2,998	73.5	4	108.3	1,875	234.7	145	5.50×19	6.00×19
5,800	3,161	80.2	4	100.8	1,730	277.5	150	5.50×19	6.00×19
4,500	2,109	67.7	5	112.0	1,893	311.7	165	5.25×17	6.50×19
5,500	3,083	71.7	4	102.3	1,680	285.7	155	5.50×19	6.00×19
5,800	3,153	93.5	4	107.2	1,625	386.5	170	5.25×17	5.25×19
5,400	3,129	86.3	4	108.3	1,620	407.4	150	6.50×19	6.50×19
4,800	2,323	75.7	5	114.6	1,847	406.1	180	5.25×19	7.00×19
5,300	3,312	66.8	4	106.0	1,655	386.7	170	5.50×18	6.00×18
5,800	3,350	92.7	4	107.2	1,650	448.5	186	5.50×19	7.00×19
5,500	3,301	93.3	4	107.2	1,650	487.3	174	5.50×19	7.00×19
5,800	2,987	91.0	4	108.3	1,810	408.8	180	6.50×18	7.00×19
5,000	2,620	86.5	5	114.6	1,847	563.1	185	5.50×19	7.00×19
5,800	3,564	95.6	4	97.0	1,570	577.1	180	5.50×19	7.00×19
5,500	3,534	101.5	4	110.1	1,770	649.7	211	5.25×19	7.00×22
6,500	2,960	116.8	4	108.3	1,940	360.8	177	5.25×19	7.00×19
7,000	3,207	140.6	5	112.2	1,875	448.0	180	5.50×19	7.00×19
5,500	2,876	49.0	4	114.0	1,905	231.0	140	5.50×18	6.50×18
6,300	3,434	120.3	4	107.1	1,720	418.6	170	5.50×19	6.50×19
8,000	3,595	152.9	5	107.4	2,160	419.4	176	5.50×19	7.00×19
7,500	3,136	148.7	4	110.2	2,030	433.5	186	5.50×19	7.00×19
7,000	3,207	162.4	5	112.2	1,875	517.3	195	5.50×19	7.00×19
7,500	3,370	162.1	5	107.4	2,005	478.8	185	5.50×19	7.00×19
7,500	2,998	164.8	5	96.5	1,582	311.0	170	5.00×17	6.00×17
6,800	3,480	144.2	4	109.8	1,725	498.6	180	5.50×19	6.50×19
8,250	3,298	186.2	5	96.5	1,600	347.5	175	5.00×17	6.00×17
7,000	3,583	147.6	4	98.4	1,390	316.5	145	5.00×17	6.00×17
7,500	3,136	185.9	4	98.6	1,540	357.1	168	5.50×17	7.00×18
7,000	2,468	150.3	5	85.1	1,545	291.3	160	5.50×16	6.50×16
7,000	3,583	174.4	4	98.4	1,390	347.1	155	5.00×17	6.00×17

Year	Marque	Model	Cyls	Bore (mm)	Stroke (mm)	Stroke/ Bore Ratio	Piston Area (sq ins)	Capacity (cc)	Super- charged	Peak Power (hp)
1949	Talbot-Lago	Type 26C	6	93	110	1.18	63.2	4,483	no	260
1950	Ferrari	125 F1	12	55	52.5	0.95	44.2	1,497	2-stage	315
1951	Alfa Romeo	Tipo 159	8	58	70	1.21	32.8	1,480	2-stage	425
1951	BRM	Type 15	16	49.53	48.3	0.98	47.8	1,489	2-stage	430
1951	Ferrari	375	12	80	74.5	0.93	93.5	4,494	no	380
1952	AFM	F.2	8	67.3	70	1.04	44.1	1,992	no	200
1952	Connaught	A-Series	4	79	100	1.27	30.4	1,961	no	140
1952	Ferrari	500	4	90	78	0.87	39.4	1,985	no	180
1952	Maserati	A6GCM	6	75	75	1.00	41.1	1,988	no	180
1953	Cooper	T23 'Mark II'	6	66	96	1.45	31.8	1,971	no	150
1953	Maserati	A6GCM	6	76.7	72	0.94	43.0	1,996	no	197
1954	Connaught	B-Series	4	93.5	90	0.96	42.6	2,472	no	250
1954	Ferrari	625	4	100	79.5	0.80	48.7	2,498	no	245
1954	Lancia	D50	8	73.6	73.1	0.99	52.8	2,488	no	230
1954	Maserati	250F	6	84	75	0.89	51.5	2,494	no	260
1954	Mercedes-Benz	W196	8	76	68.8	0.91	56.2	2,496	no	257
1955	Ferrari	555	4	100	79.5	0.80	48.7	2,498	no	270
1955	Mercedes-Benz	W196	8	76	68.8	0.91	56.3	2,497	no	290
1955	Mercedes-Benz	W196	8	76	68.8	0.91	56.3	2,497	no	290
1956	Bugatti	Type 251	8	76	68.8	0.91	56.3	2,497	no	242
1956	Gordini	Type 32B	8	75	70	0.93	54.8	2,474	no	230
1956	Maserati	250F	6	84	75	0.89	51.5	2,494	no	270
1957	BRM	Type 25	4	102.87	74.93	0.73	51.5	2,491	no	288
1957	Ferrari-Lancia	801 F1	8	80	62	0.78	62.3	2,493	no	275
1957	Maserati	250F	6	84	75	0.89	51.5	2,494	no	270
1957	Maserati	250F T2	12	68.7	56	0.82	68.9	2,491	no	310
1957	Vanwall	GP	4	96	86	0.90	44.9	2,490	no	285
1958	Cooper	T45	4	88.9	88.9	1.00	38.5	2,207	no	194
1958	Ferrari	Dino 246	6	85	71	0.84	52.8	2,417	no	285
1958	Lotus	Type 12	4	88.9	88.9	1.00	38.5	2,207	no	193
1958	Vanwall	GP	4	96	86	0.90	44.9	2,490	no	270
1959	Aston Martin	DBR4/250	6	83	76.8	0.93	50.3	2,493	no	236
1959	Cooper	T51	4	94	89.9	0.96	43.0	2,496	no	239
1960	BRM	Type 48	4	102.87	74.93	0.73	51.5	2,491	no	275
1960	Cooper	T53	4	94	89.9	0.96	0.43	2,496	no	243
1960	Ferrari	Dino 246	6	86	71	0.83	54.0	2,475	no	295
1960	Lotus	Type 18	4	94	89.9	0.96	43.0	2,496	no	243

@RPM	Piston Speed* (ft/min)	Engine hp/litre	Ratios Forward	Wheelbase (inches)	Weight (lbs)	Car hp/ tonne	Max Speed (mph)	Front Tyres	Rear Tyres
5,000	3,318	58.0	4	98.5	1,875	277.3	165	5.25x18	6.50x18
7,500	2,644	210.5	5	91.3	1,545	407.8	170	5.50x16	7.00x16
9,300	3,888	287.2	4	98.6	1,565	543.1	195	5.50x17	7.00x18
11,000	3,530	288.8	5	98.0	1,825	471.2	190	5.25x18	7.00x17
7,500	3,799	84.6	4	91.3	1,875	405.3	185	5.50x16	7.50x16
8,000	3,603	100.4	4	96.0	995	402.0	156	5.50x16	6.50x16
6,000	3,499	71.4	4	85.0	1,255	223.1	148	5.50x15	6.00x15
7,500	4,123	90.7	4	86.5	1,370	262.8	155	5.25x16	5.50x16
7,300	3,593	90.5	4	89.8	1,225	293.9	150	5.00x15	6.00x15
5,800	3,029	76.1	4	90.0	1,140	263.2	130	5.00x15	6.00x15
8,000	3,901	98.7	4	87.0	1,255	313.9	160	5.25x16	6.50x16
7,000	4,213	101.1	4	90.0	1,595	313.5	150	5.50x16	6.00x16
7,000	4,095	98.1	4	85.1	1,325	369.8	155	5.25x16	6.50x16
8,000	3,850	92.4	5	90.0	1,365	337.0	165	5.50x16	6.50x16
7,600	3,958	104.3	4	89.8	1,480	351.4	155	5.25x16	6.50x16
8,250	3,914	103.0	5	92.5	1,670	307.8	162	6.00x16	7.00x16
7,500	4,388	108.1	5	85.1	1,300	415.4	168	5.25x16	6.50x16
8,500	4,033	116.1	5	87.0	1,607	360.9	191	6.00x16	7.00x16
8,500	4,033	116.1	5	84.6	1,410	411.3	150	6.00x16	7.00x16
7,500	3,559	96.9	5	86.0	1,655	292.4	143	5.00x17	6.00x17
7,000	3,328	93.0	5	90.6	1,550	296.8	155	5.50x16	7.00x16
7,500	3,906	108.3	4	89.8	1,500	360.0	165	5.50x16	7.00x16
8,250	4,753	115.6	4	90.0	1,520	378.9	170	5.25x16	7.00x16
8,200	3,789	110.3	5	89.8	1,435	383.3	168	5.50x16	7.00x16
7,200	3,750	108.3	4	87.6	1,390	388.5	175	5.50x16	7.00x16
10,000	4,070	124.4	5	90.6	1,435	432.1	185	5.50x17	7.00x17
7,400	4,412	114.5	5	90.3	1,405	405.7	170	5.50x16	7.00x17
6,250	3,646	87.9	4	91.0	875	443.4	160	4.50x15	5.50x15
8,500	4,333	117.9	5	85.1	1,235	461.5	168	5.50x16	6.50x16
6,250	3,646	87.4	5	88.0	1,080	357.4	155	5.00x15	5.50x15
7,500	4,472	108.4	5	90.3	1,405	384.3	165	5.50x16	7.00x16
7,000	3,667	94.7	5	90.0	1,375	343.3	155	5.50x16	7.00x16
6,750	4,072	95.8	4	91.0	960	497.9	170	5.00x15	6.50x15
8,000	4,609	110.4	4 or 5	90.0	1,100	500.0	170	5.25x15	6.50x15
6,800	4,102	97.4	5	91.0	1,060	458.5	180	5.00x15	6.50x15
9,000	4,615	119.2	5	87.4	1,235	477.7	175	5.50x16	6.50x16
6,800	4,102	97.4	5	90.0	980	495.9	180	5.00x15	6.50x15

A spectator had a close-up view of Manfred von Brauchitsch and his W154 Mercedes-Benz in the 1938 Coppa Ciano at Livorno. Manfred was first over the line at the finish but was disqualified because some spectators helped his car back on to the road after an off-course excursion. Team-mate Hermann Lang was the winner.

BIBLIOGRAPHY

Many contemporary periodicals were consulted in the Ludvigsen Library during the research for this book; where relevant, they and the respective authors are referenced in the text. Of particular value to the work were: *ATZ, Auto Motor und Sport, The Autocar, Automobile Quarterly, Automobile Engineer, Automobil Revue, Autosport, Car and Driver, The Horseless Age, The Motor, Motor Age, Motor Kritik, Motor Sport, MTZ, Road & Track* and the *SAE Journal*. The annuals *Autocourse* and *Automobile Year* were also of value for the later years. Much information on the early years was gleaned from the Ludvigsen Library's holdings of the papers of an engineer with a strong interest in racing, the late Van Wyck Hewlett.

Anselmi, Angelo Tito, *Catalogo Bolaffi Delle Fiat 1899–1970*, Turin, 1970.

Bentley, W.O., *The Cars in My Life*, London, 1961.

Betts Jr, Charles L., *Auto Racing Winners*, Philadelphia, 1948.

Borgeson, Griffith, *The Golden Age of the American Racing Car*, New York, 1966.

——, *The Classic Twin-cam Engine*, London, 1981.

——, 'The 1914 Grand Prix Delage and the Signature of the Artist: Debugging the Desmodromic Dichotomy and Other Historical Fantasies', *Automobile Quarterly*, Vol. 24, No. 3, third quarter, 1986.

——, 'Of Fingers, Mushrooms and Little Buckets', *Automobile Quarterly*, Vol. 27, No. 2, second quarter, 1989.

Caracciola, Rudolf, *A Racing Car Driver's World*, New York, 1961.

Clutton, Cecil, Posthumus, Cyril and Jenkinson, Denis, *The Racing Car – Development and Design*, New York, 1956.

Conway, Hugh, *Grand Prix Bugatti*, Cambridge, 1968.

——, with Sauzay, Maurice, *Bugatti Magnum*, Sparkford, 1989.

Court, William, *Power and Glory*, London, 1966.

Davis, S.C.H. et. al., *Motor Racing*, London, 1957.

Dean, Frederick E. et. al., *Power and Speed*, Los Angeles, 1944.

Dees, Mark L., *The Miller Dynasty*, Scarsdale, 1981.

Dreyfus, René, with Kimes, Beverly Rae, *My Two Lives – Race Driver to Restaurateur*, Tucson, 1983.

Dugdale, John, *Great Motor Sport of the Thirties*, London and New York, 1977.

Earl, Cameron C., *Investigation Into the Development of German Grand Prix Racing Cars Between 1934 and 1939*, London, 1947.

Fangio, Juan Manuel, *Fangio*, London, 1961.

Ferrari, Enzo, *Piloti che gente . . .*, Bologna, 1985.

Francis, Alf with Lewis, Peter, *Alf Francis – Racing Mechanic*, London, 1957.

Frankenberg, Richard von, *Porsche – The Man and His Cars*, Cambridge, 1961.

Fusi, Luigi, *Alfa Romeo – All Cars From 1910*, Milan, 1978.

Georgano, G.N., *The Complete Encyclopedia of Motorcars – 1885–1968*, New York, 1968.

——, with Bochroch, Albert R., *The Encyclopedia of Motor Sport*, New York, 1971.

Haskell, Hugh, *Colin Chapman: Lotus Engineering*, London, 1993.

Hawthorn, Mike, *Challenge Me the Race*, London, 1958.

Heal, Anthony S., *Sunbeam Racing Cars*, Sparkford, 1989.

Hodges, David, *A–Z of Formula Racing Cars*, Bideford, 1990.

Hough, Richard, *Racing Cars*, London, 1966.

——, and Frostick, Michael, *A History of the World's Racing Cars*, New York, 1965.

Howe, The Earl et. al., *Motor Racing*, London, 1944.

Huet, Christian, *Gordini – Un Sorcier, Une Equipe*, Paris, 1984.

Jenkinson, Denis, *A Story of Formula 1 – 1954–60*, London, 1960.

——, *Racing Car Review*, London, 1948.

——, *Racing Car Review*, London, 1949.

——, and Posthumus, Cyril, *Vanwall – The Story of Tony Vandervell and his Racing Cars*, Cambridge, 1975.

Karslake, Kent, *Racing Voiturettes*, London, 1950.

Knittel, Stefan, *Auto Union Grand Prix Wagen*, Munich, 1980.

Lang, Hermann, *Grand Prix Driver*, London, 1953.

Laux, James M., *In First Gear – The French Automobile Industry to 1914*, Montreal, 1976.

Ludvigsen, Karl, *Mercedes-Benz – Quicksilver Century*, Isleworth, 1995.

——, *Ferrari: 50 Years of Innovations in Technology*, Modena, 1997.

Madaro, Giancenzo, *All the Fiats*, Milan, 1970.

Mathieson, T.A.S.O., *A Pictorial Survey of Racing Cars*, London, 1963.

——, *Grand Prix Racing 1906–1914*, Stockholm, 1965.

Mays, Raymond and Roberts, Peter, *B.R.M.*, London, 1962.

——, with May, Dennis, *Split Seconds*, London, 1951.

Merlin, Olivier, *Fangio – Racing Driver*, London, 1961.

Molter, Günther and Wörner, Kurt, *German Racing Cars and Drivers*, Los Angeles, 1950.

Monkhouse, George, *Motor Racing with Mercedes-Benz*, Los Angeles, 1945.

——, *Grand Prix Racing*, London, 1953.

Moss, Stirling and Pomeroy Jr, Laurence, *Design and Behaviour of the Racing Car*, London, 1963.

——, with Nye, Doug, *Stirling Moss – My Cars, My Career*, Wellingborough, 1987.

Neubauer, Alfred with Rowe, Harvey T., *Männer, Frauen und Motoren*, Stuttgart, 1970.

Nye, Doug, *Cooper Cars*, London, 1983.

——, *The Autocourse History of the Grand Prix Car – 1945–65*, Richmond, 1993.

——, *BRM – The Saga of British Racing Motors, Volume One: Front-engined Cars 1945–1960*, Croydon, 1994.

Orsini, Luigi and Zagari, Franco, *Maserati – A Complete History*, Milan, 1981.

Pomeroy Jr, Laurence, *The Grand Prix Car*, Abingdon-on-Thames, 1949.

——, *The Grand Prix Car, Volume Two*, London, 1954.

——, *The Evolution of the Racing Car*, London, 1966.

Pritchard, Anthony, *Lotus – All the Cars*, Bourne End, 1992.

Roberts, Peter, *Veteran and Vintage Cars*, London, 1963.

Rose, Gerald, *A Record of Motor Racing – 1894–1908*, Abingdon-on-Thames, 1949.

Rudd, Tony, *It Was Fun! – My Fifty Years of High Performance*, Sparkford, 1993.

Scott-Moncrieff, David with Nixon, St John and Paget, Clarence, *Three-Pointed Star*, New York, 1956.

Sheldon, Paul with Rabagliati, Duncan, *A Record of Grand Prix and Voiturette Racing, Volume 1: 1900–1925*, Bradford, 1987.

——, *A Record of Grand Prix and Voiturette Racing, Volume 2: 1926–1931*, Bradford, 1988.

——, *A Record of Grand Prix and Voiturette Racing, Volume 3: 1932–1936*, Bradford, 1990.

——, *A Record of Grand Prix and Voiturette Racing, Volume 4: 1937–1949*, Bradford, 1991.

——, *A Record of Grand Prix and Voiturette Racing, Volume 5: 1950–1953*, Bradford, 1992.

——, *A Record of Grand Prix and Voiturette Racing, Volume 6: 1954–1959*, Bradford, 1993.

Smith, Norman, *Case History*, London, 1958.

Spitz, Alain, *Talbot – Des Talbots-Darracq aux Talbot-Lago*, Paris, 1983.

Taruffi, Piero, *Works Driver*, London, 1964.

Thompson, Jonathan, *The Ferrari Formula One Cars – 1948–1976*, Tucson, 1976.

Tragatsch, Erwin, *Das grosse Rennfahrerbuch*, Bern, 1970.

Walkerley, Rodney, *Grands Prix – 1934–1939*, Abingdon-on-Thames, 1950.

Wood, Jonathan, *Bugatti – The Man and the Marque*, Marlborough, 1992.

Yvelin, Paul, *Cinquante Ans des Competitions Automobiles*, Paris, 1970.

ILLUSTRATION CREDITS

As noted in the Introduction, by far the majority of the illustrations in this book have been supplied from the resources of the Ludvigsen Library. Depictions of the cars of the thirties, forties and fifties have benefited from its holdings of the contemporary photography of John Dugdale, Rodolfo Mailander, Ted Eves and Karl Ludvigsen.

The two photographs on p. 48 were kindly provided by the Bugatti Trust. The superb photographs on pp. 80 and 81 were taken by George Monkhouse, as were those on pp. 89, 114 and 196. The photograph on p. 107 is by Louis Klementaski. The photograph on p. 116 is provided by Matt Spitzley. Tony Matthews made available his fine cutaway drawing of a 250F Maserati; it appears in the colour plate section.

Those who wish to contact the Ludvigsen Library with regard to its holdings are invited to do so by e-mail at library@ludvigsen.com.

INDEX

Page numbers in *italic* indicate an illustration. A suffix n indicates reference to a footnote.